My
iMac®
Mountain Lion Edition

John Ray

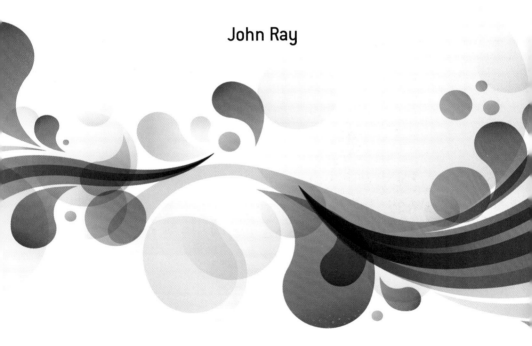

QUE®

800 East 96th Street,
Indianapolis, Indiana 46240 USA

My iMac® (Mountain Lion Edition)

Copyright © 2013 by Pearson Education

ISBN-13: 978-0-7897-5113-3
ISBN-10: 0-7897-5113-5

Library of Congress Cataloging-in-Publication Data is on file.

Printed in the United States of America

First Printing: January 2013

Trademarks

All terms mentioned in this book that are known to be trademarks or service marks have been appropriately capitalized. Que Publishing cannot attest to the accuracy of this information. Use of a term in this book should not be regarded as affecting the validity of any trademark or service mark.

Warning and Disclaimer

Every effort has been made to make this book as complete and as accurate as possible, but no warranty or fitness is implied. The information provided is on an "as is" basis. The author and the publisher shall have neither liability nor responsibility to any person or entity with respect to any loss or damages arising from the information contained in this book or from the use of the programs accompanying it.

Bulk Sales

Que Publishing offers excellent discounts on this book when ordered in quantity for bulk purchases or special sales. For more information, please contact

U.S. Corporate and Government Sales

1-800-382-3419

corpsales@pearsontechgroup.com

For sales outside of the U.S., please contact

International Sales

international@pearsoned.com

EDITOR-IN-CHIEF
Greg Wiegand

ACQUISITIONS/
DEVELOPMENT EDITOR
Laura Norman

MANAGING EDITOR
Kristy Hart

PROJECT EDITOR
Betsy Harris

INDEXER
Erika Millen

PROOFREADER
Debbie Williams

EDITORIAL ASSISTANT
Cindy Teeters

BOOK DESIGNER
Anne Jones

COMPOSITOR
Bronkella Publishing

Contents at a Glance

Table of Contents

About the Author

John Ray is a life-long fan of Apple products; he has been an avid Mac user since its inception in 1984. He relies on Mac OS X both at work and at home because it is a robust, flexible platform for programming, networking, and design. Over the past 14 years, John has written books on OS X, iOS development, Linux, web development, networking, and computer security. He currently serves as the interim director of the Office of Research Information Systems at The Ohio State University. He lives with his long-time girlfriend, their dogs, a collection of vintage arcade games, and an assortment of tech toys.

Dedication

This book is dedicated to anyone who will play #Starhawk or #NFSMostWanted (PS3) with the author. He's been writing for about eight months straight and needs a break!

Acknowledgments

Thanks to the team at Que Publishing: Laura Norman, Betsy Harris, and Bronkella Publishing for keeping the book on schedule and keeping all the parts in order. Thanks also go to Roseanne Groves for wading through the beta OS releases with me. This book takes an amazing amount of production work, and it always astounds me to see it come together.

We Want to Hear from You!

As the reader of this book, *you* are our most important critic and commentator. We value your opinion and want to know what we're doing right, what we could do better, what areas you'd like to see us publish in, and any other words of wisdom you're willing to pass our way.

We welcome your comments. You can email or write to let us know what you did or didn't like about this book—as well as what we can do to make our books better.

Please note that we cannot help you with technical problems related to the topic of this book.

When you write, please be sure to include this book's title and author as well as your name and email address. We will carefully review your comments and share them with the author and editors who worked on the book.

Email: feedback@quepublishing.com

Mail: Que Publishing
            ATTN: Reader Feedback
            800 East 96th Street
            Indianapolis, IN 46240 USA

Reader Services

Visit our website and register this book at quepublishing.com/register for convenient access to any updates, downloads, or errata that might be available for this book.

Prologue: Getting Started with the iMac

This book explains how your iMac and the latest edition of the OS X operating system, Mountain Lion, are used to create your ideal working environment. If you've never worked with a Mac before, OS X is the name applied to Apple's desktop operating system—like "Windows" on a PC. iPhones and iPads run iOS, and iMacs, MacBooks, and the like run OS X. Apple has a long tradition of naming the releases of OS X after large cats, and Mountain Lion is no exception. It certainly sounds more impressive than 10.8, don't you think?

Even though you're working with the most intuitive hardware and software platform available, there are still tips and tricks to discover. With that fact in mind, let's take a few minutes to review the hardware capabilities of your system and the prerequisites necessary to use this book.

Getting to Know the iMac Hardware

The iMac family has always included a wide array of ports and plugs for connecting to other computers, handheld devices, and peripherals such as printers and external displays. As of

2013, two different models of the iMac are available: the 21.5" iMac and the 27" iMac. These (and future) models drop support for optical drives but can easily be expanded with external CD, DVD, and Blu-ray drives. To understand the hardware options that are included in your system, let's review the different expansion options that Apple has shipped in the iMac since 2010.

- **Ethernet**—Ethernet provides high-speed wired network connections with greater speeds and reliability than wireless service. Your iMac supports a very fast version of Ethernet, Gigabit Ethernet, that makes it a first-class citizen on any home or corporate network.

- **FireWire 800**—FireWire 800 is a fast peripheral connection standard that is frequently used to connect external storage and video devices. This is dropped in 2012 models, but an adapter is available from Apple.

- **Mini DisplayPort**—The DisplayPort enables you to connect external monitors to your iMac. Although few monitors support the DisplayPort standard, you can get adapters from Apple for connecting to both VGA and DVI interface standards. DisplayPort was dropped in favor of Thunderbolt in 2011 and later iMacs.

- **Thunderbolt**—The highest-speed interconnect available on a personal computer, Thunderbolt allows monitors, storage units, and other devices to be daisy-chained together. This means that each device connects to the next device, rather than all having to plug into a separate port on your iMac.

- **USB 2.0/3.0**—Universal Serial Bus is a popular peripheral connection standard for everything from mice, to scanners, to hard drives. iMac models released in 2012 or later support USB 3.0, the next, much faster, evolution of USB.

- **SD Card Slot**—SD (Secure Digital) RAM cards are a popular Flash RAM format used in many digital cameras. Using the built-in SD RAM slot, you can create a bootable system "disk" that you can use to start your computer in an emergency.

- **Audio In**—A connection for an external microphone.

- **Audio Out**—An output for headphones, speakers, or a home theater/amplifier system.

- **802.11n**—The fastest standard currently available for consumer wireless network connections. Your iMac's wireless hardware can connect to any standards-based wireless access point for fast, long-range Internet access.

- **Bluetooth**—Bluetooth connects peripheral devices wirelessly to your Mac. Unlike 802.11n, Bluetooth has a more limited range (about 30 feet, in most cases), but it is easier to configure and doesn't require a specialized base station.

- **SuperDrive**—An optical drive that can be used to write CDs and DVDs. In 2012 and later iMac models, optical drives are no more.

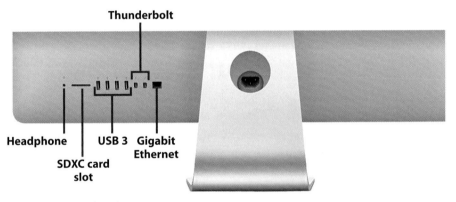

Photo courtesy of Apple Systems, Inc.

So what does your computer have? Apple's iMac lineup changes throughout the year, so your features depend on the model and the date it was made. Be sure to consult your owner's manual for a definitive description of what is included in your system.

Special Keyboard Keys

Take a look across the top of your keyboard. Notice that even though there are "F" (function) designations on the keys, there are also little icons. The keys marked with icons provide system-wide control over important Mountain Lion features.

- **F1, F2**—Dim and brighten the display, respectively

- **F3**—Start Mission Control and display all application windows

- **F4**—Open the Launchpad

- **F7, F8, F9**—Act as Rewind, Play, and Fast Forward controls during media playback
- **F10, F11, F12**—Mute, decrease, and increase volume

The Eject key is located in the farthest-right corner of the keyboard and is used to eject any media in your iMac's SuperDrive—if you have one!

Accessing the Function Keys

If you are using an application that requires you to press a function key, hold down the Fn button in the lower-left corner of the keyboard and then push the required function key.

What You Need to Know

If you're holding this book in your hand, you can see that it contains a few hundred pages packed with information about using your iMac with Mountain Lion. You might also notice books dedicated to the same topic and sitting on the same shelf at the bookstore that include a thousand pages or more! So what's the difference?

My iMac doesn't cover the basics of using a computer; you already know how to drag windows around the screen and move files by dragging them from folder to folder. Instead, this book focuses on using and configuring the core features of OS X—file sharing, Internet access, social networking, calendaring, and entertainment.

If you're switching from Windows, you might encounter a few unique features of OS X. Review these features in the next few sections.

The Menu Bar

The menu bar is universally accessible across all running applications and contains a combination of the Apple menu, which is used to access common system functions; the active application's menus; and menu items, which are global utilities for controlling and monitoring system functions.

Apple menu

Application menus

Menu items

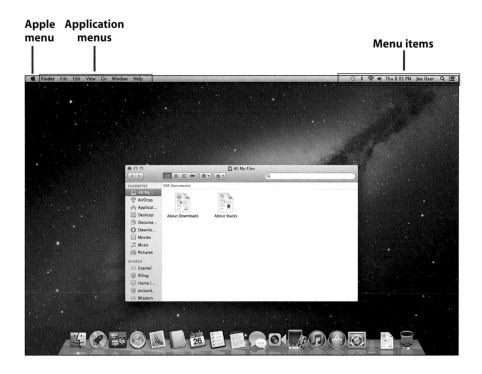

The Dock

The Mountain Lion Dock is the starting point for many of your actions when using the iMac. Part application launcher, part file manager, and part window manager, the Dock gives you quick access to your most frequently used applications and documents without requiring that you navigate the Finder to find things on your hard drive.

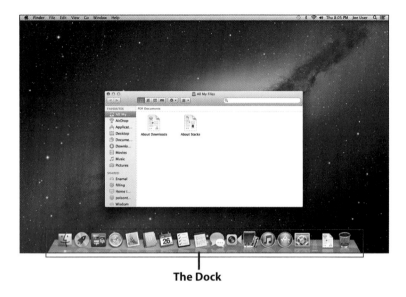

The Dock

The Finder

In Windows, Explorer provides many of your file management needs. In OS X, you work with files within an ever-present application called Finder. The Finder starts as soon as you log into your computer and continues to run until you log out.

To switch to the Finder at any time, click the blue smiling icon at the left end of the Dock.

The Launchpad

Applications are installed in folders, nested in folders, or even just lumped together with no organization at all. For simple setups, this is fine; after you've accumulated a few years of downloads, however, finding what you're looking for becomes difficult. The Launchpad offers a consolidated view of all your applications and even lets you group them logically, without having to worry about what folders they're in.

Mission Control

Mission Control is a power-user feature that is easy for anyone to use. With Mission Control, you can manage all your running applications and their windows in a single consolidated display. You can even create new workspaces to hold specific apps or navigate between existing workspaces.

Workspaces——

Current
workspace——

Application
and
associated
windows——

The App Store (and Security)

If you've used a modern smartphone or tablet, you've almost certainly used an "app store" of some sort. Mountain Lion's App Store is fully integrated with the operating system and provides fast access to screened and safe applications that are installed, updated, and even removed through a simple point-and-click process. Mountain Lion is the first release of OS X that implements security controls to prevent undesirable software installation.

The Notification Center

Does Mountain Lion need to tell you something? If so, it lets you know in the Notification Center. The Notification Center, activated by clicking the far right side of the menu bar, shows alerts from your applications that help you stay on top of important events. New mail, software updates, meeting invitations, and more are consolidated in this area and presented in a unified fashion.

Notification Center

System Preferences

Many configuration options for features in this book require you to access the Mountain Lion System Preferences. The System Preferences application (accessible from the Dock or the Apple menu) is the central hub for system configuration. You can do everything from setting your password to choosing a screen saver in the System Preferences application.

Window Controls

Mountain Lion provides up to four controls at the top of each window. On the left are the Close, Minimize, and Resize controls. The Close control shuts the window; Minimize slides the window off the screen and into the Dock; and Resize changes the size of the window to best fit the content being displayed.

On the right side of the window is the Fullscreen control. Clicking the Fullscreen control switches an app to full screen, if available. You might not expect it, but full-screen applications can take on a completely different appearance from their windowed selves.

Contextual Menus

If you're new to OS X, you might find it hard to believe that the Mac has a "right-click" (also known as the "secondary click") menu in its operating system—and it's been there for a long time! You can invoke contextual menus by right-clicking using a mouse, Ctrl-clicking with your trackpad, or clicking with two fingers simultaneously.

Contextual menus are rarely required in any application, but they can give you quick access to features that might otherwise take more clicks.

Close   Minimize   Resize   Fullscreen

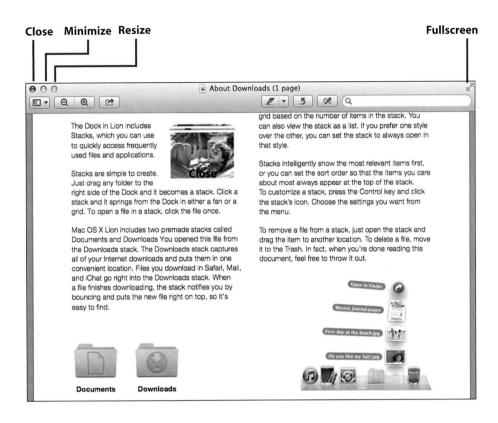

Gestures

Gestures are motions that you can make on an Apple Magic Trackpad to control your computer. In Mountain Lion, gestures are used heavily to navigate between applications and access special features. Gestures can help you navigate web pages, resize images, and do much more with just your fingertips. In fact, without a trackpad, you'll likely miss out on all Mountain Lion has to offer.

>>> Go Further

DON'T LIKE A GESTURE? CHANGE IT!

If you don't like a touch, a click, or a swipe that you find in Mountain Lion (including how contextual menus are activated), it's likely that there is an alternative. The Trackpad System Preferences panel provides complete control over your "touching" OS X experience—something you'll learn about in Chapter 10's "Changing Trackpad and Mouse Options" section.

Dictation

Don't like typing? With Mountain Lion, you don't have to. Mountain Lion supports dictation into any application where you would normally type. The only catch is that the voice recognition is performed "in the cloud," so you need an active Internet connection to use this feature. You learn more about activating dictation in Chapter 10, "Making the Most of Your iMac Hardware."

Understanding iCloud and Apple ID

Apple's iCloud and its corresponding Apple ID deserve special attention during your foray into Mountain Lion. iCloud provides services such as calendars, notes, and reminders that you can use to synchronize information across multiple Macs and multiple iOS devices. It also offers free email, a means of locating your Mac (if it is stolen, for example), and a tool for controlling your system from remote locations. You don't need to use iCloud, but you'll see references to it, like the one shown here, as you navigate the operating system.

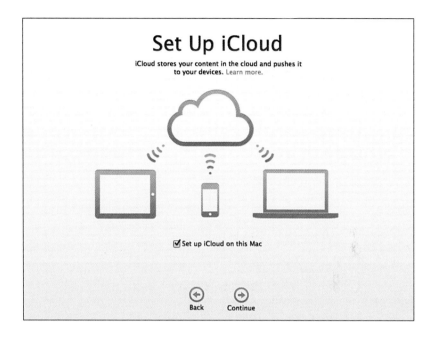

To use iCloud, you must establish an Apple ID to authenticate with the service. If you've installed Mountain Lion, chances are you've created an Apple ID in the process and already have everything you need to start using iCloud. If you aren't sure whether you have an Apple ID or you want to generate a new one, I recommend visiting https://appleid.apple.com/ and using the web tools to verify, or start, your setup.

You learn more about configuring iCloud in Chapter 4, "Accessing iCloud, Email, and the Web."

iCloud Everywhere

Because iCloud makes many of your Mountain Lion features more useful, it is referenced throughout this book. The information doesn't fit into a single category, so I discuss it in the places where I hope you'll find it most useful.

Windows Compatibility

If you have an iMac, you have a powerful Intel-based computer in your hands—a computer that is capable of natively running the Windows operating system. The goal of this book is to make you comfortable using your iMac with Mountain Lion, but I'd be remiss in my authoring duties if I didn't mention the options available for running Windows on your hardware.

Boot Camp

Boot Camp is included with Mountain Lion and gives you the capability to install and boot Windows directly on your iMac. Put simply, when you do this, your Mac becomes a Windows computer. Switching between Mountain Lion and Windows requires a reboot, so this option is best if you need to work in Windows for extended periods of time.

Apple's Boot Camp Assistant (found in the Utilities folder within the Applications folder) guides you through the process of partitioning your iMac for Windows and burning a CD of drivers for Windows, and configuring your system to boot into Windows or OS X.

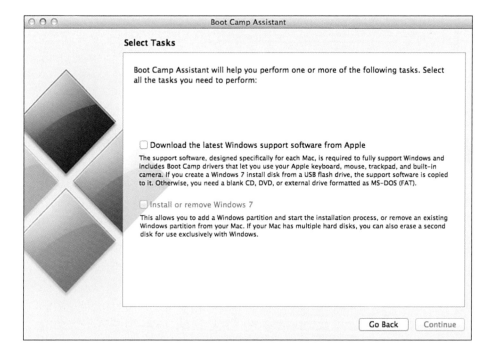

You can install Boot Camp at any time, as long as you have enough room (about 5GB) for a Windows installation. Boot Camp even works correctly with the iMac's fusion drive—just install using the Boot Camp drivers and go.

Virtualization

Another solution to the Windows compatibility conundrum is the use of virtualization software. Through virtualization, you can run Windows at near-native speeds at the same time you run Mountain Lion. Some virtualization solutions even go so far as to mix Mac and Windows applications on the same screen, blurring the lines between the operating systems.

Unlike Boot Camp, virtualization runs operating systems simultaneously. Virtualization requires more resources and has lower performance than a Boot Camp solution, but it is more convenient for running an occasional application or game.

Consider three options for virtualizing Windows on your iMac:

1. **VMWare Fusion (www.vmware.com)**—A stable solution from a leader in virtualization software. VMWare Fusion is rock solid and fully compatible with a wide range of virtual "appliances" available for VMWare on Windows.

2. **Parallels Desktop (www.parallels.com)**—The widest range of features available of any virtualization solution for OS X, including near-seamless integration with Mac applications.

3. **VirtualBox (www.virtualbox.org)**—Free virtualization software that offers many of the same features of VMWare and Parallels. VirtualBox is not as polished as the commercial solutions, but it's well supported and has excellent performance.

Other Operating Systems

Virtualization isn't limited to running Windows. You can also run other operating systems, such as Linux, Chrome, and Solaris, using any of these solutions. In fact, if you have enough memory, you can run two, three, or more operating systems simultaneously.

Use the sidebar to quickly access locations, files, and other wireless OS X users.

Navigate and customize your workspace in the Finder.

Receive important information in the Notification Center.

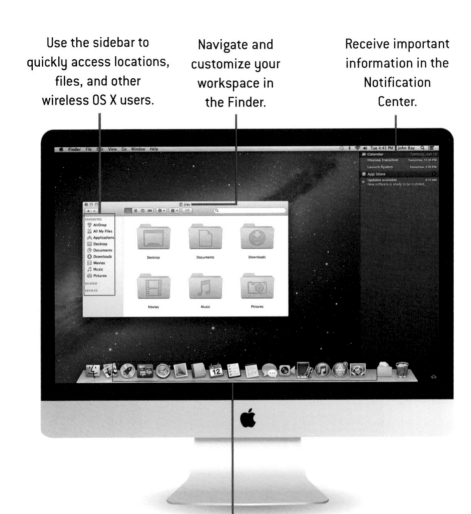

The Dock serves as a launching point for common applications and documents.

In this chapter, you learn how to make efficient use of your iMac's screen space.

→ Organizing files using the Dock

→ Navigating folders within the Dock's Grid view mode

→ Customizing the Finder sidebar and toolbar

→ Viewing the contents of files with Quick Look

→ Searching for files and information with Spotlight

→ Keeping track of application events with Notifications

Managing Your iMac Desktop

With screens up to 27", the iMac offers a huge amount of desktop real estate for all your applications, widgets, utilities, and games. With modern processors like the i7, the iMac lets you run just about anything you want—all at once. Unfortunately, with power comes complexity. If you're like me, you'll quickly find that even a 27" screen fills up with applications, icons, and general clutter.

To keep things tidy, you can take advantage of a variety of time- and space-saving tools built into Mountain Lion that will help keep your desktop clean, make working with files and applications fun and efficient, and keep you up-to-date on how your system and applications are performing. You'll see that, no matter the size of your screen, Mountain Lion can make working with your computer easier and more intuitive.

Organizing in the Dock

The Mountain Lion Dock serves as application launcher, filer, and process manager. It enables you to launch applications and documents with a single click, place documents in folders, and even navigate the contents of folders without using the Finder. It also displays running applications so you can easily switch between them. Configuring your Dock to suit your working style and habits can be a big time saver because you don't have to dig through folders within folders just to find a single file.

The Dock is divided into two parts—applications, and files and folders. Applications are on the left of the faint broken line; files and folders are on the right (or top/bottom, if the Dock is oriented vertically).

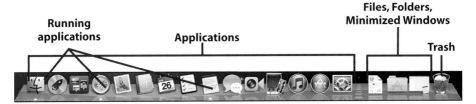

Adding and Removing Items from the Dock

Adding files and folders to the Dock is a simple process of dragging and dropping.

1. Use the Finder to locate the icon you wish to add to the Dock.

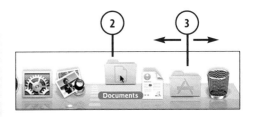

2. Drag the item from the Finder window to the appropriate side of the Dock (apps on the right, docs and folders on the left). As you drag the icon into the Dock, the existing icons will move to make room for the addition. Release your mouse when you're happy with the new location.

3. You can rearrange Dock items at any time by dragging them to another position in the Dock.

4. To remove an icon from the Dock, click and drag the icon out of the Dock.

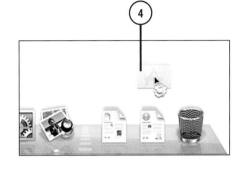

Keep Your Apps Handy

If you start an application and decide you want to keep it in the Dock, click and hold the icon of the running application, and then choose Options, Keep In Dock from the menu that appears.

Using Folders and Stacks in the Dock

Folders that are added to the Dock behave differently from files or applications. When you click a folder residing on the Dock, the contents of the folder are displayed above it in one of three different styles—a Fan, Grid, or List. Additionally, the folder icons themselves can be shown as a simple folder or a stack of files, with your most recent file at the top.

Configuring Folders and Stacks

You can dramatically change the behavior of folders and stacks in the Dock by using the configuration options.

1. After adding a folder to the Dock, right-click or Control-click on the folder to open the menu to configure its behavior.

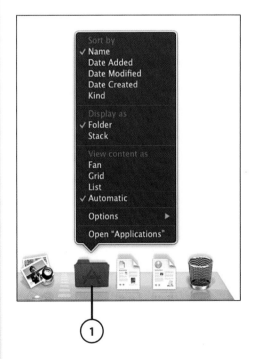

2. Choose to Display as a Folder or Stack to customize the appearance of the icon on the Dock.

3. Choose Fan, Grid, List, or Automatic to set how the content will be displayed when you click the icon in the Dock. The Automatic setting will choose the best option based on the number of items in the folder.

4. Finally, to customize the sorting of the displayed items, choose an option from the Sort By menu.

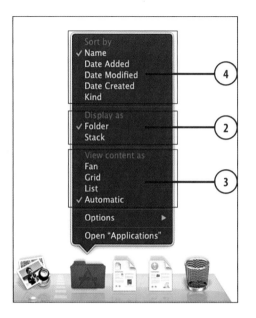

Navigating Files and Folders in Grid Mode

In Mountain Lion, the Folder Grid mode offers the most functionality for navigating your files. You can navigate through a scrolling list of files, and you can open additional folders.

1. Click a Folder in the Dock that has been configured to Grid mode. A grid popover appears above the folder icon.

2. Scroll through the available files, if needed.

3. To navigate into a folder, click the folder's icon.

4. The Grid refreshes to show the contents of the folder.

5. Click the back arrow in the upper-left corner to return to the previous "parent" folder.

6. Click Open in Finder if you wish to open the current folder as a window in the Finder.

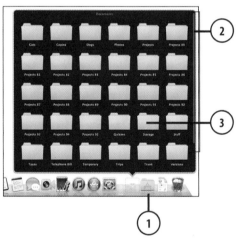

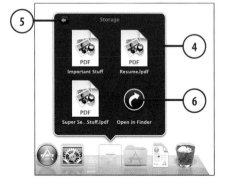

Customizing the Dock's Appearance

The Dock helps keep your desktop nice and tidy by giving you a place to put your commonly used files and folders, but it also takes up a bit of screen space. You can easily customize the Dock's appearance to make it as unobtrusive as possible.

1. Open the System Preferences panel, and click the Dock icon.

2. Use the Size slider to change the size of the Dock.

3. Click the Magnification checkbox. Use the corresponding slider to set the magnification of the icons as you mouse over them in the Dock.

4. Use the radio buttons to control the position of the Dock on the screen.

5. To control the way windows animate to and from the Dock, click the Minimize Windows Using drop-down to choose between the Genie and Scale effects.

6. Check the Minimize Windows into Application Icon checkbox to help conserve space in the Dock by putting minimized windows into their applications' Dock icons.

7. By default, application icons "bounce" in the Dock while they're opening. Uncheck the Animate Opening Applications checkbox to disable this behavior.

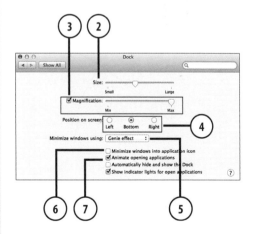

8. Click Automatically Hide and Show the Dock if you'd like the Dock to disappear altogether when you're not using it.

9. Check Show Indicator Lights for Open Applications if you'd like a dot to appear under applications that are running.

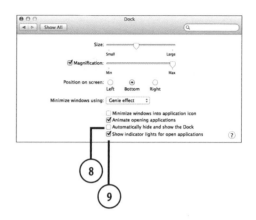

Hiding the Dock

To quickly hide the Dock, press Command+Option+D. You can also easily toggle the position and magnification of the Dock using the Dock submenu from the Apple menu.

Customizing Finder Windows

Like the Dock, Finder windows provide an opportunity to configure shortcuts to information that are accessible via a single click. The Finder sidebar and toolbar can be customized with your own files as well as default system shortcuts.

Configuring the Sidebar's System Shortcuts

To change the sidebar's default shortcuts, you'll need to use the Finder preferences.

1. Open the Finder using its icon in the Dock and choose Finder, Preferences.

2. Click the Sidebar icon at the top of the Finder Preferences window.

3. Use the checkboxes beside Favorites, Shared, and Devices to configure which folders, network computers, and connected hardware should be displayed.

4. Close the Finder Preferences window.

Manually Modifying the Sidebar

In addition to the predefined shortcuts, you can easily add your own icons to the sidebar.

1. To add an icon to the sidebar, first make sure the item's icon is visible in a Finder window.

2. Drag the icon to the Favorites area in the sidebar.

3. A blue line appears to show where the item will be placed. Release your mouse button to add the item to the list.

4. The icon appears in the sidebar.

5. Rearrange the icons in the sidebar by clicking and dragging them up and down.

6. Remove existing sidebar entries by right-clicking (or control-clicking) their icons and choosing Remove from Sidebar.

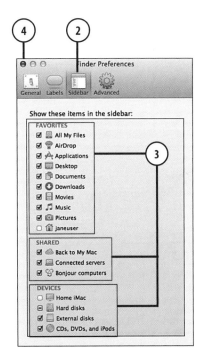

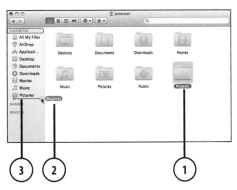

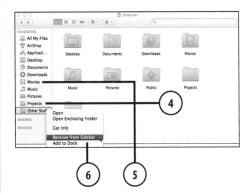

Modifying the Finder Toolbar

Like the sidebar, the Finder window's toolbar can hold shortcuts to files, folders, and applications.

1. Open the Finder window containing the file or folder you want to work with.

2. Drag the icon you wish to add into the toolbar. The other interface elements shift to make room for the new addition.

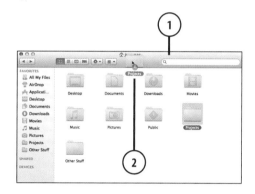

3. To move an icon to a new location on the toolbar, hold the Command key down, and then click and drag. Drag the icon off the toolbar to remove it altogether.

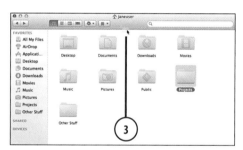

Dragging Allowed!

Toolbar and sidebar items can serve as drag destinations as well as clickable shortcuts. For example, to file a document in a folder, you can drag it to a folder in the sidebar. To save a document to a file server, you can drag it onto a shared drive, and so on.

Arranging and Grouping Files

You'll notice that this book doesn't take a bunch of time to tell you about how to sort files, open folders, and all the typical things you do on a computer. Why? Because they work exactly the way you'd expect on a modern operating system. That said, Mountain Lion introduces some interesting ways of looking at files that you might not be aware of.

Using All My Files

If you've ever wanted to view all the files you have, the All My Files group will help you out. This feature displays, quite literally, *all* your files in your personal iMac account. To view your files, follow these steps:

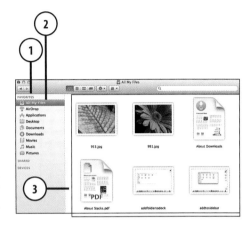

1. Make sure the Favorites section of the Finder sidebar is expanded.

2. Click the All My Files icon, or choose Go, All My Files from the menu bar.

3. All the files that belong to you are shown in the Finder window.

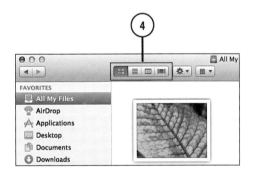

4. Use the view icons to change between icon, list, column, and coverflow views, respectively.

   Granted, this isn't the most exciting feature in the world, but when coupled with the Arrange By feature, it becomes far more interesting.

Arranging a Finder View

You're probably used to clicking a column heading and sorting files by name, date, modified, or other attributes. This is expanded in OS X with the Arrange By feature. Using Arrange By, you can view your files arranged by more "human" categories, such as the files you've opened today, in the last week, and so on.

Follow these steps to arrange any finder window, including the All My Files view:

1. Open the finder view you wish to arrange.

2. Use the Arrange By menu to select a category for grouping your files.

3. Different groups are separated by horizontal lines.

4. When in icon view mode, swipe left or right on the Magic Trackpad or Magic Mouse to scroll through a coverflow-like view of the icons within a grouping.

5. Click the Show All link to turn off the Cover Flow scrolling and show all the items within the window.

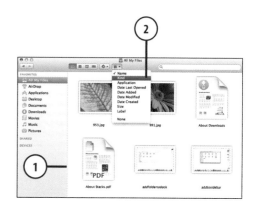

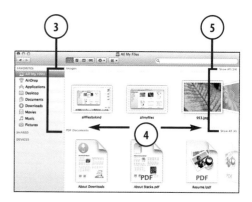

Making Arrangements

To set a default arrangement (among other things) for a folder, choose View, Show View Options from the menubar when viewing the folder.

Previewing Document Contents with Quick Look

Launching applications takes time and resources. Frequently, when you want to open a file, all you really want is to see the contents of the file. Using Mountain Lion's equivalent of X-Ray vision, called Quick Look, you can view many of your documents without the need to open an application.

Viewing a File with Quick Look

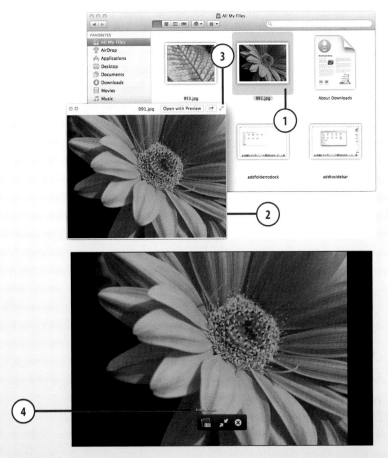

Using Quick Look doesn't require anything more than your mouse and a press of the spacebar.

1. Select a file from the Finder or Desktop by clicking once, but don't open it!

2. Press the spacebar to open Quick Look.

3. Click the double arrows to expand Quick Look to fullscreen.

4. Some files might show additional controls above the preview or below when in fullscreen mode. An image, for example, includes a button to open in the Preview application, or, when in fullscreen mode, add the file to iPhoto.

5. Press the spacebar again to exit Quick Look. Note that if you are in fullscreen mode, you need to push Escape (Esc) on your keyboard or press the onscreen X button to exit fullscreen mode before exiting Quick Look.

Instant Slideshows!

If you start Quick Look on multiple files, you can run a slideshow. The fullscreen Quick Look window includes play, forward, and backward arrows to start and control the slideshow. You can also use an index sheet icon (four squares) to show previews of all the files in a single Quick Look window (also available in windowed mode).

Quick Look even works on music and video files, enabling you to play back media without opening a dedicated application.

Previewing Files Using Finder Icons

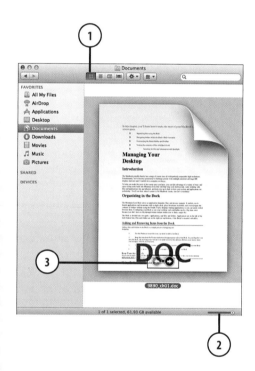

The Finder includes Quick Look-like capability for some files just by mousing over them.

1. To preview a file using icons in Mountain Lion, make sure you're in icon view mode.

2. If you're viewing an image or document file with detailed content, use the window's zoom slider to zoom in on what you want to review.

3. Mouse over the file, and use the controls that appear to navigate the contents of the file. As with Quick Look, even media files can be played in this manner.

Adjust Icon Size

If the icon size slider isn't available, choose View, Show Status Bar from the menu bar. Alternatively, you can adjust a window's icon size by choosing View, Show View Options from the menu bar.

Using Instant-Access Utilities in the Dashboard

Sometimes it is handy to be able to access information and simple utilities without moving your windows around or digging through your Applications folder to find what you need. For simple tasks, you can to use a Dashboard widget.

The Dashboard is an overlay of useful tools, called widgets, which you can call up and dismiss with a single keystroke. Widgets that you add to the Dashboard persist between reboots, so when you've configured your Dashboard the way you like it, it's there to stay!

Activating the Dashboard

The Mountain Lion Dashboard appears and disappears with a keystroke or a click.

1. To activate the Dashboard, click the Dashboard icon in the Dock (or in the Applications folder), or, even easier, swipe with four fingers to the right across your Magic Trackpad.

2. The desktop will slide out of the way and display a default set of Dashboard widgets displays.

3. You can now interact with any of the widgets, including dragging them around to rearrange them, just as you would with normal applications.

4. Exit Dashboard by clicking the arrow in the lower-right of the Dashboard or swiping with four fingers to the left.

Tweaking Your Shortcuts

To configure additional shortcuts to the Dashboard, you can visit the Mission Control system preference panel. This will be discussed further in Chapter 2, "Making the Most of Your iMac's Screen Space."

Adding and Removing Dashboard Widgets

One of the best things about widgets is that you can keep adding them to your screen, and they'll always be there until you choose to remove them.

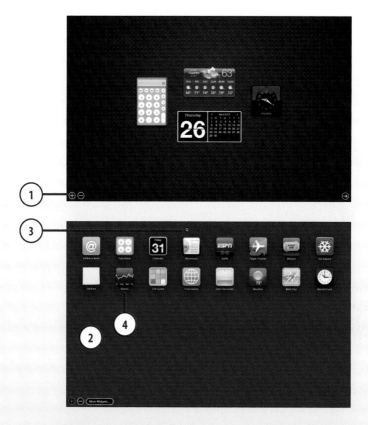

1. To add (or remove) a widget in the Dashboard, start the Dashboard and click the + icon in the lower-left corner.

2. A screen of widgets appears.

3. If you have many widgets, use the search field, if needed, to find what you are looking for.

4. To add a widget to your desktop, click its icon. The list of widgets disappears and you return to the Dashboard with the new widget visible.

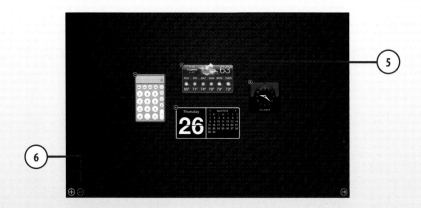

5. To remove a single widget, hold Option, position your mouse over the widget, and click the X icon in the widget's upper-left corner.

6. To remove several widgets, click the – icon in the lower-left corner, and all the widgets will display the X icon in their corner.

Configuring Dashboard Widgets

Widgets are unique applications that each behave differently; but, in general, you configure them one of two ways.

1. Some widgets, when you add them to your screen, automatically prompt you with the information they are expecting. Other widgets must be configured in order to show the proper results.

2. Mouse over a widget you want to configure. A small "i" appears in the corner of the widget. Click the "i" icon.

3. The widget flips over, revealing the configuration details.

Get More Widgets!

To find new widgets outside of the Dashboard, visit www.apple.com/downloads/dashboard/Widgets to download a file in your Downloads folder. You can install them by double-clicking their icons.

Launchpad in Disguise

The view for adding widgets to the Dashboard is really just a feature called Launchpad, but customized to only show Dashboard widgets. You can use the same techniques you'll learn about Launchpad in Chapter 2 to organize and manage your widget library.

Finding Information with Spotlight

When the Finder's file organization features can't help you find what you want, Mountain Lion's amazing Spotlight search system will make it simple. Spotlight can search across files, email messages, even the built-in dictionary to find information.

Searching for Files and Information

Spotlight searches can be started at any time, without needing to launch any additional applications.

1. To start a search, press Command+Space, or click the magnifying glass icon in the upper-right corner of your screen. A search field appears.

2. Begin typing in the search field.

3. As you type, files, images, folders, and even definitions that match your terms will be displayed in a list.

4. Hover your mouse over a result to see a preview.

5. Click a matched item in the list to open the item.

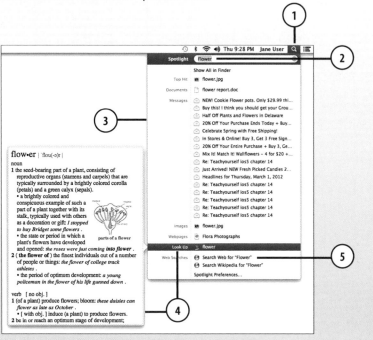

Customizing Spotlight Searching

Spotlight searches can turn up tons of information. More, perhaps, than you'd like. To choose exactly what you want to display, you need to configure the Spotlight System Preferences panel.

1. Open the Spotlight System Preferences panel.

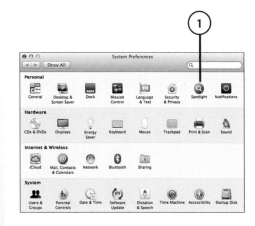

2. Within the Search Results panel, check items you want to be returned as part of the search results. Uncheck the items you want to exclude.

3. To restrict what volumes are searched, click the Privacy button. You can choose to have Spotlight ignore specific folders or disks.

4. Click the + button to choose a folder or disk that you don't want to be searchable. Alternatively, drag folders directly from the Finder into the Privacy list.

5. Use the checkboxes to change how Spotlight is started or disable keyboard shortcuts altogether.

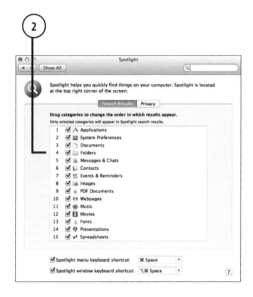

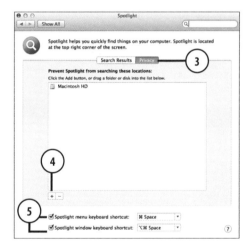

Saving Searches as Smart Folders in the Finder

Spotlight searches for files can be saved and reused in the form of Smart Folders. If you'd like to create a search that shows all your image files—regardless of where they are stored, for example—you can create and save a Show All Images search.

1. Use a Finder window's search field to type the name or content of a file you want to find.

2. Choose what the search should include (such as a file name). The default is to include file content, kinds, and other metadata.

3. Adjust whether you want to search your entire iMac (indicated by the words "This Mac") or just the folder you're currently in.

4. Use the + and – buttons below the search field to add or subtract additional search criteria lines.

5. Use the pop-up menu at the start of each search line to configure search attributes such as file, kinds, or size.

6. To add even more search criteria, choose Other. A window listing all the available search attributes displays. Choose an attribute and click OK.

7. When you're satisfied with your search, click the Save button.

8. You are prompted for a name for the search and where it should be saved.

9. Click Add To Sidebar.

10. Click Save.

11. If you choose to add the search to your sidebar, it is accessible immediately from your Finder window. Otherwise you need to navigate to the saved location and double-click the search's Smart Folder icon to run it again.

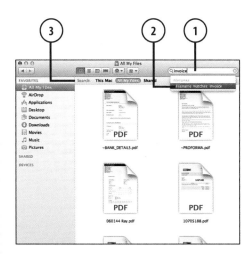

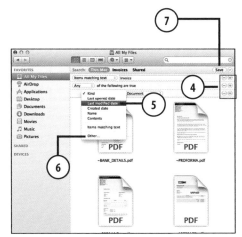

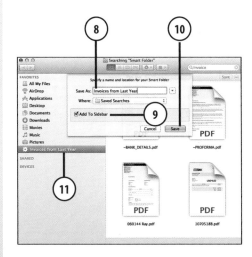

Less Is More

After you've configured a few search criteria beyond the text for the file name or file content, you can erase the search text and Mountain Lion includes all of the files that match your other criteria.

Keeping Track of Application Events with Notifications

At any given time, your iMac has quite a bit going on—mail being checked, potential FaceTime invites, software updates, and more. To keep you in the loop, applications have traditionally displayed alert messages, made sounds, or used any number of other methods to get your attention. In Mountain Lion, applications that you purchase from the App Store (and OS X itself) can present notifications to you in a simple, unified manner.

Receiving Notifications

To receive a notification, you technically don't need to do anything, but you should know what to expect:

1. Notifications, as they occur, appear along the right side of the display.

2. Most notifications go away after a few seconds and require no interaction.

3. Some may include options to immediately react to the notification. Clicking the buttons performs the action described.

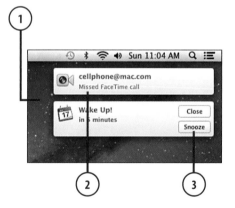

Viewing the Notification Center

If a notification "goes away" before you have a chance to read it, you can catch up with the latest notifications in the Notification Center. To access the Notification Center, follow these steps:

1. Click the bulleted list icon in the upper-right corner of the menu bar. You can also open the Notification Center by sliding two fingers to the left, starting off the right side of the Magic Trackpad.

2. The desktop slides over to reveal the Notification Center.

3. Clicking a notification reacts appropriately—clicking an event reminder, for example, opens the Calendar application and high-lights the event.

4. To dismiss an application's notifi-cations, click the X icon in the upper-right corner of its list of notifications.

5. To close the Notification Center, click on the Desktop, or slide two fingers to the right on the trackpad.

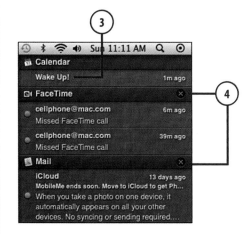

Customizing the Notification Display

How each application presents notifications (or if they present notifications at all) can be customized in OS X. To change your notification preferences, do the following:

1. Open the Notifications System Preferences panel.

2. Choose an Application to customize from the list on the left.

3. Use the App Store alert style buttons to choose from None (no visual at all), Banners (automatically close), and Alerts (can request interaction, if needed).

4. Uncheck Show in Notification Center if you prefer to not receive any notifications (visual or audio) from the application.

5. Use the Recent Items pop-up menu to choose how many notifications are shown at a time.

6. Check the Badge App Icon with Notification Count to show the count of notifications (such as new messages) on the application's icon.

7. Check Play Sound When Receiving Notifications to enable the application to provide an audio alert.

8. Select whether to Sort Notification Center manually or according to the time a notification was received. If sorting manually, you can drag the icons up and down in the application list to choose how they appear in the Notification Center.

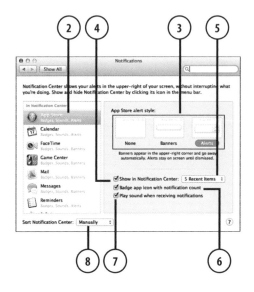

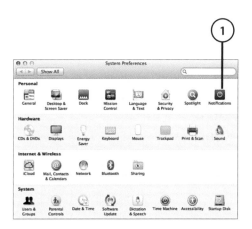

Gone but Not Lost

If you uncheck "Show in Notification Center" for an application, it disappears from the list of applications to configure. What if you want to get it back? Never fear—it didn't really disappear—it was just placed at the bottom of the app list, in a section titled "Not In Notification Center."

Quick Settings Access Within Notification Center

In the lower-right corner of the Notification Center is a button labeled with a small gear icon. Clicking this button opens the Notification Center preferences.

Activating Do Not Disturb Mode

If you're like me, you probably have a zillion different things happening on your computer and (potentially) several dozen apps wanting to tell you something via notification. For the times you'd prefer not to hear all the sounds and see the notification windows, you can activate a Do Not Disturb mode that lasts until the next morning. Begin by opening the Notification Center, and then follow these steps:

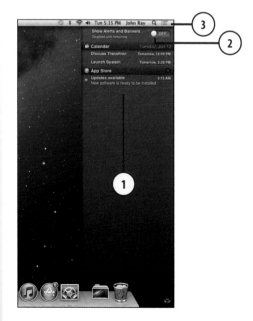

1. Scroll the Notification Center content down.

2. An On/Off button is revealed. Click Off to quiet your notifications or On to let them be seen and heard.

3. The Notification Center icon becomes dimmed when in this mode.

Navigate Desktop spaces
and applications.

Create new spaces to
make room for your work.

View active applications and
windows in Mission Control.

In this chapter, you learn how to take control of your applications and windows, including:

→ Find your way around Mission Control

→ Manage applications and windows

→ Create new spaces

→ Launch applications with Launchpad

→ Create application groups in Launchpad

→ Uninstall applications through Launchpad

→ Manage auto open and save features

Making the Most of Your iMac's Screen Space

As applications become more complex, so does the task of managing them. Software is installed everywhere, windows are spread out over your desktop, and just trying to find your way through the maze of information overload can be nightmarish. Mountain Lion attempts to bring the madness under control by way of Mission Control.

Mission Control, combined with features such as Spaces, Launchpad, full-screen apps, auto application, and window restoration, makes it easy to navigate the most cluttered computer. The biggest problem? Many of these features are hidden until you invoke them. In this chapter, you learn how to do just that!

Swimming in a Sea of Application Windows with Mission Control

One of the big benefits of modern operating systems is that they enable you to run multiple applications at once. Unfortunately, our screen real estate isn't growing as quickly as the amount of "stuff" we can have on our screen at the same time. To help manage the ever-expanding collection of windows that we need to work within, Apple provides Mission Control as part of OS X Mountain Lion. Mission Control helps you view your running apps, see the windows they have open, and even expand the amount of desktop real estate you have available.

Opening and Closing Mission Control

To manage Mission Control and access its features, follow these instructions:

1. Slide three fingers up the Magic Trackpad, double-tap two fingers on the Magic Mouse, or press the Mission Control key (F3) on your keyboard. Mission Control opens. Spaces appear on the top; the current space is in the center of the screen.

2. Slide three fingers down on the trackpad, double-tap two fingers on the mouse, or press the Mission Control key again. Mission Control closes.

In Mission Control terms, a "space" is a single screenful of information. It can be your Dashboard screen, your typical desktop, a full-screen app, or even additional desktop views that you create.

Docking Mission Control

If you prefer to start Mission Control by clicking, you can use the Mission Control icon (found in the Dock).

Navigating Applications and Windows

When you start Mission Control, your current space (probably your desktop, if you're starting Mission Control for the first time) is front and center, along with representations of each app running in the space and its windows.

To switch between applications and their windows, do the following:

1. Start Mission Control.

2. Click an application icon to exit Mission Control and bring the application to the front.

3. Click a window to exit Mission Control and bring the chosen window to the front.

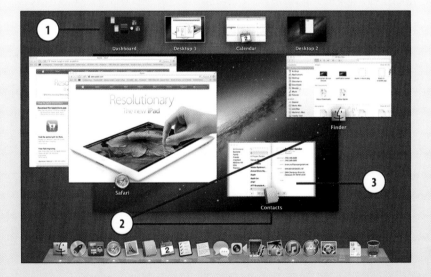

4. To preview the contents of a window, position your pointer over the window and then press the spacebar. Press the spacebar again to hide the preview.

Creating and Populating a New Space

Modern applications look like the cockpit controls of advanced aircraft; it can be overwhelming finding your way around a single application—let alone 10. With Mission Control, however, you can create new desktop spaces dedicated to whatever applications you'd like. To do so, start Mission Control and follow these steps:

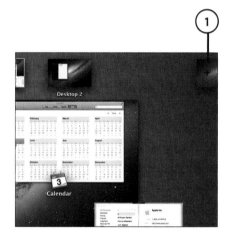

1. Move your mouse to the upper-right corner. A "+" button appears as your mouse approaches the corner; click it.

2. A new space is created and a thumbnail of its contents is added to the top of Mission Control.

3. Drag application icons or even individual windows from the current space to the thumbnail of the new space.

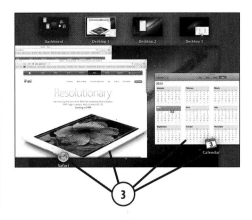

Switching Between Spaces

After you've created a new space, you can switch to it via Mission Control or using a trackpad gesture:

1. Start Mission Control.

2. Click the space thumbnail you want to display, or swipe left or right with three fingers to move between spaces.

3. Click on the background to exit Mission Control.

Even Faster Space Switching

The fastest way to switch between Mission Control spaces is without even starting Mission Control. Swipe left or right with three fingers on your Magic Trackpad (or two fingers on the Magic Mouse) at any time to move between spaces.

Closing a Space

It's so easy to create spaces, you might find yourself with some extra ones you need to get rid of. To close out a space, follow these steps:

1. Start Mission Control.

2. Position your cursor over a space.

3. After a few seconds, an X appears in the upper-left corner of the space thumbnail. Click the X to close the space. Any windows within it move back to the primary desktop space.

Creating Full-Screen Application Spaces

Spaces are great for providing more, um, space for your windowed applications, but they also serve as a "container" for your full-screen apps. Rather than a full-screen application eating up one of your desktop spaces, it automatically creates a new dedicated space when it starts and removes it when it stops.

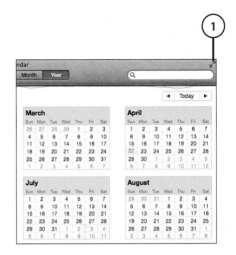

1. Click the double-arrow icon in the upper-right corner of the application window to enter full-screen mode.

2. A new space is created and is visible in Mission Control.

3. Switch to and from the space exactly as you would any other. When you're done using the full-screen app, either quit the application or exit full-screen mode. The space is automatically removed from Mission Control.

Choosing Between Application Windows

When you just need to navigate your windows, the Mission Control Application windows option comes in handy. Using this, you can show all your application windows, or just the windows for a specific program, with a single click.

1. To display all the windows open within an application, click and hold an active application's icon in the dock and choose Show All Windows. Alternatively, press Control+down arrow.

2. The screen refreshes to show miniature versions of your windows. Minimized windows appear in the bottom portion of the display; active windows appear at the top.

3. Press the Tab key to switch between active applications, limiting the miniaturized windows to the highlighted application.

4. Click a window to select it and move it to the front.

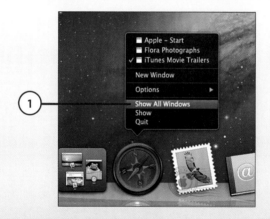

Showing the Desktop

Sometimes you need quick access to the files on your desktop, and rearranging windows (or using the Finder's Hide menu) isn't very efficient. Mission Control's Show Desktop feature comes in handy here:

1. To clear all the windows off the screen so that you can temporarily work with the desktop, press F11 (you need to hold down the function key).

2. You can now work within the desktop with no obstructions. Press F11 again to return the windows to their original positions.

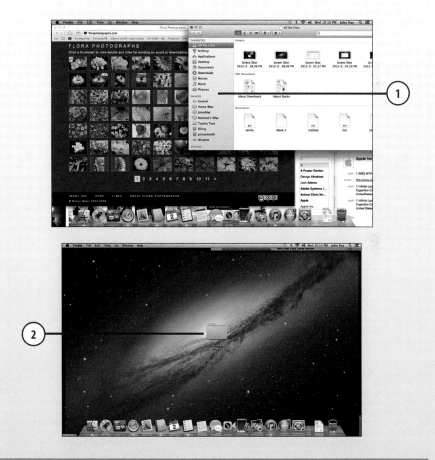

If Only Real Life Were So Easy...

To quickly drop a file from the Finder into another application (such as an attachment into an email message), start dragging a file while the desktop is cleared, press F11 to return the windows to the screen, and then finish dragging and dropping the file into an application.

Configuring Mission Control Features and Shortcuts

If you have a specific way of working and want to customize how Mission Control or any of its features is activated, just follow these steps:

1. Open the System Preferences application, and click the Mission Control panel icon.

2. If you'd like Dashboard to appear on top of your current space rather than in its own space, uncheck Show Dashboard As a Space.

3. Uncheck Automatically Rearrange Spaces Based on Most Recent Use if you prefer that Mountain Lion keep your spaces in the same order you add them, regardless of your usage patterns.

4. In most cases, leave When Switching to an Application, Switch to a Space with Open Windows for the Application checkbox checked. This indicates that when you switch to an application (using the Dock or Command+Tab), you automatically switch to the space that contains its open windows.

5. If you prefer application windows to not be grouped under their application icon in the Mission Control display, uncheck Group Windows by Application.

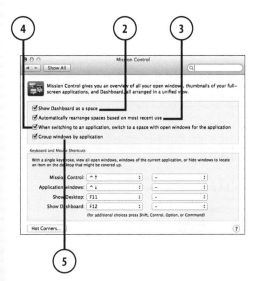

6. At the bottom of the panel, use the pop-up menus to configure keyboard and mouse button combinations to invoke the Mission Control features and Dashboard.

7. To trigger these features by moving the mouse to the screen corners, click the Hot Corners button.

8. Use the pop-up menus beside each screen corner to choose among the different options. After you've made a selection, just move the mouse into that corner to invoke the feature.

9. Click OK when finished.

10. Close the system preferences.

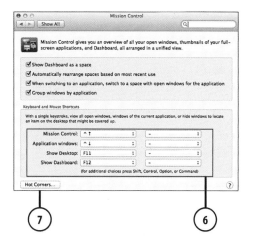

Remember Your Gestures!

As you know, you control Mission Control through gestures, and these aren't set in stone! Use the Trackpad or Mouse System Preferences panels to configure the gestures used by Mission Control.

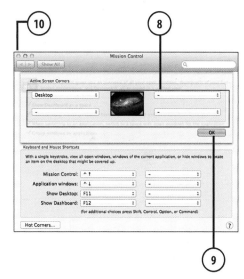

Managing and Launching Applications with Launchpad

Whereas Mission Control helps you find your way through your windows, Mountain Lion's Launchpad eliminates the need to open them. Launchpad brings iOS application management to your Mac. Instead of digging through folders to launch an application, you simply start Launchpad and all your installed apps are visible in one place. No digging required.

Starting Launchpad

Like Mission Control, Apple wants to keep Launchpad at the ready. Unlike other applications, it takes no time to start and can be invoked through a gesture:

1. Open Launchpad by performing a pinching gesture with your thumb and three fingers on the Magic Trackpad. Alternatively, press the Launchpad key (F4), or click the Launchpad icon in the dock or in the Applications folder.

2. The Launchpad appears, blurring out your background.

3. Reverse the pinching gesture, or click on the background to exit Launchpad.

Navigating Launchpad

If you've used an iPad or an iPhone, you immediately know how to navigate Launchpad. If you haven't, don't worry—it takes about a minute to learn everything you'll need to know.

1. Open Launchpad to access your applications.

2. Click an application icon to launch it.

3. Click a folder icon to open it.

4. Click outside the folder to close it.

5. There can be multiple pages of icons, represented by the dots at the center bottom of the screen.

6.   Move between pages by swiping left or right with your fingers, clicking the dots, or clicking and dragging left or right.

Searching Launchpad

If you can't find an application you're looking for, you can easily search for it directly in Launchpad.

1. Open Launchpad.

2. Click to type in the search field.

3. Enter a few characters of the name of the application you're looking for.

4. Launchpad refreshes to show the search results. The best match is highlighted.

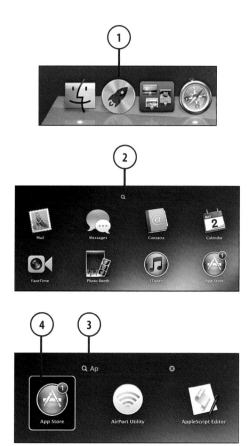

Rearranging Icons

The Launchpad display is completely customizable. To rearrange the icons on your screen, follow these instructions:

1. Open Launchpad.

2. Click and drag the icon to a new location—even a new page. Release the mouse to place the icon.

It's Not All Good

A MAC DISGUISED AS AN iPAD

Launchpad suffers from a bit of an identity crisis. It follows the same "click and hold to enter icon wiggle mode," just like iOS. This behavior, however, isn't necessary for rearranging or even deleting icons as it is in iOS. Whether you use it is up to you and completely superficial. You can even make the icons wiggle manually by pressing and holding the Option key on your keyboard.

Creating New Folders

Unlike folders in the Finder, Launchpad folders are created on the fly and automatically disappear when all their contents are removed. To create a folder in Launchpad, follow these steps:

1. Open Launchpad.

2. Drag an icon on top of another icon that you want to group it with.

3. A new folder is created and opened, and the icons are added.

4. Click the title of the folder to rename it.

5. Click on the background outside the folder to close it.

The Folder That Wasn't There

Folders you create or delete in Launchpad do not alter your file system. They are purely logical groupings and do not affect the location of your actual files.

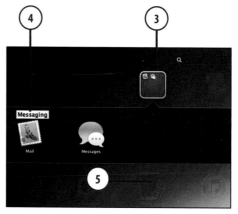

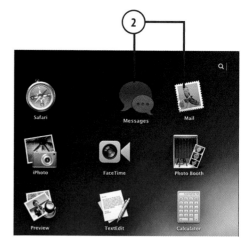

Deleting Folders

To remove a folder from Launchpad, follow these instructions:

1. Open Launchpad.

2. Click the folder that you want to remove.

3. The folder opens.

4. Drag each item out of the folder.

5. When you reach the last item, the folder vanishes automatically.

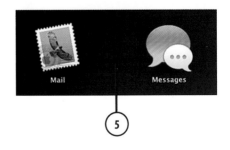

Deleting Applications

In addition to providing a quick way to access your applications, Launchpad offers an easy way to uninstall applications that you've installed from the Mac App Store. (See Chapter 9, "Installing and Managing Software on Your iMac," for details.)

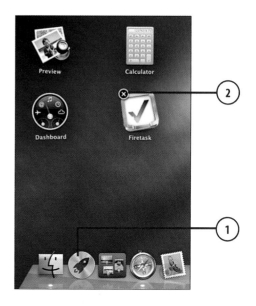

1. Open Launchpad.

2. Drag an application you want to uninstall to the trash. Alternatively, click and hold on the icon until an X appears in the upper left, and click the X.

3. You are prompted to confirm the deletion.

4. Click Delete. The application is uninstalled from your system. You can reinstall it through the App Store if needed.

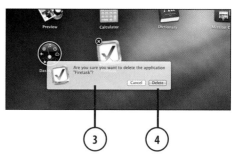

It's Not All Good

THE NOT-SO-UNIVERSAL UNINSTALLER

You can only use Launchpad for uninstalling applications you've added through the Mac App Store. To remove other apps, you need to revert to the old-school method of using an uninstaller (if one came with the application) or manually dragging the application files to the trash.

Managing Auto Open and Save Features

Mountain Lion offers some unique features that save you time when you're booting your system after some downtime, starting an application you use frequently, or even just saving files. Although these can be useful, they can also be disconcerting to users who expect more conventional behavior— such as explicitly choosing when to open applications and save files.

Toggling Application Auto Open

By default, applications and windows open at login exactly as you had them when you shut down your computer. This is a nifty feature, but it also means you might have software starting at boot that you didn't intend. You can toggle this feature on and off by following these steps:

1. Choose Log Out from the Apple menu.

2. Uncheck Reopen Windows When Logging Back In to disable automatic application startup, or check the box to re-enable it.

3. Click Log Out or Cancel. Your preference will be maintained.

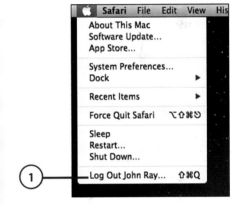

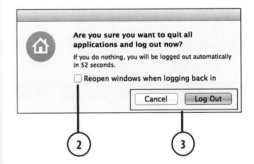

Setting Window Restoration

In addition to restoring applications, Mountain Lion can restore the open files and windows that you were using when you quit an application. By default, this feature is turned off, but you can easily toggle it on.

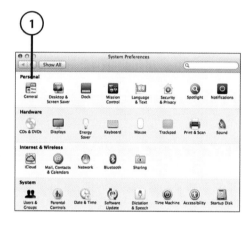

1. Open the System Preferences application and click the General icon.

2. Uncheck Close Windows When Quitting an Application. This causes your applications to save their current state when they quit. Check the box to disable the behavior.

3. Close the system preferences.

Temporarily Enable or Disable Window Saving

If you're not sure you want to use the window restoration feature, or you don't want to use it with specific applications, you can temporarily toggle it on and off. To do this, just hold down the Option key when quitting your application. The Quit menu selection changes to Quit and Keep Windows or Quit and Close All Windows, depending on your setting in the general preference panel.

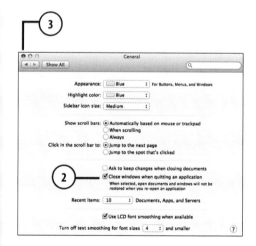

Enabling Manual File Saving

When you start working in Mountain Lion, you'll notice something "missing" when you work with files: Frequently, you aren't asked to save them when you close them. Mountain Lion automatically saves your files, even if you prefer that it didn't. To change this, complete these steps:

1. Open the System Preferences application and click the General icon.

2. Check Ask to Keep Changes When Closing Documents.

3. Close the system preferences.

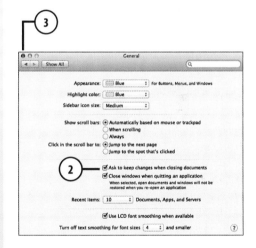

Use the Wi-Fi
status menu to find
and join wireless
networks.

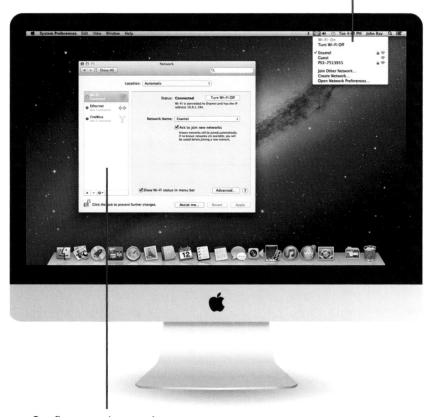

Configure and control your
iMac network interfaces in
the Network System
Preferences panel.

In this chapter, you learn how to get your iMac online, including tasks like:

→ Connecting to wired networks
→ Connecting to secure wireless networks
→ Configuring network address, DNS, and routing information
→ Verifying network connections
→ Creating VPN connections
→ Managing multiple connections with Locations

Connecting Your iMac to a Network

Being connected to a network gives you access to information, files, and services such as email or the web. Your iMac comes with the latest networking technology—802.11n Wi-Fi and gigabit Ethernet, making it a snap to connect to existing wired or wireless networks.

In this chapter, we explore the connection options available to you on your iMac.

Connecting to a Wired Network

The most common type of network connection in the business world is a wired Ethernet connection. The cables used to connect to the network look like oversized phone connectors and, as luck has it, plug directly into your iMac's Ethernet port. iMac supports gigabit Ethernet—capable of exchanging information at extremely high speeds.

It's Not All Good

There aren't many things that upset a network administrator more than a person who attempts to guess at the proper configuration of his computer when attaching it to a network. An improperly configured computer can potentially disrupt an entire network, so please make sure you have all of the information you need from your administrator or ISP before attempting the things in this chapter!

Making an Ethernet (Wired) Connection

On a network that is set up to automatically configure your computer using DHCP, the most complicated thing you need to do is plug in the network cable!

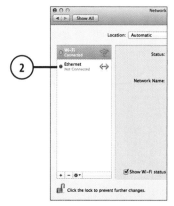

1. Open the System Preferences panel and click the Network icon.

2. The network preference panel displays. All of the active network interfaces are listed here. Red dots indicate that no connection is present on the interface.

3. Plug the network cable into the back of your iMac. After a few seconds, the interface should update, showing a green dot for an active connection. The pane to the right of the interfaces displays the information that your computer is using to communicate online.

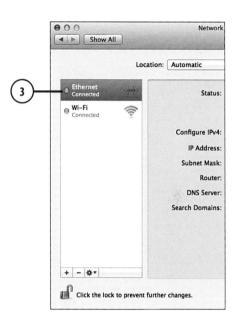

Things Not Working?

If your network connection is showing a yellow dot, you might have to configure your settings manually, or if you're using a DSL connection, you might have to use PPPoE to make your connection. If this is the case, skip ahead to "Manually Configuring Network Settings."

If, however, you see a red dot, you need to check your cable or the device you're plugging into because your Macintosh can't detect *any* type of network.

Connecting to a Wireless Network

When wireless network cards first started appearing, they were limited to portable computers. Over the past decade, however, Wi-Fi has taken off as a networking standard for both laptops and desktop computers. Current wireless network speeds are approaching wired connections, so, slowly but surely, wireless is taking over.

Using the built-in AirPort wireless card in your iMac, you can connect to almost any type of wireless network.

>>> Go Further

WHAT TYPE OF WIRELESS NETWORKS CAN MY iMAC USE?

The latest iMacs can make use of 802.11n, 802.11a, 802.11b, and 802.11g networks! This represents the full range of consumer and business wireless networking standards. Your iMac is also capable of talking to a wide range of 802.1x authentication protocols and encryption methods. Setup is usually automatic, so you won't need to know the specifics unless your administrator tells you otherwise.

To learn more about wireless security, read http://en.wikipedia.org/wiki/Wireless_security.

Making a Wireless Connection

Apple makes life easy. Your iMac comes ready (and able) to connect to wireless networks with a minimal amount of fuss.

Finding and Connecting to a Network

If you haven't already made a wired connection, your iMac's Wi-Fi (wireless) card will be active and searching for networks that it can connect to.

1. If your iMac finds an available network, it prompts you to make a connection.

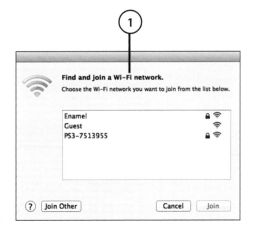

①

Find and join a Wi-Fi network.
Choose the Wi-Fi network you want to join from the list below.

Enamel	🔒 📶
Guest	📶
PS3–7513955	🔒 📶

⑦ Join Other   Cancel   Join

2. Choose the network name to connect to. Note that the network signal strength and security are denoted by icons to the right of the name. If a lock is present, the network requires authentication. This is covered in "Authenticating on a Wireless Network" later in this chapter.

3. Click Join to connect to the selected network.

4. If you've been given the specific name of a network (called an SSID) by a network administrator and it doesn't appear in the available networks list, click the Join Other button to enter the name and attempt to find the network.

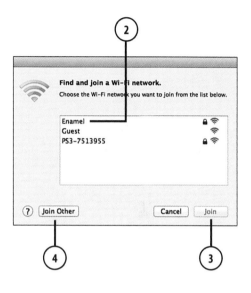

Things Not Working?

If you've successfully connected to a wireless network, but it doesn't seem to work, you may need to configure the network settings manually. Keep in mind that you need to get those settings from your wireless network administrator.

If this is the case, skip ahead to the "Manually Configuring Network Settings" task.

Manually Choosing a Wireless Connection

If you want to manually choose a wireless network connection, you can use the Wi-Fi menu in your menu bar.

1. The Wi-Fi menu displays a list of all of the available wireless access points, their signal strengths, and their security requirements.

2. Choose the network name to which you want to connect from the list. If you're connecting to a network that shows a lock icon, it requires authentication. This topic is covered in "Authenticating on a Wireless Network" later in this chapter.

3. If you want to connect to a network using only its name, choose Join Other Network to enter the name and attempt the connection.

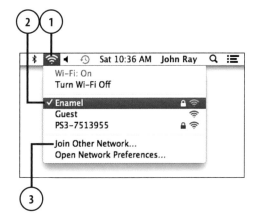

Alternate Wi-Fi Configuration

If you'd prefer to manage all your network connection information in one place, you can access these same options by opening the Network System Preference panel and selecting the Wi-Fi interface.

You can also use the Show Wi-Fi Status in Menu Bar checkbox to remove or add (if it's missing) the Wi-Fi status menu item.

Authenticating on a Wireless Network

When your iMac connects to an open (unsecured) network, it works immediately. If you're connecting to a network that is secure, however, you need to authenticate, which means you need to provide a password or other identifying information. This requirement is usually denoted by a lock icon in the Network panel.

1. If you attempt to connect to a network that has a security requirement, you are prompted for a password.

2. Enter the password (or other information, depending on the security settings).

3. Click Show Password if you'd like to see the password instead of dots while you type.

4. To make sure that the network can be used again in the future without requiring that you retype the password, check the Remember This Network button.

5. Click Join to finish and authenticate to the network.

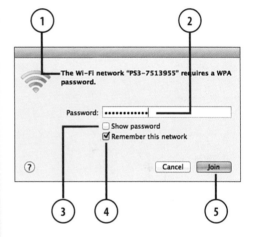

Disabling (and Enabling) Wireless Networking

Not everyone *wants* to have wireless networking always enabled. It can potentially open you up to network attacks on poorly secured wireless networks. Disabling the Wi-Fi network interface, and re-enabling it, is just a menu option away.

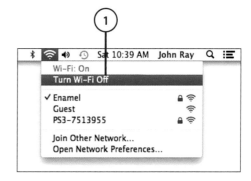

1. To disable the Wi-Fi card, choose Turn Wi-Fi Off from the Wi-Fi status menu.

2. The Wi-Fi menu updates to an outline of the usual multiline symbol. The Wi-Fi hardware is now powered down.

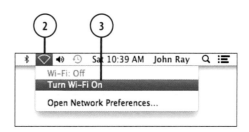

3. To re-enable the Wi-Fi card, choose Turn Wi-Fi On from the Wi-Fi status menu.

Manually Configuring Network Settings

Network connections, when automatically configured, seem to work almost like magic. Your computer finds a signal (wired or wireless), makes a connection, and everything just "works." Behind the scenes, however, there are a handful of network settings that make this happen. If a network doesn't support auto-configuration, using a protocol known as DHCP, you need to make these settings manually.

Your network administrator needs to provide the following settings in order to manually set up your network:

- **IP Address**—A numerical address that uniquely identifies your computer.

- **Subnet Mask**—A value that helps your computer determine what network it is on.

- **Router**—The address of a device that moves network traffic between other local computers and remote networks (such as the Internet).

- **DNS**—The address of a device providing domain name lookups to your network. This service translates human-readable names (such as www.apple.com) into IP addresses and vice-versa.

- **Proxy Settings**—A device that sends and receives network traffic on your behalf, acting as a middleman for services.

Configuring TCP/IP and Proxy Settings

To manually change your TCP/IP and Proxy settings, follow these simple steps:

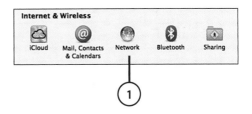

1. Open System Preferences and click the Network panel icon.

2. The network panel opens, showing all the available interfaces. Click the interface you wish to configure (usually Ethernet or Wi-Fi).

3. Click the Advanced button to view the full manual interface for network settings.

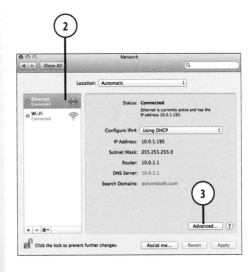

4. The Advanced configuration screen appears. Click TCP/IP in the button bar to access the common TCP/IP network settings.

5. Use the Configure IPv4 drop-down menu to change your settings to be configured Manually.

6. Enter the IP address, Subnet Mask, and Router, as provided by your network administrator.

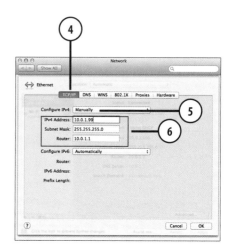

7. Click DNS in the button bar to change your domain name server settings.

8. Click the + button below the DNS Servers list to add a new server to the list. Your ISP or network administrator usually provides at least two addresses to use; be sure to type it exactly as provided. (Use the – button to remove unused DNS Servers. Search Domains are not required unless specified by your administrator.)

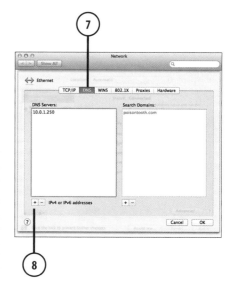

9. If your network requires the use of a proxy, click the Proxies button in the button bar. If not, skip ahead to step 13.

10. Click the checkboxes beside the protocols that you want to configure.

11. Click the protocol names to configure each proxy. Setup fields appear to the right of the protocol list.

12. Enter the proxy information as provided by your network administrator.

13. Click OK to exit advanced setup.

14. Click Apply to activate and begin using your new network settings.

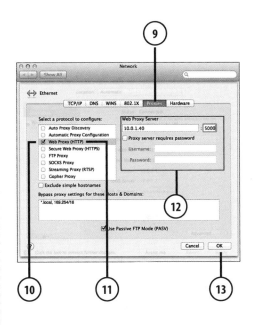

Switching to Automatic Configuration

To revert back to the default "automatic" configuration of a network interface, you need to select Using DHCP from the Configure IPv4 drop-down menu.

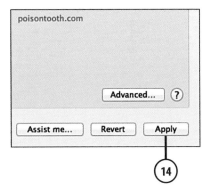

Activating PPPoE for DSL Connections

In some cases, most typically when using a DSL modem, you need to activate PPPoE (Point-to-Point Protocol over Ethernet) in order to make a connection.

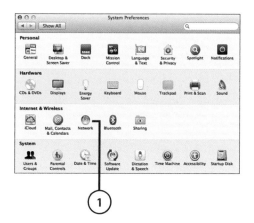

1. Open System Preferences and click the Network panel icon.

2. Select your active Ethernet Interface.

3. Choose Create PPPoE Service from the Configure IPv4 drop-down menu.

4. Choose a name for the connection. (The default, PPPoE, is fine.)

5. Click Done.

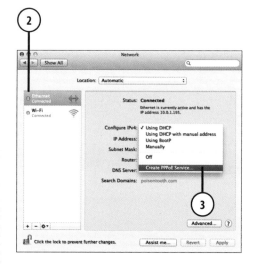

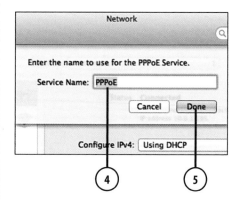

6. Enter the PPPoE information as provided by your ISP. Choose to remember the password if desired.

7. Click the Show PPPoE Status in Menu Bar checkbox to add a convenient menu option for connecting and disconnecting to the service.

8. Click the Advanced button.

9. Click PPP to open a variety of options for configuring your connection.

10. To help maintain a stable connection, check Connect Automatically When Needed and uncheck the Disconnect checkboxes if desired.

11. If required by your ISP, configure the TCP/IP settings manually as described in the "Configuring TCP/IP and Proxy Settings" task.

12. Click OK to close the Advanced settings.

13. Click Connect to begin using the PPPoE interface you've configured.

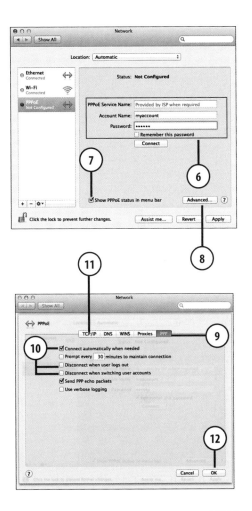

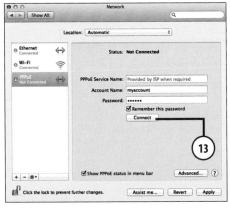

Creating Virtual Private Network Connections

In the modern world, it's difficult not to bring your work home with you. Your iMac makes an excellent workstation for both business and school use and is more than capable of handling serious tasks. Unfortunately, network security requirements frequently force businesses and schools to disable direct access to their networks. This limits your ability to access printers, file servers, and other critical resources that you might need to work remotely.

Thankfully, many organizations also provide Virtual Private Network (VPN) servers. Using a VPN server, your iMac can use its current network connection (wired or wireless) to securely connect to your company's network. You can access all of the same resources that you see when you're sitting in your office chair.

Creating a VPN Connection

Mountain Lion supports three types of VPN connections—L2TP, PPTP, and Cisco IPSec. You need to find out from your network administrator which option is right for you, along with the settings you need to make the connection.

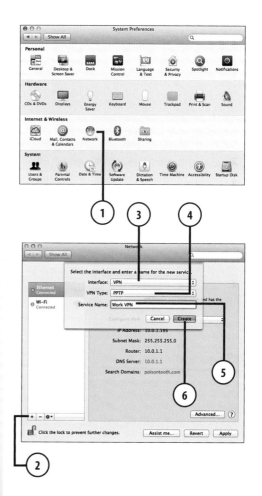

1. Create a new VPN connection by opening the System Preferences and clicking the Network icon.

2. Click the + button at the bottom of the interfaces pane.

3. Choose VPN as the interface.

4. Set the VPN type to the type specified by your network administrator.

5. Enter a meaningful name for the VPN service, such as "Work VPN."

6. Click Create.

7. A new VPN interface is created and added to the list of network interfaces. Make sure the VPN interface is highlighted.

8. Configuration options appear on the right side of the network preference panel. Enter the server address and account information provided by your network administrator.

9. Click the Show VPN Status in Menu Bar checkbox. This adds a menu item to the menu bar so you can quickly connect and disconnect from a VPN.

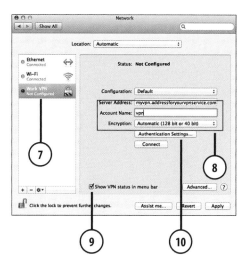

10. Click the Authentication Settings button.

11. You are prompted for a method of authentication. Enter a password or choose one of the other available options as directed by your network administrator

12. Click OK.

13. If you have been given specific network settings by your network administrator, click the Advanced button and enter the options as described in "Manually Configuring Network Settings."

14. Click the Connect button to connect to the VPN.

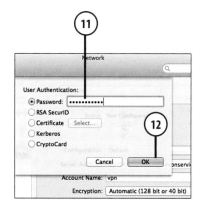

Managing Your VPN Connection

If you've chosen to show the VPN status in your menu bar, you can use the menu item to quickly connect and disconnect at any time. In addition, you can show the amount of time you've been connected, in case connection charges apply.

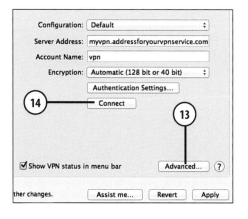

Managing Multiple Connections with Locations and Configurations

If you work in a business or academic environment, you might find that you need to juggle network settings depending on what you are trying to accomplish. My workplace, for example, includes a wired network and three wireless networks—each providing a different level of access and a different way of viewing network resources. Depending on the day, I might need to connect to the intranet wireless, guest wireless, or just use a wired connection.

To help keep things straight, Mountain Lion includes Configurations and Locations—two important tools for keeping multiple sets of network information.

Creating Configurations

To create a configuration, do the following:

1. To create a configuration (if supported by your network interface), first open the System Preferences and click the Network icon.

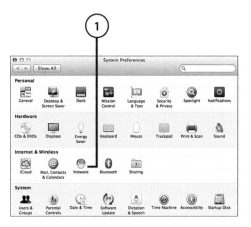

2. Click the interface for which you want to create a new configuration.

3. Using the Configuration pop-up menu, choose Add Configuration.

4. Enter a name for the configuration.

5. Click Create. You may now configure the network interface as described in the chapter.

6. Your new settings are stored and accessible under the configuration name you provided so that you can easily switch from one to another. (You can also remove or rename configurations under this menu.)

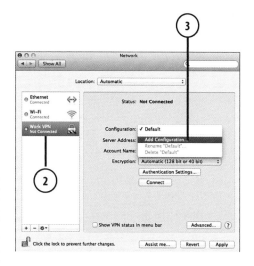

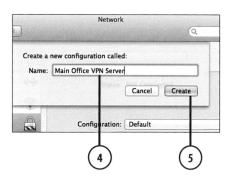

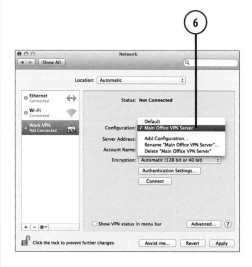

Adding and Using Locations

Locations are like configurations on steroids. Lots of steroids. Using locations, you can create entirely new sets of network interfaces and options and switch between them easily.

1. Open the System Preferences and click the Network icon.

2. The default location of Automatic is set at the top of the network panel.

3. Choose Edit Locations from the Location drop-down menu.

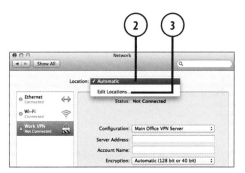

4. A dialog box that lists any configured locations displays.

5. Click the + button to add an entry for a new location. (Use – to remove locations you no longer want.)

6. Type a name to describe the location, such as "Office Intranet."

7. Click Done.

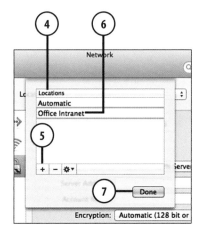

8. All your network settings are now set to their defaults for the new location. All VPN connections and other interfaces are gone. You are, in effect, starting fresh with configuring your iMac network setup.

9. Configure your network settings as described in this chapter.

10. After you've completed your setup, you can switch between locations using the Location drop-down menu within the System Preferences Network panel. Remember that you can return to your original network settings by choosing the location named "Automatic."

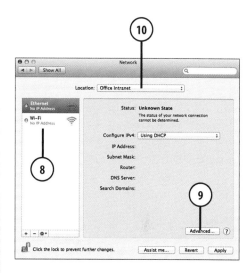

Seeking Automated Network Assistance

The Mountain Lion operating system provides a few automated tools to help you configure and diagnose your iMac's network settings. Be aware that the automated tools might not be able to fully set up your connection; and if you have complicated network configurations, you might want to manage the settings manually anyway. Let's review what you need to do to use these tools.

Launching Diagnostics

To launch the diagnostics system, follow these steps:

1. Open the System Preferences panel and click the Network icon.

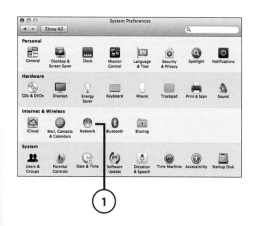

2. Click the Assist Me button at the bottom of the window.

3. Click Diagnostics in the dialog box that displays.

4. Choose the Network interface to run diagnostics on. If you've configured locations, you are first prompted to choose your location.

5. Click Continue.

6. Review the results and follow the onscreen instructions.

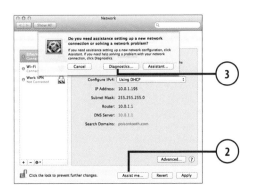

Launching the Setup Assistant

To launch the setup assistant, follow these steps:

1. Open the System Preferences panel and click the Network icon.

2. Click the Assist Me button at the bottom of the window.

3. Click Assistant in the dialog box that appears.

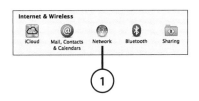

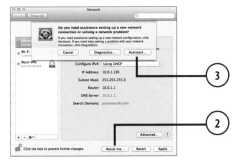

4. Provide a location where you will be using the network connection. This process creates a new location, as described in the previous "Adding and Using Locations" section.

5. Click Continue.

6. Choose the type of connection you are making.

7. Click Continue.

8. Follow the onscreen instructions to let Mountain Lion attempt to configure your network settings for you.

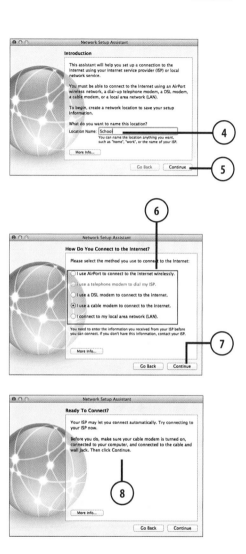

It's Not All Good

DON'T DISCOUNT YOUR ADMIN!

It is impossible for me to stress this enough: Your network administrator or ISP is your best resource for correcting network problems. Using Mountain Lion's assistant tools is not a silver bullet; if you don't have the information required to make a network connection (IP address, and so on), it won't "just work"!

Read your email in
the Mail application.

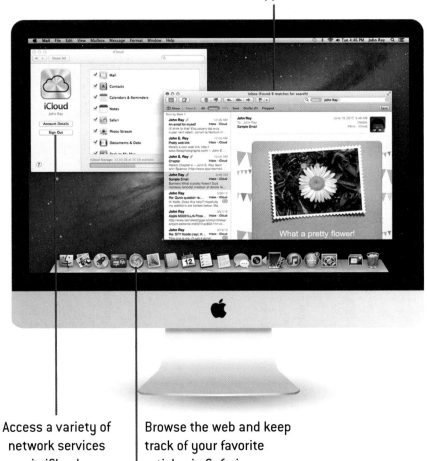

Access a variety of
network services
in iCloud.

Browse the web and keep
track of your favorite
articles in Safari.

In this chapter, you learn how to use your iMac to access online services, including:

→ Connecting to email servers
→ Using VIP and Smart Mailboxes
→ Browsing the Web using Safari 5.x
→ Creating web clippings
→ Using Safari extensions

Accessing iCloud, Email, and the Web

The Internet (for better or worse) is everywhere we turn. To be effective in our professional (and frequently social) lives, we need best-of-breed Internet tools on our iMac. The good news is that we've got 'em.

In this chapter, you learn how to use some of the unique features of Mountain Lion's Mail and web applications as well as how to establish and configure iCloud accounts. Even if you're working in a Microsoft-centric environment, you'll find that your iMac's tools are up to the job.

Setting Up iCloud

One of the most convenient features of using multiple Apple devices is the difficult-to-describe iCloud service. iCloud provides data syncronization between your computers and iOS devices (such as syncronizing your web browser bookmarks), and also gives you free email, contact storage, and even the ability to connect to your home Macintosh from your work computer. Best of all, all you need to do to use iCloud is establish an account and click a few checkboxes.

Integrated iCloud

I'll mention iCloud where relevant throughout this book, but keep in mind that Apple is continuously upgrading iCloud services and adding new features. The goal is for your computing life to be more intuitive and seamless without having to worry about what is going on in the background.

Configuring iCloud for the First Time

The first step in using iCloud is configuring your iMac to log into your account. If you have an Apple ID, chances are you already have an iCloud account. If not, the setup process will guide you along the way. Note that you will only need to follow these steps once—after that, you'll remain logged in even if you reboot your iMac.

To access your iCloud account, follow these steps:

1. Open the iCloud System Preferences panel.

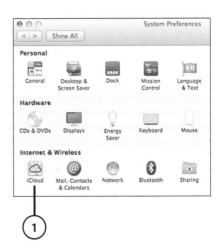

2. A Sign-In window appears. Enter your Apple ID and Password, or Click Create an Apple ID to generate a new safe ID.

3. Click Sign In to log in to the iCloud service.

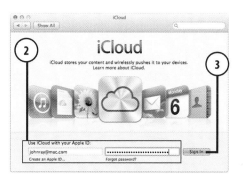

4. iCloud prompts to automatically install basic services—contact, calendar, and bookmark syncing as well as Find My Mac. You can either enable these now, or by following the instructions in "Activating iCloud Services."

5. Click Next.

6. If prompted to allow Location Services and you want to be able to locate your Mac on a map, click Allow. You can always change this later in the Security & Privacy System Preferences panel.

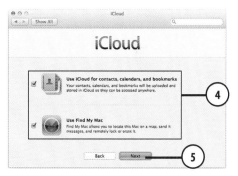

7. You are shown the list of active iCloud services. Close the System Preferences, or proceed to the next section to learn more about the available services.

Activating iCloud Services

Your iCloud account comes with many free services that work across your OS X systems and iOS (iPhone/iPad) devices. A summary of the available services at the time of this writing is available here:

- **Mail**—When activated, Mail sets up a Mountain Lion email account associated with your iCloud account. This will be an "@me.com" address that you established when registering for an Apple ID. (Discussed later in "Using Mail.")

- **Contacts**—Moves your contacts to iCloud storage, making them accessible and editable on any device that has iCloud configured. (See Chapter 6, "Keeping Contacts, Appointments, Reminders, and Notes," for more details.)

- **Calendars & Reminders**—Sets up shared calendars and to-do lists (reminders) that, once again, are shared between all iCloud devices and available online. (See Chapter 6 for more details.)

- **Notes**—Connects your Notes application to iCloud storage, making all your notes available across your iMac, portable Mac, and iPhone/iPad. (See Chapter 6 for more details.)

- **Safari**—Enables syncing of your Safari bookmarks and your reading list across devices as well as providing a list of open Safari tabs on other devices. This makes it possible to start browsing in one location and finish in another. (Discussed later in "Continuing Browsing with iCloud Tabs.")

- **Photo Stream**—If you have iPhoto installed on your iMac, Photo Stream automatically makes the photos you take on your iPhone or iPad available on your Mac. It also transfers imported photos from your Mac to your iOS devices. (Discussed later in "Using Photo Stream.")

- **Documents & Data**—This makes it possible to save files to iCloud rather than your local hard drive. Using this feature, you can start editing a document on one machine and finish it up on another. (Discussed later in "Using Documents and Data.")

- **Back to My Mac**—When activated, this unique iCloud feature makes your computer visible to any other computer where you have activated Back to My Mac. Using this, you can access your home computer from any other network-connected Mac—no network configuration required. (See Chapter 7, "Sharing Devices, Files, and Services on a Network," for details.)

- **Find My Mac**—If your iMac is lost or stolen, Find My Mac will attempt to locate it. Using the icloud.com website, you can track your iMac on a map and even lock or erase it. (Discussed later in "Using Find My Mac.")

To activate an iCloud service, first make sure you have completed the task "Configuring iCloud for the First Time," and then follow these simple steps:

1. Open the iCloud Preferences panel.

2. Click the checkboxes in front of the services you want to use. If prompted to provide access to additional system services (Find My Mac requires you to grant access to your location, for instance), click the appropriate response.

3. Close System Preferences when satisfied with your selections.

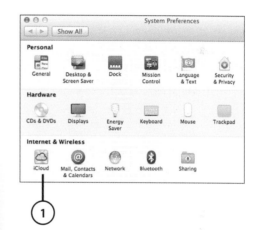

More Storage Is a Click Away

At the bottom of the service list is a bar showing how much storage you have left. By default, iCloud includes 5GB of storage—but storing documents and data, backups of your iOS devices, and other information can eat the space up quickly. Click the Manage button to buy more storage if needed.

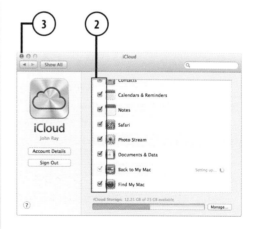

Exploring Unique iCloud Services

It's pretty easy to describe the use of features like Contacts and Safari bookmark syncing, and they fall neatly into place in many of this book's chapters.
There are a few "unique" iCloud services, however, that are important to cover,
but don't quite fit as cleanly elsewhere. One such service, for example,
enables you to find your iMac on a map, should it be lost or stolen. Another
provides direct access to your contacts, events, and mail from a web interface
no matter where you are. Rather than leave these topics out, they are covered
in the following tasks.

Accessing iCloud Applications Online

After you activate iCloud services like
Mail, Calendar, and Reminders, you can
log into Apple's online iCloud service
and use web applications that resemble
their iMac counterparts. To access iCloud
applications, do the following:

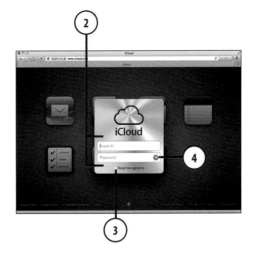

1. Open a current version of a web
    browser (Safari, Internet Explorer
    8+, Firefox, or Chrome) and
    browse to http://www.icloud.com.

2. Click the Sign In button (if it
    appears) and enter your Apple ID
    and Password.

3. Click the Keep Me Signed In
    checkbox if you'd like to be able
    to access iCloud from your com-
    puter without logging in again.

4. Click the arrow to log in.

5. Once connected, click the icon of
    the application you wish to
    launch.

6. Use the web application as you would the desktop version. As you make changes, they will be pushed out to all your iCloud-connected devices.

7. Click the Cloud button to exit back to the main menu.

8. Close your browser when finished.

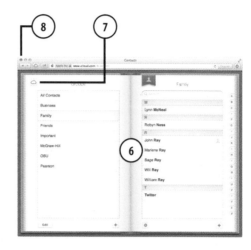

Using Find My Mac

To turn on Find My Mac and make your iMac location available via the iCloud website, follow these steps:

1. If you haven't already, activate Find My Mac using the technique described in "Activating iCloud Services," earlier in this chapter.

2. If prompted, click Allow on the Allow Find My Mac to use the location services dialog.

3. Choose the option to Allow guests to log into your system if it's lost, to improve recoverability. This makes it possible for a user to get online through a guest account (that has no access to your data) without a password. Enabling this makes it possible for your iMac to signal its location if the thief takes it online.

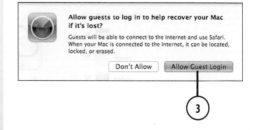

4. If you need to find your Mac, go to iCloud.com in your browser and log in. Click Find My iPhone.

5. Click the Devices button.

6. Find your iMac and click it in the devices list.

7. The iMac's location is shown on the map.

8. The web app displays options for sending a message/playing a sound on the computer, locking it, or wiping the contents of the hard drive.

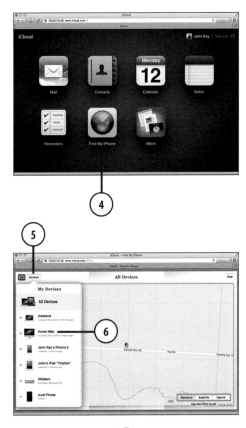

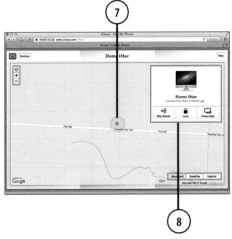

Using Documents and Data

The Documents and Data feature of iCloud is meant to make it easy to work on a document in one location, and then open it again in another.

It's Not All Good

WHERE DID I PUT THAT?!

In your author's opinion, the Mountain Lion implementation of Documents and Data leaves a bit to be desired. While this feature sounds like a useful tool, it requires that you have the same application on all the machines that need to edit an application's files.

For example, assume you edit a file on your iMac using an iCloud-enabled word processor and save the document to iCloud. You then go to your desktop, which has a different, but compatible, word processor installed. Surprise! You won't be able to see the file. You can only open iCloud files in the applications that created them.

Before starting, be sure to activate Documents and Data using the steps described at the end of the "Activating iCloud Services" section, earlier in this chapter.

Saving Files to iCloud

To store a file in iCloud, do the following:

1. Edit the file as you normally would in an application of your choice (be aware that not all applications support iCloud at this time).

2. Choose File, Save from the menu bar.

3. When prompted for a file name, set the "Where" location to iCloud.

4. Click Save to save the file to iCloud.

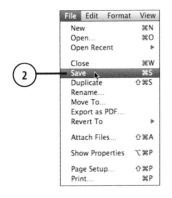

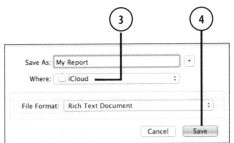

Opening Files from iCloud

To open a file that you've saved in iCloud (from any iCloud-connected device), first open the same application you used to create the file, and then follow these steps:

1. Choose File, Open.

2. In the dialog box that appears, make sure iCloud is selected.

3. Use the icon and list buttons at the bottom of the dialog to switch between icon and list views.

4. Click the file you want to work with.

5. Click Open. The file opens and you can begin working with it wherever you left off, no matter which device you were using.

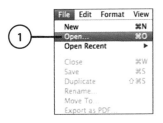

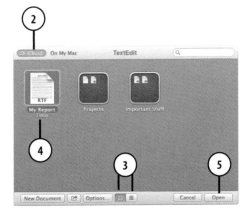

When It's in iCloud, It's in iCloud

When you open and edit a file in iCloud, it stays in iCloud. You don't need to worry about moving it from your local computer to iCloud after editing it, or anything of the sort. Just think of iCloud storage like any other disk, except that you have access to it no matter where you are or what iCloud-enabled device you are using.

It's Not All Good

USE THE CORRECT APP!

Documents can only be opened (at this time) in the application that created them. You won't even see the files on another device unless the device is running the app that was used to create it. You also won't see it in the open file dialog of any other iCloud application. In other words, if you want to share files created in Pages across systems with iCloud, both systems *must* have Pages available for editing the file.

Moving Existing Files to and from iCloud

If you create a document locally (such as on your desktop) and want it to be available everywhere, you need to move it to iCloud. Similarly, if you want to take a document that has been shared via iCloud and move it so only a single copy exists on your iMac, you need to move it locally. To move in either direction, first open the file in your application of choice, and then follow along:

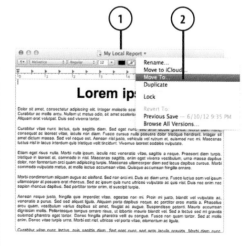

1. Click the file name in the window's title bar.

2. Choose Move To from the pop-up menu.

3. Click the Where pop-up menu to view the locations where you can send the file.

4. To move a local file to iCloud, choose iCloud or a folder within iCloud.

5. Choose a local destination to move the file to your local machine.

6. Click Move to finish moving the file.

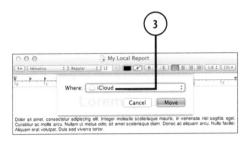

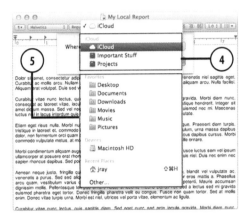

>>> Go Further

ORGANIZING YOUR iCLOUD

If you find yourself using iCloud as an integral part of your document workflow, you'll notice that it quickly becomes full of files with no organization. Unlike OS X, iCloud won't let you create zillions of nested folders. In fact, it uses a completely different interface for organizing files, but, thankfully, one you're probably used to.

When viewing files in the iCloud Open File dialog, you can create whatever file organization you like, just by dragging the icons around—it works *exactly* like the Launchpad organization covered in Chapter 2, "Making the Most of Your iMac's Screen Space." Drag a file onto another file, and a folder/group is automatically created. Drag files out of the folder, and the folder disappears. If you're used to working with Launchpad or iOS, you'll have no problem organizing your iCloud documents.

Using Photo Stream

Another extremely useful (and fun) feature of iCloud is Photo Stream. Photo Stream automatically keeps copies of your most recent 1000 photos taken using iOS devices and makes sure that your iMac has copies of them all. To enable and use Photo Stream, follow these steps:

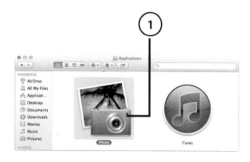

1. Open iPhoto from the Launchpad or Applications folder. (If you do not have iPhoto, it can be purchased from the Mac App Store.)

2. Choose iPhoto, Preferences from the menu bar.

3. Click the Photo Stream button.

4. Click the My Photo Stream checkbox.

5. Choose whether your Photo Stream photos should automatically be imported to the Events, Photos, Faces, and Places categories in your library.

6. Select Automatic Upload to send any photos added directly to iPhoto on your Mac to your iPhone and iPad devices through Photo Stream.

7. Click Shared Photo Streams to access photo streams from other people or share your stream with others.

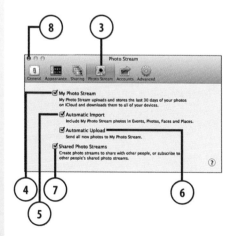

8. Close the Preferences window.

9. Now when you take photos with your iPhone or iPad, they automatically appear in Photo Stream when your iOS device connects with Wi-Fi. Alternatively, you can drag photos from your iPhoto library (or image files from the Finder) into the iPhoto Photo Stream group to send them to your iOS devices (not shown).

iPhoto Preferences Are All You Need

Notice that you didn't use System Preferences to configure the iCloud Photo Stream? The iPhoto preferences automatically turn on the iCloud Photo Stream service.

Getting Started with Accounts

For all the fun and information the Internet has brought us, it has also created a mess in terms of managing all the accounts we use to communicate online. If you're like many people, you have multiple email accounts—possibly one through iCloud, one from work, and one at home. You have accounts for chatting with instant messenger. You have accounts for sharing contacts and calendars. In other words, you've got multiple usernames and passwords that all need to be configured in different applications, just so you can be connected.

In OS X, Apple has recognized the problem of account overload and worked to consolidate all your online account management in a single centralized preference panel—Mail, Contacts, & Calendars. Here you can set up email, instant messenger, Exchange, Calendar, and other account types—without needing to figure out where they're managed in your individual applications.

I'll be showing the use of this panel as needed in the relevant chapters, but let's take a very brief look at how you'll interact with this tool on your iMac.

More iCloud Settings?

When you use the Mail, Contacts & Calendars panel to manage your accounts, you'll notice that it also includes iCloud. The iCloud settings in this panel are identical to what you configured in the iCloud panel shown earlier in this chapter—this is just a different way to access them.

Adding an Account

To add an account for an online service (email, contacts, calendars, Exchange, etc.), follow these steps:

1. Open the Mail, Contacts & Calendars System Preferences panel.

2. Choose an online service provider that you want to configure by clicking its name on the right. Select Add Other Account from the bottom of the list to pick from additional service types.

3. Fill in the requested information in the setup wizard that appears.

4. The completed account is listed in the preference panel with its settings available on the right.

5. Close System Preferences when finished.

Exploration Is Rewarded!

While the Mail, Contacts & Calendars panel is a great place for establishing new accounts and performing high-level configuration, you may still find yourself needing to dig for various esoteric settings (such as specific server addresses, proxies, and other technical tweaks) within your individual Internet applications.

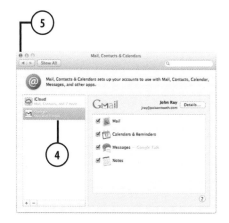

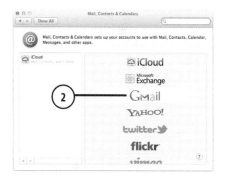

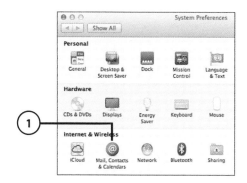

Using Mail

The first thing that many of us do when we have an Internet connection is check our email. Email is now a way to exchange rich media—such as photos, files, and movies—in addition to a way to exchange written messages. The email application, Mail (found in the Applications folder by clicking the Mail icon), is provided with your iMac. With Mail, you can connect to a variety of different mail servers, including Microsoft Exchange, with only a few clicks of your mouse.

Things You Need Before Setting up an Email Connection

As with the networking information in the last chapter, configuring your email account isn't a matter of guessing. Apple's Mail application can automatically set up several popular email services (such as Google and Yahoo), but if you're connecting to a corporate email server, you should collect as much information as possible from your email system administrator or ISP before proceeding. This includes your email address, password, email server, email server type (POP, IMAP, or Exchange), and SMTP server:

- **Incoming Mail Server**—The server that you connect to when retrieving your email.

- **Incoming Mail Server Type**—The type of server that you're connecting to. Apple's Mail application supports Exchange, IMAP, and POP servers.

- **Outgoing (SMTP) Server**—The server that sends your messages.

- **Authentication**—Typically, a username and password required to retrieve or send messages.

Adding an Email Account (Simple)

If you have an email account that Mountain Lion recognizes, configuration couldn't be easier—you just need your email address, name, and password to make a connection. Mountain Lion attempts to identify and configure your account. If for some reason it fails, you can continue with an advanced manual configuration (see the next task).

Note that if you've already activated iCloud email, your account is already set up. You don't need to do anything else.

1. Open the Mail, Contacts & Calendars System Preferences panel.

2. Choose an email service that you want to configure by clicking its name on the right.

3. The Add Account window displays. Type your name (as you want it to appear in outgoing messages), email address, and password for the account.

4. Click Set Up.

5. Mountain Lion attempts to automatically configure your account. If additional features are determined to be available from the email provider, they are listed in the window. Choose which services you want to use by checking/unchecking the checkboxes.

6. Click Add Account to finish adding the account.

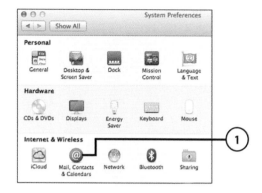

7. If it's successful, the newly configured email account appears in the
   account list. If the setup fails, cancel setup and skip ahead to the
   next section, "Adding an Email
   Account (Advanced)."

8. Clicking the account name in the
   list displays the account details on
   the right.

9. You can click Details to edit the
   basic account settings if, for example, you want to change your display name or the name of your
   account.

10. You can now close System
    Preferences and begin using your
    account in Mail.

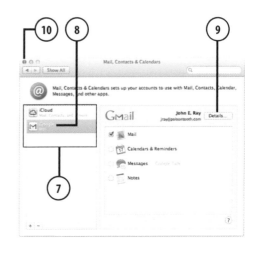

Adding an Email Account (Advanced)

Email accounts that aren't immediately recognized by Mountain Lion
require more information to be
entered before they can be used. This
is the case for some ISP email
accounts, corporate, and educational
systems. Be sure you have all the
information listed previously under
"Things You Need Before Setting Up
an Email Connection."

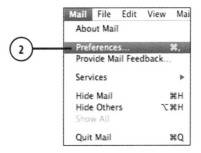

1. Open the Mail application from
   the Dock or Applications folder.

2. Choose Preferences from the Mail
   menu.

3. Click the Accounts button within the Mail preferences window.

4. Click + to add a new account.

5. Provide the basic account information when prompted and click Continue.

6. When Mail cannot automatically configure the account, it displays a new dialog to collect information about your incoming mail server.

7. Enter the account information provided by your system administrator or ISP (the incoming mail server, username, and password). Use the description field to name the account with something meaningful that helps you differentiate it from other accounts.

8. If you are setting up an Exchange account, click the Contacts and Calendars checkboxes if you would like your iMac to have access to your Exchange-based address book and calendars directly within Contacts and Calendars (discussed in Chapter 6).

9. Click Continue. Mail automatically tests the information you've provided. If a failure occurs, recheck your information. After it is correct, click Continue again.

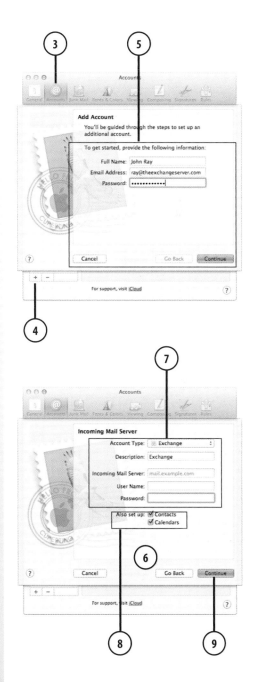

10. Mail displays the security settings for your incoming mail server. Typically, you are prompted for whether or not to use Secure Sockets Layer. If it's available, this option is recommended.

11. Use the Authentication drop-down menu to choose how you authenticate with the server. Typically you choose Password (some complex configurations might use more advanced authentication methods).

12. Click Continue.

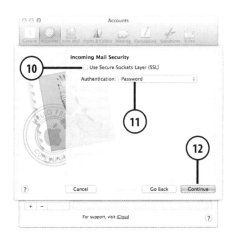

13. Mail displays the outgoing mail server settings, known as the SMTP server settings. You should enter the information provided by your system administrator or ISP, or choose an existing outgoing server from the Outgoing Mail server drop-down menu. Again, use the description field to provide a meaningful name for the mail server.

14. If your outgoing mail server requires authentication (many do!), click the Use Authentication checkbox and then provide a username and password.

15. Click Continue.

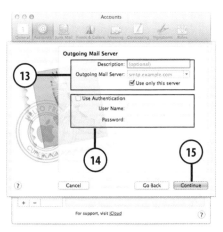

16. Now you are prompted for whether or not to use Secure Sockets Layer for outgoing mail, as well as the authentication type. (Again, you would typically choose Password here.)

17. Click Continue to review your final settings. If an error occurs, check your settings, or click Continue to proceed with the settings you provided.

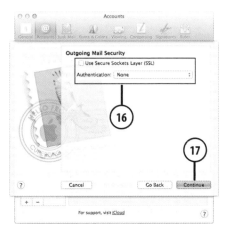

18. Make sure the Take Account Online checkbox is selected so that you can begin using your account.

19. Click Create to finish setting up the account.

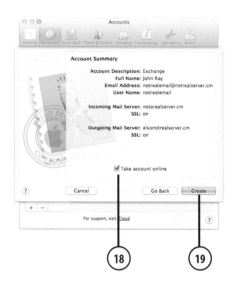

Troubleshooting Your Connection

To troubleshoot your account settings, from within Mail choose Window, Connection Doctor. Your iMac tests all your email account settings and shows you exactly where any errors are occurring.

Multiple Email Addresses, One Account

It isn't uncommon for one email account to have multiple addresses associated with it. I might have a single account with addresses, such as *myimac@placeforstuff.com* or *johnray@me.com*, which I want to appear when I send a message. To configure multiple addresses for a single account, open Mail's preferences, click Accounts, and then click the account you want to add an alias to. Enter the alias email addresses, separated by commas, in the Email Address field in the account details. The email addresses are then available in a pop-up menu when you compose a new message.

Finding Your Way Around Mail

After your email account is configured, Mail connects and retrieves your messages. The Mail application workspace is split into three columns, from left to right: mailboxes, a message list, and message content.

On the left, the mailbox list shows different mailboxes (or folders) for categorizing your messages. In Mountain Lion, Apple has decided to conserve as much space as possible by hiding the mailboxes by default. They've also given us a quick hide/show mailboxes button to show the mailbox column and links to the important mailboxes (Inbox, Sent, and so on) directly below the toolbar.

When a mailbox is clicked, the message list refreshes to show all of the email within the mailbox, including a several-line preview of the contents. Any message that you click in the Message list is displayed in the message content area on the right.

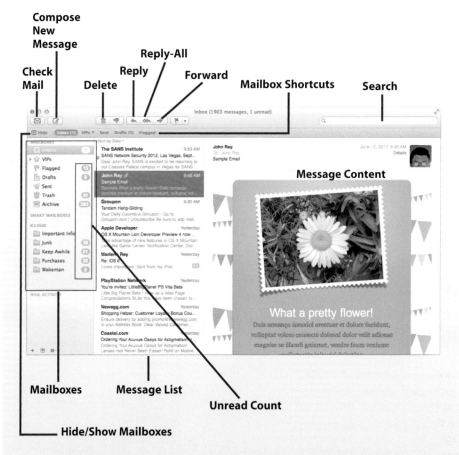

Compose New Message

Reply-All

Check Mail   **Reply**   **Forward**

Delete   **Mailbox Shortcuts**   **Search**

Message Content

Mailboxes   **Message List**

Unread Count

Hide/Show Mailboxes

Now that you know the basics of finding your way around Mail, let's take a look at the common tasks you should familiarize yourself with.

Out with the New, In with the Old

If you've been using Apple Mail for the past decade, you'll recognize the OS X Mail layout is a dramatic departure from earlier versions. If you'd prefer to live in the past, you can change to the older style layout by checking the Use classic layout option found within the Viewing section of the Mail preferences (choose Mail, Preferences from the menu bar).

Reading Email

Reading messages is typically a matter of finding a message in the message list, clicking it, and reading. Even so, you can improve the experience by taking advantage of several tools built into Mail.

Sorting Mail

You're certainly used to sorting information by clicking column headings, right? In Mountain Lion's Mail application, however, the message list doesn't have columns, so you'll need to follow this approach:

1. Use the Sort By drop-down menu above the message list to choose a message attribute to use as your sorting criteria.

2. Use the same menu to choose Ascending or Descending to set the order of your sorting preferences.

Viewing Additional Attributes

Much as you can set the mail attributes you want to use for sorting, you can also set the attributes displayed in the message list. Use the View, Message List menu to set which attributes will be visible in the message list items.

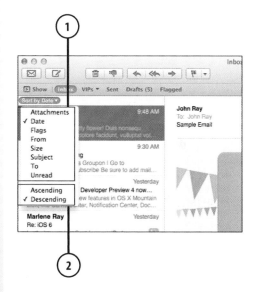

Previewing Attachments

In Chapter 1, "Managing Your iMac Desktop," you learned about the Quick Look system for previewing files in the Finder. In Mail, if your message contains an attachment, you can also use the Quick Look system.

1. Choose a message with an attachment—represented by a paperclip in the message list.

2. Click the Details link at the top of the message content to show buttons for saving and viewing attachments.

3. Click the Quick Look button at the top of the message content area.

4. A Quick Look window appears, displaying the selected content.

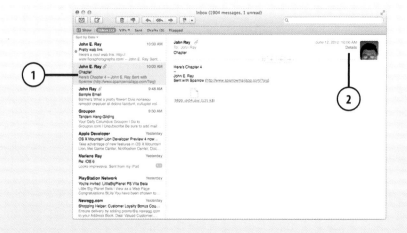

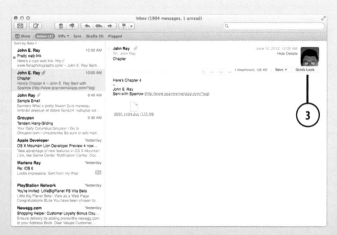

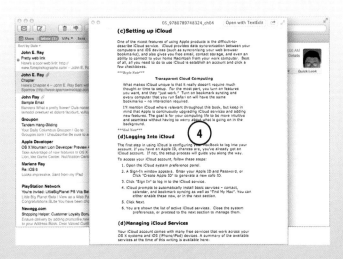

Saving Attachments

You can easily save one or more attachments to your iMac's hard drive, and even add images to iPhoto, directly from Mail.

1. Choose a message with an attachment—represented by a paperclip in the message list, then click the Details link at the top of the message content as described in the previous task.

2. Click the Save button at the top of the message content area.

3. A menu appears, enabling you to Save All, choose an individual file to save, or, if applicable, add the file to iPhoto.

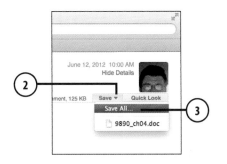

WORKING WITH ATTACHMENTS

If you prefer a more Finder-like approach to dealing with attachments, you can also work with attached files as icons. Scroll through your email and you'll see the attached files represented as icons in the message (usually at the bottom). You can drag these icons to your desktop (or anywhere you'd like to store them). You can also click an icon to immediately open it in a compatible Mountain Lion application.

Viewing Web Pages within an Email

Have you ever gotten a link to a web page in email and wanted to view it without having to launch Safari? In Mountain Lion, you can. To preview a web link directly in Mail, follow these steps:

1. Position your cursor over the link within the message content, but do not click!

2. A small downward-pointing arrow appears to the right of the link. Click it.

3. A popover window appears displaying the web page.

4. Click Open with Safari to open the full page in your web browser, or Add to Reading List to save the page to your Safari reading list.

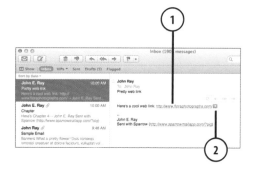

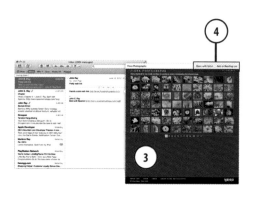

Using Data Detectors

The icon that appears at the end of a web link in mail (and the subsequent preview of the page) is an example of a Mountain Lion "Data Detector" in action. You may notice other icons beside dates, addresses, phone numbers, and so on. Clicking these icons will do similar helpful actions, such as setting appointments, adding information to a contact, or tracking shipments.

Organizing with Email Conversations

Email conversations can grow quite lengthy with back-and-forth replies. To help keep long conversations under control, Mountain Lion's Mail, by default, collapses your conversations into a single entry in your message list. You can expand the entry to show the individual messages whenever you need to see one.

1. Conversations are denoted by a number within an entry in the message list.

2. Click the message list entry to show all the messages in the conversation within the content area.

3. Messages are numbered at the top to show the order in which they were received.

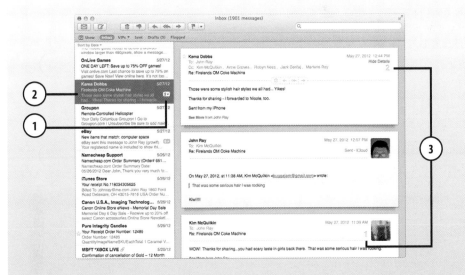

4. To focus on a single message, click the arrow beside the number in the message list to show a list of individual senders and dates.

5. Click the individual name/date to show only that message.

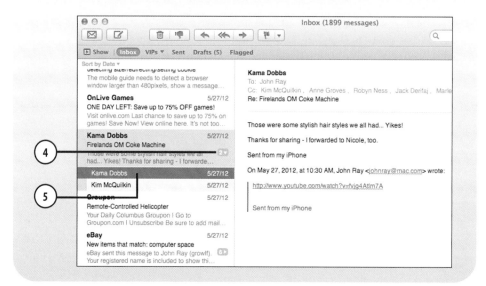

It's Not All Good

SILENCE THE CONVERSATION!

Many people find the conversation view to be disorienting in Mail. If you're one of those people, you can turn it off entirely by choosing Organize by Conversation from Mail's View Menu.

See My Smiling Face!

To see your friends' (and other contacts') photos beside each message summary in the message list, open Mail's preferences (Mail, Preferences from the menu), and within the Viewing section, click the Show contact photos in the message list checkbox.

Managing Spam Filtering

Mail can learn (with some help) which messages in your inbox are spam and then filter similar messages so you don't have to see them. To manage your spam filtering, follow these steps:

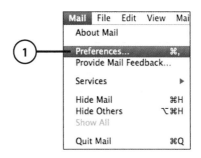

1. Choose Mail, Preferences from the menu bar.

2. Click the Junk Mail toolbar icon.

3. Click Enable Junk Mail Filtering to turn on spam filtering. You can disable it by unchecking this box at any time.

4. Choose where Mail should file spam messages. Moving messages to the Junk mailbox is a good choice.

5. To help prevent getting false positives, use the spam exemptions to identify types of messages that you don't consider to be spam.

6. If your ISP offers spam filtering (and you trust it), make sure the Trust Junk Mail Headers in Messages option is set.

7. Close the Mail Preferences.

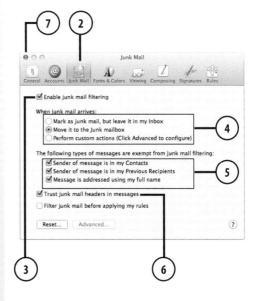

Classifying Spam

If you receive spam mail, select it and click the Junk icon (thumbs down) in the Mail toolbar. This classifies messages as spam. When new messages recognized as spam come in, they are automatically placed in the Junk folder. If *good* mail is accidentally classified as spam, use the thumbs up icon in the toolbar to tell Mail it made a mistake.

Changing How Often Mail Is Retrieved

You can force Mail to retrieve messages using the Get Mail toolbar button, but to change the frequency with which it forces a check you need to access the preferences.

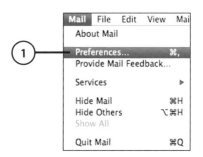

1. Choose Mail, Preferences from the menu bar.

2. Click the General icon in the Preferences Toolbar.

3. Use the Check for New Messages pop-up menu to set how frequently Mail looks for new messages.

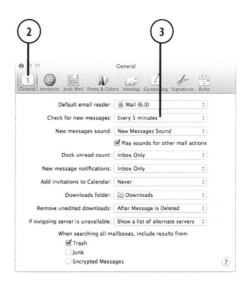

Composing Email

Email today is a bit more than just typing a message—it can include sending photos, files, or even professionally designed invitations and announcements. Mountain Lion's Mail on your iMac enables you to do all of these things.

Let's take a look at what you can do beyond simple text.

Sending Messages with Attachments

Mail can attach virtually any type of file to your messages with ease. Follow these steps to add Windows-compatible attachments to a mail message.

1. Start a new message by clicking the new message icon (pencil and paper) in the Mail toolbar.

2. Click the Attach icon (paperclip) in the New Message window.

3. Choose the files or folders to send from the file chooser dialog. Select multiples by holding down the Command key and clicking.

4. Check the Send Windows-Friendly Attachments checkbox to ensure that anyone (regardless of their platform choice) can open the attachments.

5. Click Choose File to add the attachments.

6. Compose the message as normal and then click the send icon (paper airplane).

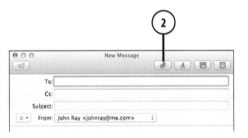

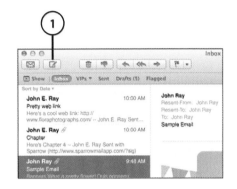

Attaching Pictures from iPhoto

To quickly attach photos from iPhoto, click the Photo Browser button to open a small window that shows your iPhoto galleries. Choose your photos and drag them into the message to attach them!

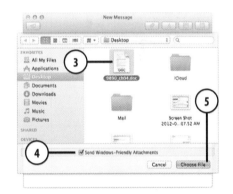

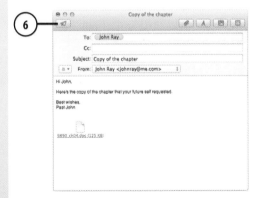

Using Stationery Templates

If you'd like to send an invitation or a fancy greeting, you can make use of prebuilt templates, called "Stationery," that come with Mountain Lion's Mail application. Stationery is available whenever you're composing a message:

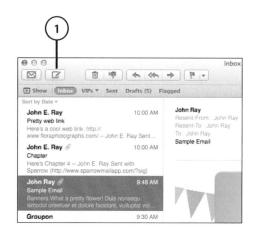

1. Start a new message by clicking the new message icon (pencil and paper) in the Mail toolbar.

2. Click the Show Stationery icon (paper with dots) in the New Message toolbar.

3. Choose a category of templates on the left side of the Stationery bar.

4. Click the thumbnail of the template you want to apply.

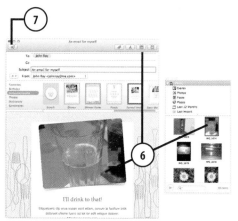

5. Click to edit the text within the template.

6. If the template contains images, replace them by dragging photo files from the Finder onto the template image or use the Photo Browser button to locate an image and drag it in.

7. Click the send icon (paper airplane) when you are finished with the message.

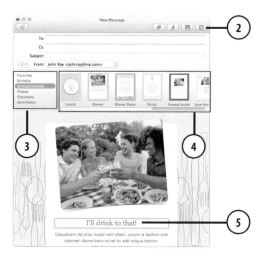

Changing Templates

After you change the content of a template, you can choose another template and your changes will be maintained as much as possible.

Creating Signatures

When you send a lot of email, you probably get a bit tired of typing the same thing at the end of each message—your name, email, and other contact information. To add this information automatically to the end of each message you write, create a signature.

1. Choose Mail, Preferences from the menu bar.

2. Click the Signatures icon in the preferences toolbar.

3. Choose an account that the signature should be used with, or choose All Signatures to not associate the signature with a specific account.

4. Click + to add a new signature.

5. Type a name for the signature.

6. Enter the text for the signature in the space to the right.

7. Click Always Match My Default Message Font so that the signature always matches the font you're using.

8. If you're adding the signature to an account, use the Choose Signature pop-up menu to choose which signature is automatically added when you write a message. You can also manually choose a signature using the Choose Signature pop-up menu in the message composition window.

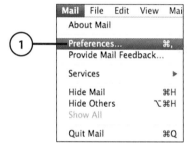

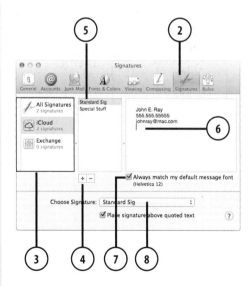

9. Click Place Signature Above Quoted Text to have Mail position your signature above earlier (quoted) text when replying to messages.

10. Close the Mail Preferences window.

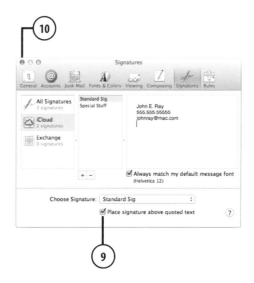

Adding a vCard

To attach your personal information to your signature as a virtual business card, you can drag a card out of your Address Panel (Window, Address Panel) into the signature.

Managing Your Email

Email can be overwhelming, especially if you have several different accounts and dozens of incoming messages each day. To help you cope with the incoming mail, you can create mailboxes in which to file or copy messages. You can also set up smart mailboxes that automatically display messages that match certain criteria.

Creating Mailboxes

To create a new mailbox, follow these steps:

1. Click the + button at the bottom of the Mailbox list.

2. Choose New Mailbox.

3. Using the Location pop-up menu, choose where the mailbox should be stored. You see all of your existing Mailboxes in the menu, as well as On My Mac. Choosing an existing location creates the new mailbox inside of that location.

4. Enter a name for the new mailbox.

5. Click OK.

6. The new mailbox is created and displayed in the Mailbox list.

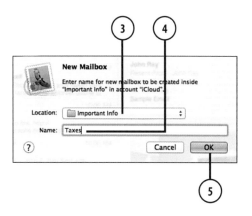

Make Room for Your Mail

Remember: Because the mailbox display eats up a bunch of room on your screen, Apple has made it simple to hide and show the mailbox column using the Hide/Show disclosure button in the upper-left corner of the Mail window. In addition, you can quickly change between your Inbox, Sent, Drafts, and Flagged folders using the links directly in the Mail toolbar.

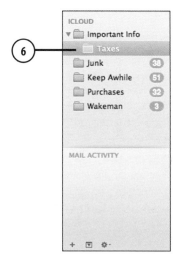

Deleting and Renaming Mailboxes

If you find yourself with extra mailboxes or mailboxes that are no longer serving their original purposes, you can delete or rename them.

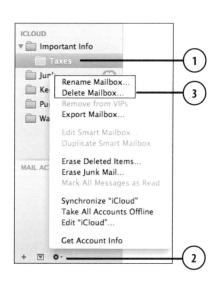

1. Select the mailbox you want to change in your mailbox list.

2. Click the Action icon (the gear) at the bottom of the mailbox list.

3. Choose Delete Mailbox or Rename Mailbox as needed. Any messages stored in a mailbox being deleted are also deleted.

Nesting Folders

Even though you chose where to put your mailbox when it was first created, you can move it within your mailbox hierarchy easily. Mailboxes can be moved inside of other mailboxes by clicking and dragging their folder icons into (or out of) another mailbox.

Filing Messages in Mailboxes

Mailboxes are only useful if you file your messages in them. You can either copy or move messages one at a time or en masse to a mailbox. This can be done either manually, as described here, or automatically using Smart Mailboxes or Email Rules, discussed in the tasks following this one.

1. Select a message by clicking it in the message list. You can select a contiguous range of messages by holding down Shift and clicking another message, or select several scattered messages by holding down the Command key and clicking multiple messages.

2. Move the messages to a mailbox by dragging them onto the desired mailbox. To copy—rather than move—the messages, hold down the Option key while you're dragging the messages. The messages are moved (or copied) to the other mailbox.

Filing without Dragging

If you have a large number of mailboxes, or just find the process of dragging to the mailbox list to be cumbersome, you can select the messages, then use Move To or Copy To from the Messages menu to file the email without any dragging required.

Automatic Email Organization with Smart Mailboxes

Much as Smart Folders in the Finder can help you keep track of files that share certain attributes, Smart Mailboxes can do the same for your email. Using information such as the sender, recipient, and even attachment names, you can group messages together in a Smart Mailbox, regardless of what mailbox, or even what email account, they're associated with. Apple includes one Smart Mailbox by default—"Today"—showing all the messages you've received today.

1. To create a new Smart Mailbox, click the + button at the bottom of the Mailbox list and choose New Smart Mailbox.

2. Type a name for the mailbox.

3. Choose whether the mailbox should match any or all conditions.

4. Configure your search criteria. Use the first pop-up menu to choose a message attribute (such as Subject), the second to choose a comparison, and the field (where applicable) to provide the value that you are comparing against.

5. Use the + and – buttons to add or remove additional criteria.

6. To include messages from the Trash mailbox or Sent mailbox, click the appropriate Include Messages checkboxes.

7. Click OK when you're finished configuring the Smart Mailbox.

8. The new mailbox is created and displayed in the SMART MAIL-BOXES section within the Mailbox list.

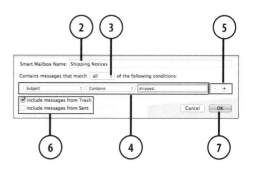

Nesting Smart Mailboxes

Smart Mailboxes can't be arranged hierarchically inside one another as normal mailboxes can. To create a hierarchy of smart mailboxes, you must create a Smart Mailbox Folder (Mailbox, New Smart Mailbox Folder). This special folder will be added to the SMART MAILBOXES section and can be used to organize any Smart Mailboxes you create.

Keeping Track of Your Very Important People with VIP Mailboxes

New to Mountain Lion is a feature that makes it very simple to track and view all messages from a specific person—the VIP Mailbox. VIP Mailboxes are like smart folders, but with a very targeted purpose—showing you all messages from an individual person. To create a VIP mailbox, follow these steps:

1. Choose a message from a sender you want to designate as a VIP.

2. Position your mouse beside the sender's name in the content window and click the star that appears.

3. The sender is added to a new VIP mailbox.

4. Clicking the VIP mailbox shows all messages from the sender.

5. Click the star in the content view again, or select the new VIP mailbox and choose Remove from VIPs from the Action pop-up menu (gear) to remove VIP status (and the corresponding VIP mailbox).

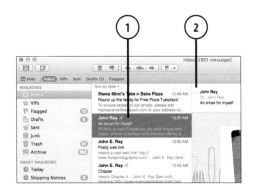

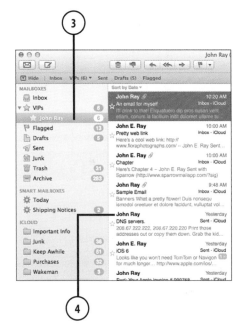

Searching for Messages

Mail makes it easy to quickly search all of your email for particular content, and to turn that search into a Smart Mailbox for future reference. To search your mail, follow these steps:

1. Type the text you are looking for into the search field in the upper-right corner.

2. Using the links below the toolbar, click the mailbox where the search should be performed.

3. Potential search options appear in a drop-down list for matched people, mailboxes, subjects, and message content. Choose what best matches what you want to find.

4. The results appear in the message list.

5. Click Save to save the search as a Smart Mailbox. (See steps 2-8 of the "Automatic Email Organization with Smart Mailboxes" task.)

6. Alternatively, click the X button in the search field to clear the search results.

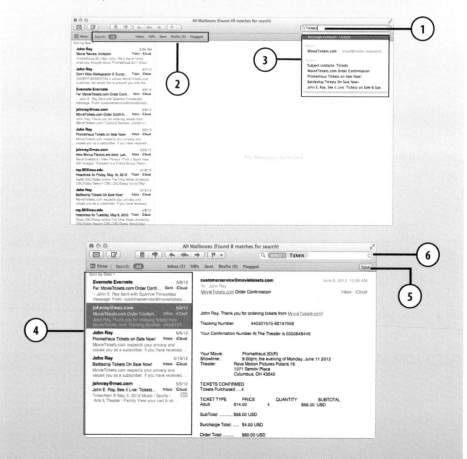

Writing Email Rules

If you'd prefer to have messages filed to actual mailboxes rather than Smart Mailboxes, you can write email rules. Email rules can file messages, highlight messages in the message list, and even forward them to another account. To write a rule, follow these steps:

1. Choose Mail, Preferences from the menu bar.

2. Click the Rules icon in the Preferences toolbar.

3. Click Add Rule.

4. Enter a description for the rule so that you can identify it later.

5. Use the Any from the pop-up menu to choose where any or all rules must evaluate as "true" in order for the rule's actions to be carried out.

6. Configure the conditions under which the rule executes. The first pop-up menu chooses what is evaluated, the second the comparison to be made, and the third field is the value that should be used in the comparison.

7. Use + or – to add or remove additional conditions.

8. Configure the actions that are performed when the conditions are met.

9. Use + or – to add or remove actions.

10. Click OK to save the rule.

11. Close the Mail Preferences.

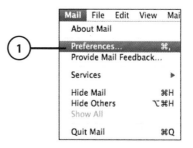

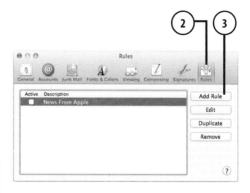

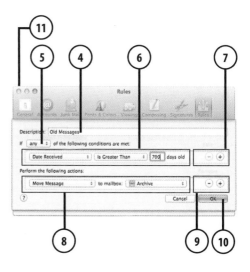

Web Browsing in Safari

Although similar in many ways to other web browsers, Safari offers a few unique features that set it apart. You can open Safari from its icon on the Dock or Launchpad, or in the Applications folder.

Safari has seen dramatic improvements over the past few years. Safari uses a web browsing engine called Webkit that was, although not an Apple product, engineered by mostly Apple developers. This engine is the same engine found in Google Chrome and on iOS, HP WebOS, and Android platforms. This means that Safari is quickly becoming a web browsing standard, rather than an exception.

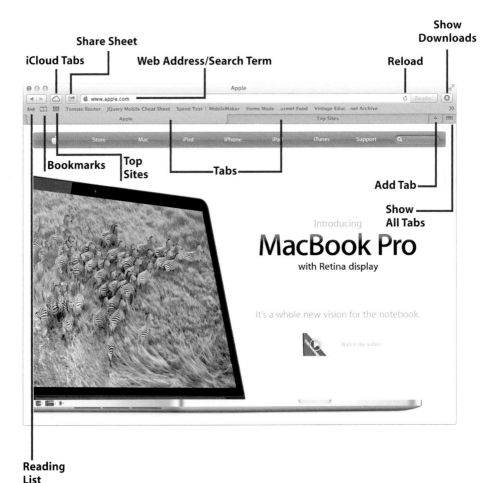

BRING YOUR OWN FLASH

If you're browsing with Safari and your web pages seem a bit "bare," it might be because Mountain Lion doesn't include Adobe Flash by default. To add the Flash plug-in to your browser, visit http://www.adobe.com/products/flashplayer/ in Safari.

Managing Your Bookmarks, Top Sites, and Reading List

In Safari, there are four primary areas where you can store sites for easy access: the bookmark menu, which appears under the bookmarks menu item; the bookmarks bar, displayed under the URL; the top sites screen, which shows the sites you (or Safari) have identified as being frequently visited; and, new in Mountain Lion, the Reading List. The Reading List (denoted by an icon of eyeglasses) holds pages and links that you want to visit at a later time, but aren't planning to keep as a permanent bookmark.

It's Not All Good

SEARCHING FOR SEARCH?

The first time you start Safari in Mountain Lion, you may notice something is missing—the search field. Apple has taken the approach of many other browsers and combined the search with the URL field. To go to a particular URL, type in a URL. To perform a search, type in the search. It can be a bit disconcerting at first, but it works just fine.

Adding a Bookmark

To add a bookmark to Safari, you need to know what site you want to bookmark, and where the bookmark should be stored:

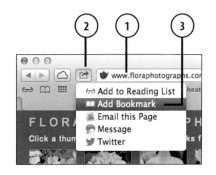

1. Visit the site you want to bookmark by typing its address into the URL field.

2. Click the Share Sheet button in the Safari toolbar.

3. Choose Add Bookmark from the Share Sheet pop-up menu.

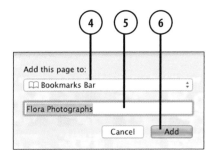

4. Choose where to file the bookmark (Top Sites, Bookmark Menu, Bookmarks Bar, Reading List, or a folder within one of these areas).

5. Enter a name for the bookmark so you can identify it later.

6. Click Add.

Previewing Bookmarks

Amassing a huge collection of bookmarks can make it difficult to find what you're looking for. With Safari you can quickly preview the websites in your bookmarks or history.

1. Click the Show Bookmarks button.

2. Choose a collection of bookmarks from the left-hand pane.

3. Select a folder of bookmarks (if any) or individual bookmark from the bookmark list.

4. Drag the handle to resize the preview Coverflow pane so that you can get a clear preview of the pages.

5. Use the scrollbar below the preview area to flip through the sites in the folder.

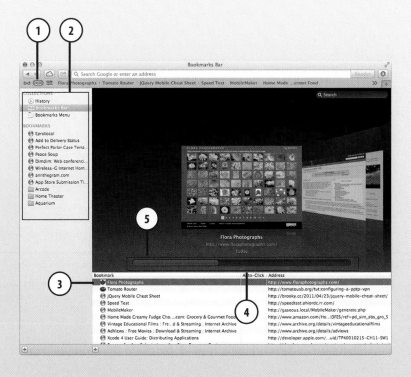

Organizing Bookmarks

After you've added a few bookmarks to the bookmark menu or bookmark bar, you can re-categorize them using these steps:

1. Click the Show Bookmark button.

2. Click the collection with which you want to work.

3. Navigate the folders and individual bookmarks as you would navigate a Finder window.

4. Click and drag bookmarks between folders or collections to organize them.

5. Click the + buttons to add new bookmark collections or folders for additional filing options.

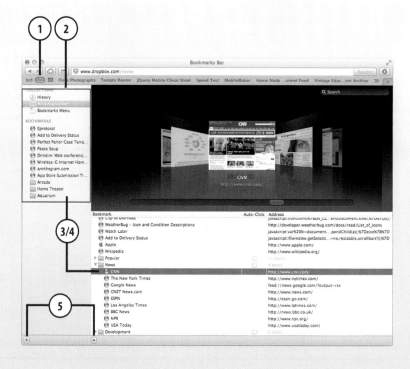

Organizing Top Sites

As you browse, Safari identifies your "top sites." The Top Sites button switches to display previews and marks sites that have updates with a star. Clicking a site opens it in Safari.

To manage the ordering and display of the top sites in Safari, follow these steps:

1. Click the Top Sites button.

2. Click Edit.

3. Click the X button by a site to remove it, or the "pin" button to make sure the site stays on the screen.

4. Rearrange the sites by clicking and dragging their preview images.

5. Add new sites by dragging their URLs into the top sites window.

6. Click Done.

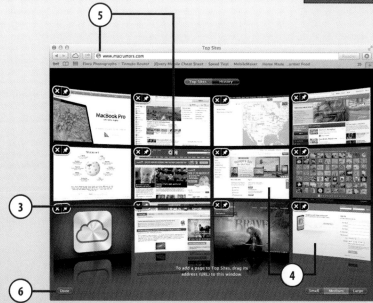

A History Lesson

When viewing Top Sites, you'll see a History button at the top of the display. Clicking History will take you to a coverflow view of your browsing history.

Adding to Your Reading List

The Reading List is a simple feature that holds links and pages until you have a chance to go back and read them. If you have an iCloud account shared between your iOS devices and your Mac, you'll even see the same synced reading list between all of them.

To add to your reading list in Safari, first browse to a web page that you want to view later, and then do the following:

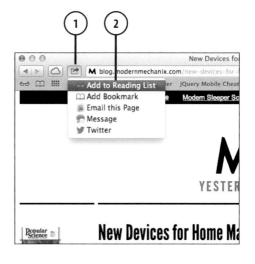

1. Click the Share Sheet button in the Safari toolbar.

2. Choose Add to Reading List from the Share Sheet pop-up menu.

Paneless Reading List Additions

In addition to the steps described here, you can also Shift-click links to add them to the Reading List, or press Shift-Command to add your current page to the list. If you're more of a click and drag person, you can drag individual links to the Reading List pane or to the Reading List icon to add them to the list as well.

Managing Your Reading List

After you add things to your list, you want to read them, right? To manage your list, just follow these steps:

1. Open the Reading List by clicking the Reading List icon.

2. Click All or Unread to limit your view of the list to all pages, or just pages you haven't finished reading.

3. Click a Reading List entry to load the page in Safari.

4. Click the X icon in the upper-right corner of an entry to remove it from the list.

5. Click Clear All to remove all items from the list.

6. Click the Reading List icon again to hide the list when you're finished.

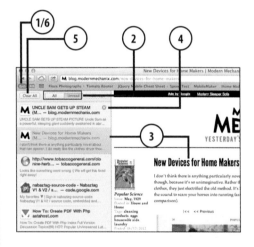

Reading List on the Ready

Your reading list icon in the Safari toolbar occasionally acts like a progress bar, slowly changing color. While this is happening, Safari is fetching the articles in your list so they are ready to read immediately as soon as you click them.

Advanced Browsing Features

Although "web browsing" as a pastime is only a little more than a decade old, it's a skill that it almost seems that we were born with. Little by little, browser developers have been refining the process to add additional features. Safari is no different.

Using Tabbed Browsing

Originally, web browsers created a new window for each page you visited. In Safari, all these windows can be combined under a single window with tabs representing individual websites within that window. To use tabbed browsing in Safari, follow these steps:

1. Click the + button near the far right of the Safari toolbar.

2. A new tab is added.

3. Enter a URL (or choose a bookmark) to browse to a new site in that tab.

4. Use the tabs to quickly switch between web pages. Note that while you're browsing, you can hold down Command as you click links. The links create a new tab in the Safari browser window.

Fine-Tune Your Tabs

To fine-tune your tabbed browsing behavior (or disable it entirely), use the Tabs section of the Safari Preferences. (Choose Safari, Preferences, from the menu bar.)

Viewing All Tabs

If you find yourself lost in tabs, not knowing what they all are, you can view all the tabbed web pages at once in a pretty scrolling view. To do this, follow these steps:

1. Perform a pinch gesture (Magic Trackpad only) within a web page or click the Show all tabs icon at the far right of the Safari toolbar.

2. The tabs appear in a horizontally scrolling list. Use two fingers (Magic Trackpad) or one finger (Magic Mouse) to swipe side to side and view, or click the small circles underneath the web page images.

3. Click within a page to go to that page, or reverse your pinch (Magic Trackpad only) to return to your standard tab view.

Viewing PDFs Online

In Mountain Lion, Apple has included a helpful PDF viewer that makes reviewing PDF documents a breeze. When you click a PDF link, the viewer opens. To control the viewer, follow these steps:

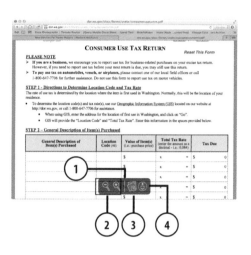

1. Position the cursor near the bottom center of the browser window to show the PDF controls.

2. Click + or – to zoom in and out.

3. Click the Preview icon to open the PDF in the Mountain Lion Preview (an Image/PDF viewer) application.

4. Click the Download button to save the PDF to your Downloads folder.

Distraction-Free Reading with Reader

Web pages, unfortunately, are rarely dedicated to getting you just the information you need. They are filled with ads and other distracting content, and frequently require you to click multiple links to get the whole story. To provide a distraction-free reading experience, Apple includes a Reader feature with Safari that strips out all the unnecessary cruft. To use Reader, follow these instructions.

1. When viewing a web page with a story you want to read, check to see if the Reader button is lit up at the far right of the URL field. Click it.

2. You are now viewing a clean version of the content.

3. Position your pointer near the bottom of the Safari window to show additional controls, which enable you to change the font size, email or print the article, or close the Reader session.

4. Click the X to close Reader and return to a normal browser.

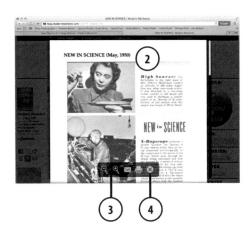

Disabled Reader Button?
C'est la vie!
The Reader feature of Safari does not work with all articles—only those that it can correctly identify and reformat. If the button is disabled, Reader can't work with the content you're viewing and no amount of reloading or fiddling with settings is going to help.

Continuing Browsing with iCloud Tabs

Ever start reading something on one computer or iOS device and want to pick it up somewhere else? Instead of having to remember to add things to your reading list (or email yourself a bookmark), you can use the iCloud tabs button. This simple feature makes it easy to see what tabs are open on your other devices and quickly open them wherever you are.

1. Click the iCloud button in the toolbar.

2. A popover appears showing all your open tabs, by device.

3. Click an entry to open it in your local browser.

Enable the Safari iCloud Service

This feature requires the Safari service to be active on your iCloud account, as described earlier in this chapter.

Sharing with Others

To share the page that you are currently reading with someone else via email or Messages, you can use the Safari Share Sheet. We discuss more about Share Sheets in Chapters 5 and 7. For now, follow these steps:

1. Click the Share Sheet icon when browsing a page you like.

2. Choose to share the page via email or messages.

3. When sharing via email, a new email is created and you can choose whether to share a reader version of the page, the full web page, a PDF of the page, or just the link!

Social-Ready Sharing

In Chapter 5, "Being Social with Messages, FaceTime, Twitter, Facebook, and Game Center," you learn how to add Twitter and Facebook to the Share Sheet, making it simple to quickly tweet or post the current URL to your favorite social networking site.

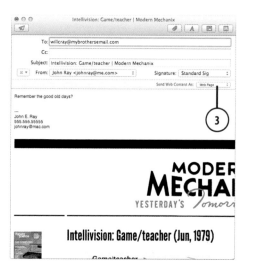

Enabling Private Browsing

If you share a computer with other people, and there's a chance that they might stumble upon something in your web history that you'd prefer they didn't (holiday gift orders, for example), you can enable private browsing.

When private browsing is enabled, no website content is saved to your iMac—it's as if you were never there:

1. Choose Safari, Private Browsing from the menu bar.

2. Click OK when prompted to verify whether private browsing should be enabled.

3. You can now use Safari as you would normally, but your session is private—as indicated in the URL field.

4. Choose Safari, Private Browsing again to disable private browsing.

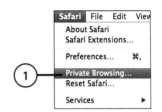

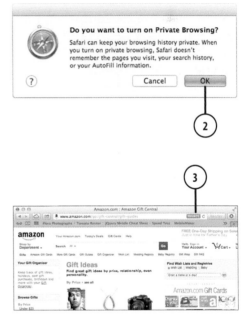

Protecting Your iMac and Yourself Online

Safari offers several tools to help protect you from fraudulent activity online. To ensure that you have the most secure browsing experience possible, complete the following configuration:

1. Choose Safari, Preferences from the menu.

2. Click the Security toolbar icon.

3. Check the checkbox beside Warn When Visiting a Fraudulent Website.

4. Check the checkbox beside Block Pop-up Windows.

5. Click the Privacy toolbar icon.

6. Be sure that the Block cookies option is set to from third parties and advertisers.

7. Choose whether Safari should deny all access to your location information, or to prompt you if a website requests it. Note that some online services can provide valuable customized information using your location.

8. Click Ask Websites Not to Track Me to request that your website visits be logged as little as possible. Note that web service providers may not pay attention to this setting.

9. To remove all information stored on your computer by the sites you've visited, click "Remove All Website Data." You may want to repeat this from time to time.

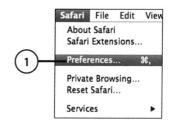

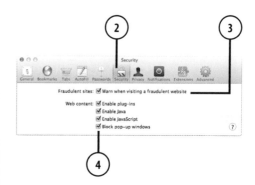

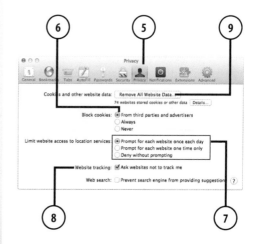

10. Use the Notification Preferences section to manage which web-sites can post notifications to the Mountain Lion Notification Center.

11. Close the Safari Preferences.

Go with What You Know

As a general rule, you should never download files online unless you trust the source. By default, Safari opens files that it has identified as safe. If you prefer to prevent Safari from opening any file it downloads, you can find this option under the General Safari Preferences.

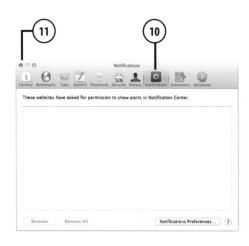

Adding Web Content to the Dashboard

Many of us visit a web page just to see a tiny piece of content, such as the latest weather report or breaking news. With Safari and Mountain Lion's Dashboard, you can create your own widget, called a web clipping, that is accessible directly from your iMac's dashboard. This gives you instant access to information you like without needing to open Safari. The content even updates automatically as long as you are connected to the Internet.

1. Visit the web page with the content you want to add to the dashboard.

2. Choose File, Open in Dashboard.

3. Position the box on the page so that the content you want to capture is highlighted as best possible, then click your mouse.

4. Fine-tune the selected area by dragging it within the Safari window and using the handles on the sides to resize it.

5. Click Add when you are satisfied with the results.

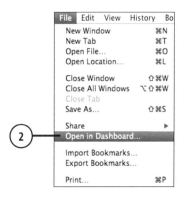

Changing the Clipping Appearance

To customize the web clipping even more, click the "i" icon in the lower-right corner of the widget in Dashboard. You are given the option of several different borders that can be applied to stylize the clipping.

6. The Dashboard opens and the new web clipping widget is displayed.

Extending Safari's Capabilities with Extensions

Safari supports developer-created extensions that can add additional functionality to your browsing experience—such as the ability to quickly access Twitter, eBay, and other services without leaving your current web page. Safari extensions are supported by the individual developers, so after you install one, you will need to refer to their documentation for further support.

Installing an Extension

Installing extensions doesn't require anything more than clicking a link on a website.

To find and install Safari extensions, follow these steps:

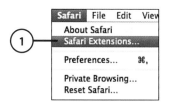

1. Choose Safari, Safari Extensions from the menu bar.

2. An Apple website opens listing all registered extensions.

3. Use the website to browse to an extension you are interested in, and then click the Install Now button beside the extension.

4. After a few seconds, the extension is installed and activated. Depending on how it works, you may see a new button or area added to the Safari toolbar. Follow the developer's instructions to use the extension.

Managing Extensions

To manage the extensions you've installed—including configuring them, if configuration is necessary—use Safari preferences. Follow these steps to access your extension preferences:

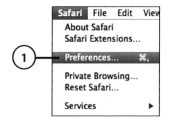

1. Open the Safari preferences by choosing Safari, Preferences from the menu bar.

2. Click the Extensions button in the top of the Preferences window.

3. Click an individual extension to view its configuration options.

4. Use the Enable checkbox to enable or disable individual extensions.

5. Click Uninstall to remove the extension entirely.

6. Use the On/Off switch to disable all extensions.

7. Click the Updates button to look for and install updates to any installed extensions.

8. Close the Preferences panel when finished.

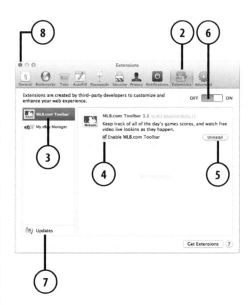

Practice your game in Game Center.

Chat with friends and
family in Messages.

Be social with Twitter and Facebook.

In this chapter, you learn how to use your iMac to be social online, including:

→ Configuring instant messaging in Messages
→ Conducting video and audio chats
→ Chatting across computers and iOS devices
→ Sending Tweets and Facebook Updates from applications throughout OS X
→ Setting up Game Center
→ Comparing gaming stats with your friends

5

Being Social with Messages, FaceTime, Twitter, Facebook, and Game Center

In addition to providing methods of sending and consuming content, the Internet (and Mountain Lion) gives us new ways to be social. Using the tools built into OS X, you can send instant messages, conduct video chats, send tweets, and play games with your friends.

In this chapter, you learn how to use many of the features of Mountain Lion's Messages, Web, FaceTime, and Game Center applications. These will help you stay on top of current events in your friends' lives and interact with people around the world—without driving up your phone bill.

Instant Messaging with Messages

When email isn't conversational enough, instant messaging can take over. Your iMac comes with a first-rate instant messaging application called Messages (found in the Applications folder). You can use Messages for text messaging, audio conferencing, video conferencing, and even screen sharing. If you have an iCloud, GoogleTalk, Jabber, or AIM (AOL Instant Messenger) account, you're ready to go.

There are two ways to use Messages, although both are integrated (somewhat poorly) into the same interface. First, you can use Apple's unique iMessage protocol to send and receive messages on all your iOS devices and Macs simultaneously. Using this approach, you can start a conversation on Messages on your iPad and then pick it up immediately on your iMac just by starting Mountain Lion's Messages app. Best of all, after you enable an iMessage account, you don't even have to *start* Messages to receive notifications. As long as your iMac is online, you will receive your iMessages.

The second way to use Messages is with a traditional instant messaging account, such as AIM, Yahoo! Messenger, or GoogleTalk. The process is pretty similar, regardless of your approach, and when you've started a messaging session, you'll be using the same interface regardless.

To keep things straight in your mind, remember that if I talk about using an iMessage account or sending an iMessage, I'm referring to Apple's Mac and iOS messaging system. I'll be as specific as possible as I describe the features in Messages.

Adding Accounts to Messages

Apple simplifies the process of configuring Messages by emailing you to create an iMessage account *and* a traditional account the first time you run the app. After that, however, I recommend that you manage your accounts in different locations.

Configuring Your Accounts During Startup

Unlike other accounts, to configure iMessage within Messages, you need to use the application itself. This is likely to change in the future, but for now, don't expect too much consistency in the interface. The easiest way to configure Messages with an iMessage account (and an IM account) is to do so during the first run, like this:

1. Start Messages from the Dock, Launchpad, or Applications folder.

2. Click Continue at the Welcome to Messages screen.

3. Enter the Apple ID (and password) you want to use with the iMessage protocol.

4. Click Sign In.

5. Choose whether you want your contacts to view when you read messages sent using the iMessage protocol.

6. By default, the email address associated with your Apple ID can receive iMessages. To add other addresses, click the + button or the Add an Email line and type a new address.

7. Click Continue.

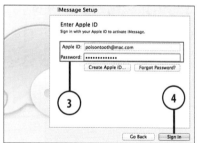

8. If you want to configure a traditional IM account, choose the account type from the drop-down menu; otherwise, go to step 10.

9. Enter your IM username and password.

10. Click Continue.

11. Click Done to begin using Messages

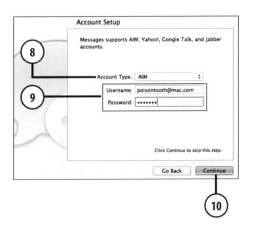

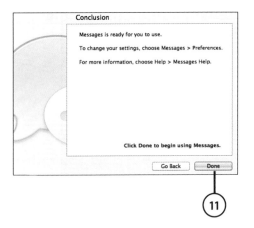

Accessing Your iMessage Account Settings

To manage an iMessage account after you've first started the Messages application, you need to use the Messages preferences. Follow these steps to manage your settings:

1. Choose Messages, Preferences from the menu bar.

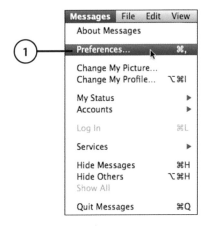

2. Click the Accounts toolbar.

3. Select the iMessage account entry.

4. Use the Enable This Account check box to enable or disable the account.

5. Uncheck Send Read Receipts if you don't want your contacts to see when you've read their messages.

6. Choose a location for your account.

7. Click + or Add an Email… to add a new account that can receive iMessages.

8. Close the preferences when finished.

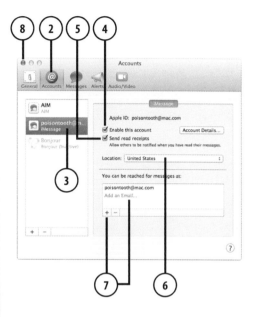

Adding a Traditional IM Account to Messages

If you want to configure IM after running Messages for the first time, I recommend using the central Mail, Contacts & Calendars preference panel. You need to know your account type, username, and password before continuing.

1. Open the Mail, Contacts & Calendars System Preferences panel.

2. Choose the online service that provides your IM account by clicking its name on the right. If your service only provides IM and not mail or calendaring, click Add Other Account to directly configure an IM account.

3. If you chose Add Other Account, select Add a Messages Account.

4. Click Create.

5. Fill in the requested information in the setup wizard that appears.

6. Click Create.

7. Close the System Preferences window.

Multiple IM Accounts? No Problem!

Adding multiple IM accounts to Messages is no problem. The Messages buddy list window combines your buddy lists into a single consolidated list. You can log in and out of the different services using the availability controls for each account (they are stacked on top of each other), as described in the "Logging into (and out of) Your IM Account" task.

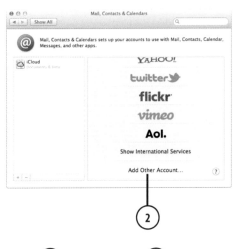

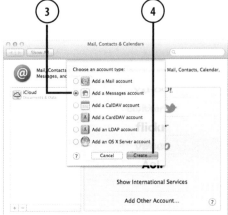

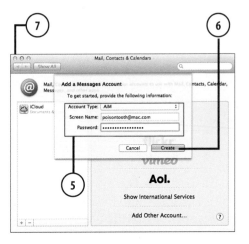

Logging into (and out of) Your IM Account

When Messages has an account configured, you're ready to start Messages and begin chatting immediately. No "logging into" iMessage accounts is required; your IM account is automatically logged in when you start the application. To manually log out of or into your IM accounts, you simply need to set your status.

1. Click the status message in the lower-left corner of the Messages window.

2. To keep your status in sync between accounts, make sure Use Same Status for All Accounts is checked.

3. Choose Offline to log out.

4. Choose any other status to log back into your IM account.

5. Choose Invisible to log in but hide your availability from other people.

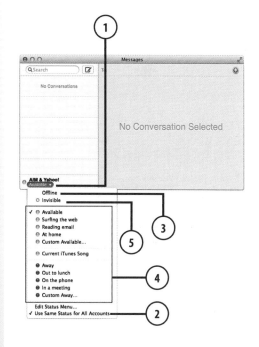

Adding a Messages Status Menu

To add a Messages status menu to your menu bar, open the Messages Preferences and click Show Status in Menu Bar within the General settings. This gives you the ability to log in and out of your IM accounts when Messages isn't running. Remember, however, that you can't log out of your iMessage account; it is always active unless you explicitly deactivate it in the Messages preferences.

Configuring Your IM Identity

If you're using traditional IM services (AIM, Yahoo!, and so on), you should customize your identity to better represent your online presence. With Messages, it's
simple to set custom status messages and pictures to reflect your current mood.

It's Not All Good

IM BUT NOT iMESSAGE

Things get a bit confusing here. These features are not available for iMessage
accounts; they apply to traditional instant messaging only. I do hope (and
suspect) that Apple will add these features later.

Setting the Messages Picture

Because your iMac has a camera built
in, you can swap your IM picture
whenever you want. Just smile and
click, and instantly your buddies are
seeing a new image.

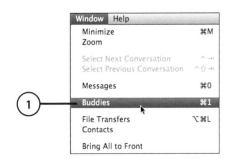

1. Choose Window, Buddies to open
   the IM buddy list.

2. Click the picture in the upper-
   right corner of the Messages
   buddy list.

3. Choose from a Recent picture or
   Default IM pictures, or click
   Camera to use your iMac's
   camera.

4. Click the Camera icon to take a
   new picture, or drag a picture
   from the Finder into the Recents
   section to use it.

5. Set cropping and size for the picture by dragging it within the preview window and adjusting the
   zoom slider.

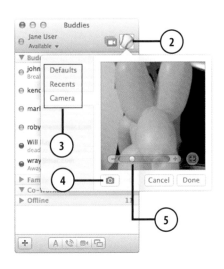

6. Apply effects, if desired, using the Effects button.

7. Click Done to start using the new picture.

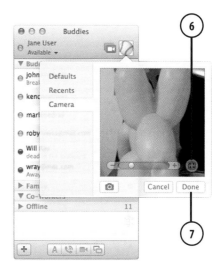

Configuring Custom Status Messages

Your status message can convey your state of mind, ask a question, or present some other information to your buddies. To configure a new status message, follow these steps:

1. Click the status pop-up menu either in your buddy list or in the main messages window.

2. Choose Edit Status Menu.

3. Click + or – under the Available or Away lists to add or remove status messages.

4. Click OK to save your status message settings.

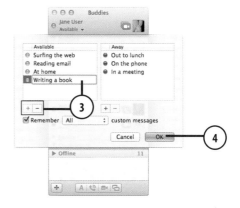

Managing Your IM Buddy List

Sending iMessages to your friends on Macs and iOS devices requires that you know their iMessage address or have it listed in your Contacts application. If you're using an IM account, however, you need to make sure that your buddy list is kept up-to-date with the people you want to chat with.

As you probably know, a buddy list contains all the people you want to chat with (and possibly some you don't). With each buddy is a display of his status (Away, Available, Idle, and so on) and an icon to indicate his chat capability.

Cross-Platform Video Conferencing

Messages can carry out cross-platform A/V chats with Windows users using AIM, Google Talk, or Yahoo!.

Adding Buddies

To initiate an IM chat with someone, you must first add her to your buddy list.

1. Click the + button at the bottom of the buddy list.

2. Choose Add Buddy.

3. If you have a contact card for the person you want to add, click the disclosure arrow in the lower-right corner of the window to display your contacts, and then find and click the person's name.

4. Choose the IM service your buddy uses and select her screen name.

5. Enter a first and last name for your addition, and choose a group, if any are available. Think of groups as a "folder" for your buddy.

6. Click Add.

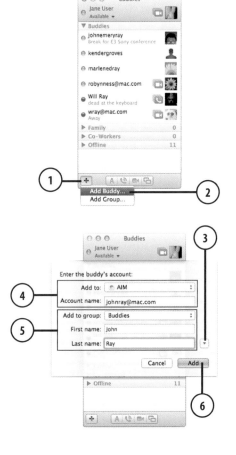

Adding Groups

As your IM buddy list grows, you might want to consider organizing your buddies into groups, such as friends, family, coworkers, and so on. Adding new groups is similar to adding new buddies.

1. Make sure View, Use Groups is selected in the Messages menu bar.

2. Click the + button at the bottom of the buddy list.

3. Choose Add Group.

4. Enter a name for the new group.

5. Click Add.

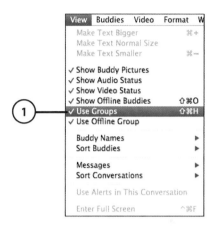

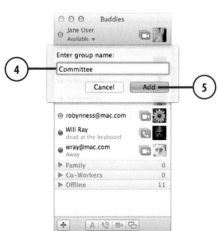

6. Drag buddies within the buddy list into the group where you want them to appear.

Recent Buddies

By default, a group called Recent Buddies is added to your buddy list after you start chatting to people. This group contains all the new contacts you've communicated with recently. You can disable this group within the Messages IM account settings.

Communicating with IM and iMessages

Messages, through an iMessages account, can communicate with your friends and colleagues using text and file attachments, such as images.

When using IM accounts, Messages supports a number of communications methods, including text, audio, and video. Messages Theater even makes it possible to share visual media from your iMac across a chat session. For example, you might review an upcoming presentation with colleagues to fine-tune the content or present a slideshow of a vacation to friends and family.

Responding to an Incoming Chat Request

After you've configured Messages and given your iMessages address screen name to your buddies, chances are, you'll start getting a few messages. To respond to an incoming chat request, follow these steps:

1. If you're in another application with no windows open, the Messages icon updates with a count of the messages you have waiting.

2. Open Messages and make sure the main window is visible. If it isn't, choose Window, Messages from the menu bar.

3. The Messages window shows all your current and new conversations.

4. To accept a conversation request, just click the entry in the list on the left and begin chatting.

5. If you don't know the individual or don't want to hear from him, just hover over his appropriate entry in the conversation list and click the X button that appears.

6. When you're finished chatting, close the Messages window.

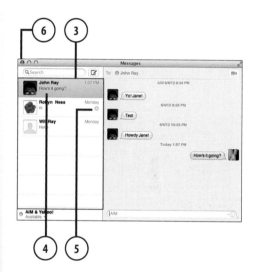

Starting a Chat

To initiate an IM or iMessage chat with one or more buddies, make sure the Messages window is visible (Window, Messages) and follow these steps:

1. Click the New Chat button.

2. Click the + button to choose from a list of your contacts (useful for iMessaging) or your IM buddy list.

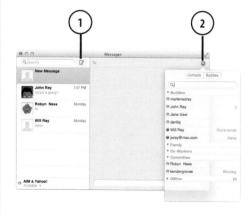

3. Alternatively, begin typing in the To field. Messages autocompletes as you type and shows you the different accounts you can use to communicate with someone. Click the contact (and communications method) you want.

4. Type to your friend, press Return, and wait for a response.

Double-Click to Chat

If you're viewing your buddy list, you can also initiate an IM chat by double-clicking a buddy or clicking his name and then clicking the A (for text chat) button at the bottom of the buddy list.

Consolidate or Separate Messages

Messages automatically consolidates your chats into a single window. To move a chat to a separate window, double-click one of the conversations in the Messages window. It becomes its own standalone chat window.

Starting an IM Audio or IM Video Chat

A/V chats require significantly more bandwidth than text chats. Messages automatically senses the capabilities of your machine and Internet connection, and that of the people involved in your conversations. Messages does not allow chats unless it thinks they will be successful. Using IM, you can chat with up to 3 other people via video and 10 via audio, depending on your connection and assuming that they have microphone- or camera-enabled systems. When chatting with iMessage, you are able to launch a FaceTime conversation with one other individual.

The good news is that, regardless of your system capabilities or those of your chat partners, Messages shows only the relevant options.

1. Begin a chat with the individuals you want to include in an audio or video session.

2. Click the camera icon in the upper-right corner of the chat window.

3. You see the available audio and video chat options listed. Choose one. Note that choosing a FaceTime option (if available) launches the FaceTime application, which we discuss next in this chapter.

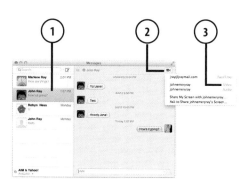

4. Your audio/video chat begins. Click the + button to add members to the chat. A three-way video conference with a balloon dog is shown here.

5. Toggle mute on the chat by clicking the microphone.

6. When conducting a video chat, click Effects to apply real-time video effects to your onscreen image.

7. Click the double arrows during a video chat to expand the video to full screen.

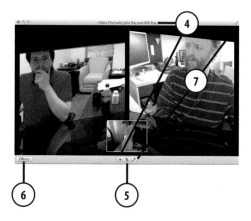

Be Heard with a Headset

If you find yourself using video or audio chat frequently, you might want to invest in a microphone or headset. To change the Messages microphone and set up a headset, open the Audio/Video section of the Messages preferences.

Sharing Files, Photos, and Your Screen

In addition to being a great communications tool, Messages can serve as a collaboration platform or even a way to interact on the same desktop. If you've ever found yourself in the position of having to talk through a document long distance or troubleshoot technical problems remotely, you'll appreciate the additional functionality built into Messages.

Presenting Files, Photos, and Web Pages in Messages Theater (IM Only)

Using Messages Theater, you can share the content you've created on your iMac—photos, videos, and even web pages. You can share these items with any buddy whose connection supports video chats. Unfortunately, this is limited to traditional IM accounts—iMessage is not supported.

1. Initiate a video chat with the individuals with whom you want to share a file.

2. Click the + button in the video chat window and then choose Share a File with Theater to share an individual file, Share iPhoto with Theater to share an iPhoto album, or Share a Web Page with Theater to share a page from Safari.

3. Choose the file, album, or web page you want to share.

4. Click the Share button.

5. When the sharing session begins, use the onscreen controls to move through the presentation. Text and PDF files display page controls, video files include typical video controls, and so on.

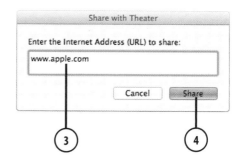

6. Click the X button in the upper-right corner of the shared file's display to stop sharing and return to the video chat.

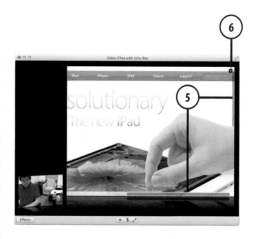

Transferring Files over Messages

Messages provides a convenient mechanism for sending files while chatting. You can send individual files or even entire folders (IM only) just by dragging them into Messages.

1. Find the file or folder that you want to share.

2. To transfer to an online buddy you aren't currently chatting with, drag the file to her name in your buddy list (IM only).

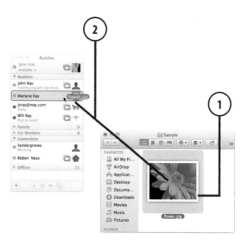

3. To transfer a file within an active chat session, drag the file to the chat window. Files such as images are displayed inline in the chat and can be previewed without opening the file.

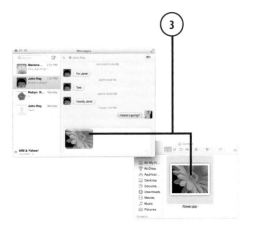

Confirming File Transfers

If someone attempts to transfer a file to you over Messages, you must click the download within the chat window to accept the file. By default, all transferred files are saved in the Downloads directory.

Starting a Screen-Sharing Session (IM only)

A unique Mac-only feature of Messages is the capability to share someone else's screen. Using this tool, you can control the other person's computer as if you were sitting directly in front of it.

1. Begin a chat with the individuals you want to include in a screen-sharing session.

2. Click the camera icon in the upper-right corner of the chat window.

3. Choose whether you want to request access to your buddy's screen or if you want to share your screen.

4. After the request is accepted, you (or your buddy) have access to the remote screen. You can interact with the desktop as if you were sitting in front of the computer.

5. Click the miniaturized version of the screen to switch between viewing the local screen and viewing the remote screen.

6. Click the X on the miniature screen to close the session.

Remote Support via Messages

When screens are being shared, Messages also starts a simultaneous audio chat, which makes it easy for you to talk through issues with the remote party.

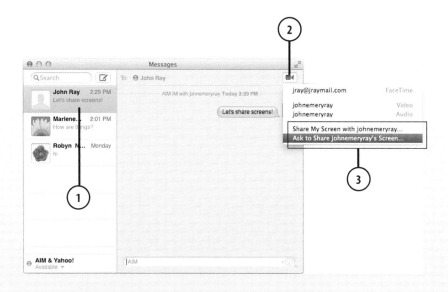

Video Calls with FaceTime

Similar to an iMessage account in Messages, FaceTime is an always-running video chat service that bridges your iOS devices and your Macs. FaceTime starts automatically if someone places a FaceTime call, and it simultaneously rings on as many Macs, iPhones, and iPads as you want.

Also as with iMessage, FaceTime requires zero configuration beyond providing an email address that your friends can "call."

Setting Up FaceTime

The first time FaceTime starts, you need to provide it with an Apple ID for registration. After the initial ID is provided, you can associate as many email addresses as you want with a given install. Follow these steps to add FaceTime addresses:

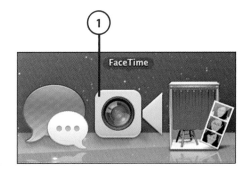

1. Open FaceTime from the Dock, Launchpad, or Applications folder.

2. Enter your Apple ID and password.

3. If you do not have an ID, click Create New Account to walk through an ID creation wizard.

4. Click Sign In.

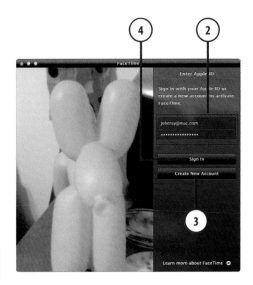

5. Provide the primary email address you want to use for FaceTime.

6. Click Next.

7. FaceTime logs in, and you're ready for calls.

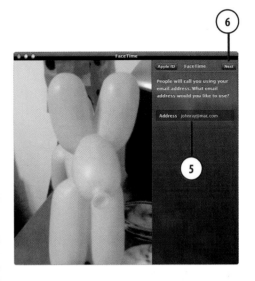

Placing FaceTime Calls

To place a call with FaceTime, you need to have the address or phone number of a FaceTime-compatible contact in your address book. In other words, make sure your family and friends have an iOS device or a Mac and have configured FaceTime. You also need to be sure you've stored their contact information in the Contacts application. (See Chapter 6, "Keeping Contacts, Appointments, Reminders, and Notes," for more information.)

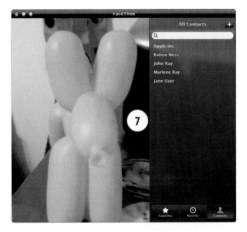

Placing Calls from the Contacts List

When you've got yourself a few equipped friends, follow these steps to call them over FaceTime:

1. Click the Contacts button at the bottom of the FaceTime window.

2. Browse your contacts. When you find the person you want to call, click his name.

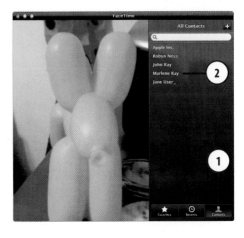

3. The contact information for your friend appears.

4. If you want to call the person frequently, click the Add to Favorites button to add a shortcut for future use.

5. Click the phone number or email address you want to call.

6. If the call is connected, you are able to see and talk to the other person. Otherwise, skip to step 9.

7. Use the button at the bottom-left corner of the window to mute the call, or use the button at the bottom-right corner to go fullscreen.

8. Click End to hang up when you are finished talking.

9. If the call does not connect, you're given the options of cancelling the call or calling back (redial).

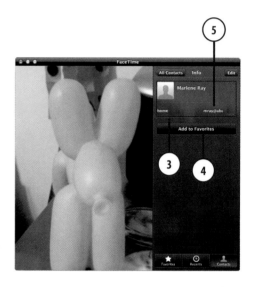

See Your Surroundings

By default, the FaceTime camera takes a portrait image. If you want to see more of your surroundings, you can rotate to landscape mode by choosing Video, Use Landscape (Command+R) from the menu bar.

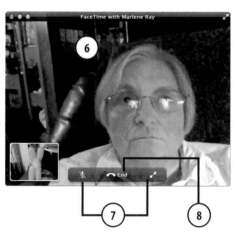

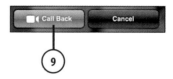

Placing Calls from the Favorites List

To place a call to someone you've marked as a favorite, complete these steps:

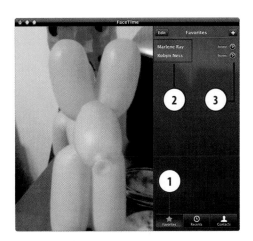

1. Click the Favorites button at the bottom-right corner of the FaceTime window.

2. Click a name in the Favorites list to place a call.

3. Click the arrow at the end of a favorite to open that individual's contact information.

4. The star beside the entry indicates it is used as the FaceTime address for a call from the Favorites list.

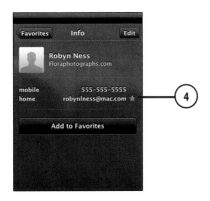

Receiving a FaceTime Call

If you've ever received a call on an iPhone, you'll be right at home receiving FaceTime calls on your iMac:

1. When an incoming call registers, FaceTime automatically starts with no user intervention.

2. Click Decline to ignore the call.

3. Click Accept to begin talking.

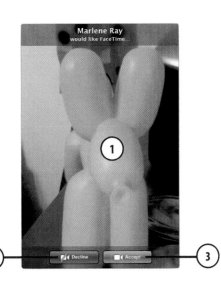

Did I Miss a Call?

If you're wondering whether someone tried to contact you while you were away, the FaceTime icon shows a count of your missed calls. You can find out details about the missed calls by accessing the call list, our next task.

Accessing Your Call List

FaceTime keeps a list of all incoming and outgoing calls, even if you aren't around your computer when a call comes, so that you can check later to see who called.

1. Click the Recents button at the bottom-right corner of the FaceTime window.

2. Click All to show all incoming and outgoing calls. Missed calls display in red.

3. Click Missed to filter the list to missed incoming calls.

4. Click an entry in one of the lists to place a call.

5. Touch the arrow at the right side of an entry to view that person's address book information and a full call history.

6. Click Clear to remove the call history.

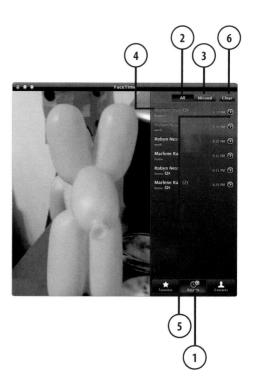

Disabling FaceTime

FaceTime is great, but as with a phone, sometimes you want to just ignore it. If you're having one of those days, you can disable FaceTime on your iMac so that it won't ring if someone tries to call.

1. Choose Turn FaceTime Off (Command+K) from the FaceTime menu.

2. FaceTime is now disabled on your iMac.

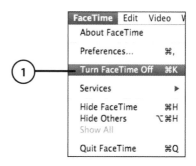

Updating Account Information and FaceTime Addresses

If you've registered several FaceTime accounts and want them all to ring on your iMac, you need to edit the preferences to list all the email addresses you have. To do this, follow these steps:

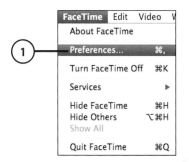

1. Open the FaceTime Preferences by choosing FaceTime, Preferences from the menu.

2. Click the Account line if you want to change the Apple ID associated with your account.

3. Click Add Another Email to add an alternative email account. If you have not registered that address with Apple, you need to look for an email with a clickable link for verifying your address.

4. Repeat step 3 for as many addresses as you want to use with your FaceTime installation.

5. Click the Caller ID line to display all addresses associated with your FaceTime.

6. Click a line to set that address as your caller ID.

7. Click the Preferences button to return to the main preferences.

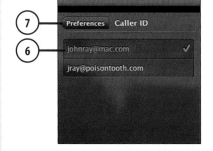

8. Click Done to finalize your
   preferences.

Using the Mountain Lion Twitter and Facebook Posting Support

Mountain Lion has baked-in Twitter support to make sending tweets as easy as clicking a button in many of your favorite applications. Facebook users can also get in on the fun by posting to their wall and photo albums in the same way. In this section, we look at how to enable Twitter and Facebook support throughout OS X and how to make use of them.

Enabling Twitter

To see the tweeting options in Mountain Lion, you must first enable Twitter. To do this, follow these steps:

1. Open the Mail, Contacts & Calendars System Preferences panel.

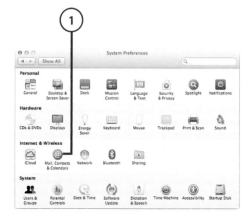

2. Click the Twitter service link on the right.

3. Enter your twitter username and password.

4. Click Sign In.

5. On the Summary screen, click Update Contacts to pull Twitter usernames and photos into your system-wide Contacts list.

6. Check or uncheck Allow Others to Find Me by Email to enable other Twitter users to find you online using your email address.

7. Close the System Preferences.

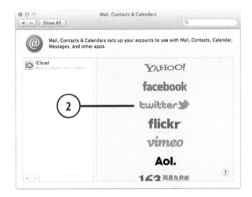

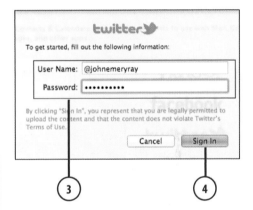

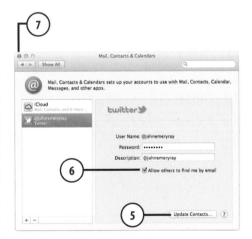

Enabling Facebook

To enable Mountain Lion to post Facebook updates, follow these steps:

1. Open the Mail, Contacts & Calendars System Preferences panel.

2. Click the Facebook service link on the right.

3. Enter your Facebook username and password.

4. Click Next.

5. Read the Facebook conditions and click Sign In.

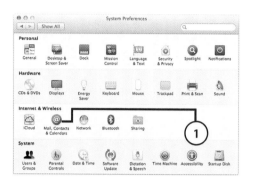

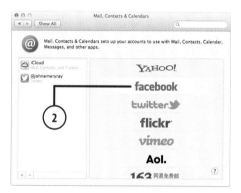

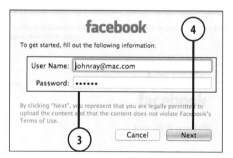

6. On the Summary screen, click Update Contacts to pull Facebook usernames and photos into your existing system-wide Contacts list.

7. Click the Contacts check box to add Facebook contacts as a new network contact list in the Contacts application.

8. Close the System Preferences.

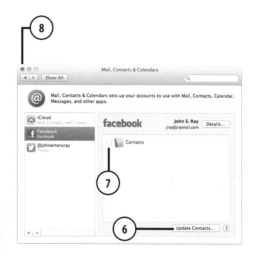

Posting Tweets and Facebook Updates

You can send tweets and post Facebook updates from any application that has been updated to support Mountain Lion's social networking implementation, such as the Finder or Safari. For example, suppose you want to post a photo from the Finder. To compose the update, do the following:

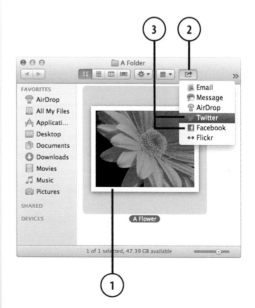

1. Select or open an image (if you want to attach an image to the tweet or Facebook update).

2. Click the Share Sheet button.

3. Choose Twitter or Facebook from the drop-down menu. (This example uses Twitter.)

4. A composition window appears with the attachment (if any) in the upper-right corner. Enter your tweet/update here.

5. Click the Add Location button to add your current location to the post.

6. Click Send to send a tweet, or click Post to post to Facebook.

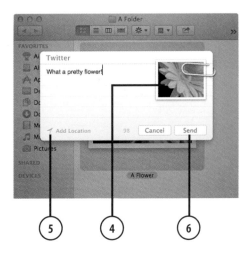

Being Social Is a Two-Way Street

You know how to post to Facebook and Twitter from Mountain Lion, but that's only part of social networking; you also need to be able to read posts that others send to you. To receive updates from your friends and followers on Facebook and Twitter, configure the Notification Center, as described in Chapter 1, "Managing Your iMac Desktop." Apple has included Notification Center settings for Twitter and Facebook that let you receive and view updates right on your desktop. Of course, you'll still want a browser handy to access all the features of these popular sites, but OS X has you covered for the basics.

Post from Anywhere with Notification Center!

If you're suddenly struck with a fantastic idea for a tweet or Facebook post, you can instantly access a composition window by clicking the Notification Center icon in the menu bar and then clicking the Twitter or Facebook buttons at the top of the Notification Center area. These buttons become visible only after you've enabled Twitter and/or Facebook.

Getting Your Game on with Game Center

New to Mountain Lion is Game Center, a social gaming system similar to Xbox Live and the Playstation Network. With Game Center, you can create lists of friends, compare games and game achievements, discover new games, and launch games that you have installed on your iMac. What's more, Game Center is fully integrated with iOS, so you can keep track of your friends (and frenemies) wherever you are.

Cross-Device Play—Sometimes

You might have heard that the OS X version of Game Center enables you to play games on your iMac against friends on their iPhones and iPads. It's true that this feature is available, but it's on a per-game basis for the developers to enable—it doesn't just start working if you have the same games installed on different devices.

Signing into Game Center

The first step to using Game Center is signing in. This requires an Apple ID, so it's a good idea to have one before starting. If you don't have one, however, it can guide you through the setup.

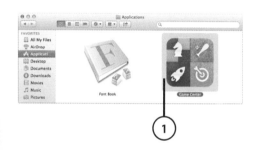

1. Open Game Center from the Launchpad or Applications folder.

2. Click Create Apple ID to get a new Apple ID, if needed.

3. Enter your Apple ID and Password in the provided fields.

4. Click Sign In. If this is your first time using Game Center, complete steps 5–8.

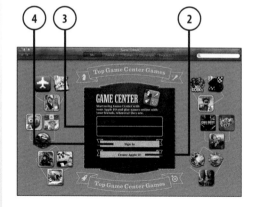

5. Enter a Nickname on the screen that appears.

6. Click the Public Profile if you want others to be able to search and find you within Game Center.

7. Click Use Contacts for Friend Suggestions if you want Game Center to use your Contact list to try to find new friends.

8. Click Continue.

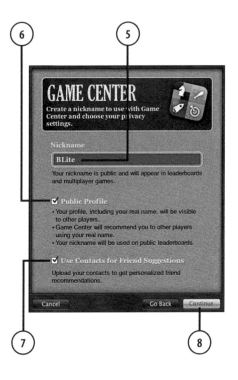

Navigating the Me Screen

After logging into Game Center, you are taken to a screen that describes your account status and provides some additional features.

1. A summary of the games you have installed (across all your devices), points you have accumulated, and friends is shown in banners near the center of the screen.

2. Click the field under the banners to set your current status, or what is displayed to your friends in their Game Center.

3. Click Change Photo (or your photo) to take a new picture of yourself.

4. Click your account name to log out if you share your computer account with other people.

Managing Friends and Friend Requests

After getting into Game Center, it's a good idea to start adding and managing friends—otherwise, you'll be lonely. Let's review the process for sending friend requests, reviewing friend recommendations, and responding to requests that have been sent to you.

Sending a Friend Request

How do you get a new friend? By sending a request. To send a friend request to someone you know, follow these steps:

1. Click the Friends button at the top of the Game Center window.

2. Click the Add Friends button on the left side of the window.

3. A friend request dialog box appears. Enter the email address for the person you want to add.

4. Type a message to your potential friend, or use the default.

5. Click Send. A request is sent to your friend, who can respond on her Mac or iOS device.

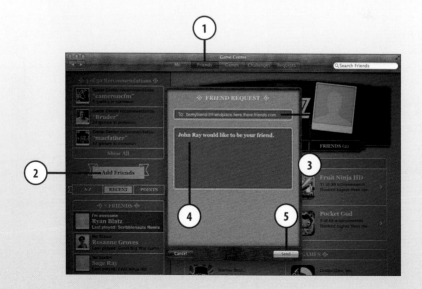

Responding to a Friend Request

When a friend request comes in, you can respond wherever you are by clicking a link in email. You can also respond directly in Game Center.

1. The Requests button updates with the number of pending requests beside the name. (The Game Center icon also shows this count.) Click the Requests button.

2. Choose the friend request you want to view.

3. Click Ignore to ignore the request, or click Accept to make the person your friend.

4. If you clicked Accept, the person is added to your Friends list.

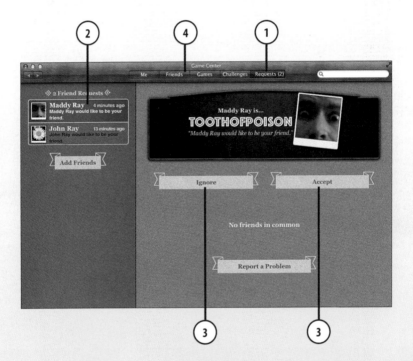

Getting Friend Recommendations

Not sure who you should add as a friend? Game Center can give you recommendations based on your contacts and the games you have installed. To see the recommendations, follow these steps:

1. Click the Friends button.

2. Click the Friend Recommendations box at the top-left of the window.

3. The left side of the window changes to a list of recommendations.

4. Choose an individual from the list to view her information on the right.

5. Click Send Friend Request to send a friend request to the individual.

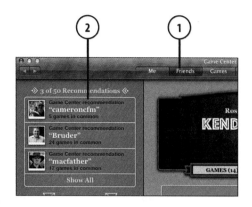

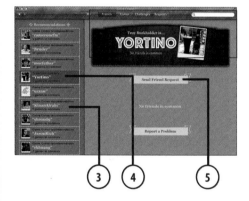

Sizing Up Your Friends

After you have established a few friends, you probably want to see how your gaming skills compare to theirs. Game Center enables you to drill down to view a number of different stats about your friends and their games. To see a few, follow these steps:

1. Click the Friends button.

2. Choose how your friends are sorted using the buttons at the top of the Friends list.

3. Filter your list down to a specific friend using the Search field, if desired.

4. Click an entry in the list to select a friend.

5. A summary of your friend's game-playing activity is shown on the right.

6. Click a game to drill down to more information.

7. The window refreshes to show the achievements that you and your friends have earned, as well as a summary of your overall scoring. (Note that we haven't earned any achievements in this screenshot.)

Lost? Just Go Back

It's easy to drill down to a great detail of information in Game Center. If you ever feel lost, you can use the forward and back arrows in the upper-left corner; they work just like the arrows in a web browser.

Browsing by Game

In the previous step, you located a friend and used her as the starting point for browsing to a game and showing a comparison of activity. You can also take a more game-centric approach.

1. Click the Games button at the top of Game Center.

2. The window refreshes to list all your games across all devices. (New game recommendations appear at the top but are not visible here.)

3. Search for individual games using the Search Games field.

4. Click a game to view information about it.

5. Use the Achievements button (the default) to show your personal achievements in the game.

6. Click Leaderboards to show how you compare against players worldwide.

7. Use the Players button to display any friends who have recently played the game.

8. Click the Tell a Friend button to email your friend and convince her to download the game.

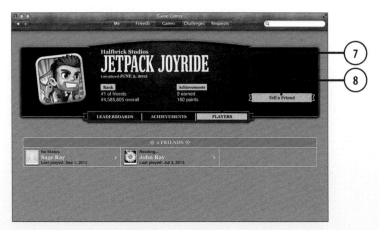

Making and Taking a Challenge

Within Game Center, you can challenge your friends to beat your achievements or game scores. For some games, you can even challenge them to a live match.

To send (or receive) a challenge, follow these steps:

1. Navigate to the game you want to challenge your friend in.

2. Click the achievement (or a score from the leaderboards) that you want to base the challenge around.

3. In the popover that appears, click Challenge Friends.

4. Pick the friends you want to challenge.

5. Click Next.

6. Enter a message (if desired) to go with the challenge.

7. Click Send. Your challenge will now be sent, and you'll be notified if your friends meet (or beat!) your results.

8. Click the Challenges button at the top of the Game Center window to view any Challenges your friends have sent you in return.

Manage your business
and personal contacts
in Contacts.

Use Calendar
to schedule
appointments.

Keep Reminders on
all your devices.

Write Notes.

In this chapter, you learn how to use your iMac to manage your contacts, calendars, and appointments, including:

→ Adding contacts to Contacts
→ Organizing contacts into groups
→ Creating calendars in Calendar
→ Adding appointments to calendars
→ Inviting contacts to meetings
→ Making lists in Reminders
→ Keeping your thoughts in order with Notes

6

Keeping Contacts, Appointments, Reminders, and Notes

OS X Mountain Lion gives you the tools to organize contacts and tie into enterprise personnel directory systems. It also works with your company's scheduling system to track calendars, meeting invitations, reminders, and even organize notes. What's more, it can make all this information available on all your iOS devices. In this chapter, you learn about Contacts, Calendar, Reminders, and Notes—your iMac's personal information management utilities.

THE INVISIBLE, EVER-PRESENT, iCLOUD

>>> Go Further

The apps in this chapter share a unique characteristic that can be a bit confusing to new users—where they store their information. If you've never set up iCloud, Exchange, or a Google account on your computer, you probably aren't connected to any form of network storage. In this case, the data created in each application is stored locally on your iMac.

In practice, however, it's pretty difficult to get through setting up a Mac with Mountain Lion *without* establishing a (thankfully free!) iCloud account. If you've established an iCloud account (see Chapter 4, "Accessing iCloud, Email, and the Web," for details), chances are that the information in the applications discussed in this chapter is synced with an iCloud server. What makes this confusing is that the applications provide very little in terms of visual cues to show that you are using iCloud services for your data. The good news is that it really is transparent, and using iCloud means you can access this information from a web browser wherever you are! If you aren't sure if you're using iCloud, now is a good time to jump back to Chapter 4 so you can ensure you're making the best use of this important suite of Mountain Lion utilities.

Managing Contacts in Contacts

Many of the applications you use on your iMac send information to, or receive information from, other people. Mountain Lion offers a central contact database that you can access in Mail, Calendar, Messages, FaceTime, and other programs. Appropriately enough, you manage this database through an application called Contacts (found in the Applications folder).

Contacts acts as a digital rolodex, pulling together personal and business contacts. With it you can also connect to enterprise directory servers for accessing centralized company personnel listings. The Contacts application is similar to many other Mountain Lion applications, providing a drill-down view from a group list, to a contact list, and, finally, to contact details.

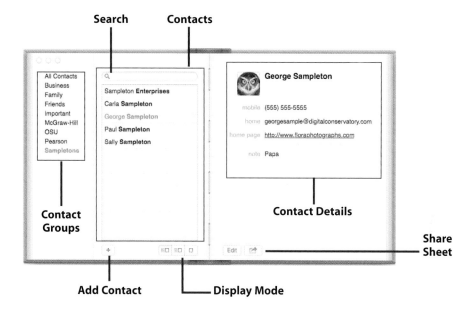

Search   Contacts

Contact Groups

Contact Details

Share Sheet

Add Contact   Display Mode

Adding Groups

When you first start Contacts, there is a single pseudo-group available: All Contacts. The group displays any contact available in Contacts. To make the most efficient use of Contacts, you should add groups for the different types of contacts you use—businesses, coworkers, family, friends, doctors, and so on. Like Mail, Contacts can use rules to create Smart Groups.

Emailing to a Group

Contacts groups are more than just organizational tools; they also add functionality to applications that support them. After you've defined a group, you can use it in Mail as your message recipient, effectively sending the email to everyone in the group!

Creating a Group

To create a new group, decide what you'd like it to be called, and then follow these steps:

1. Open Contacts from the Dock, Launchpad, or Applications folder.

2. Click the display mode button at the bottom of the window to show the group list or choose View, Groups from the menu bar.

3. Choose File, New Group from the menu bar.

4. A new "untitled group" is added. Type to change the name of the group.

Creating a Smart Group

If you'd like to use search criteria to
define your Contacts groups, you're
in luck! Contacts supports Smart
Groups, capable of pulling contacts
together from multiple different
groups and even network accounts:

1. Choose File, New Smart Group
   from the menu bar.

2. Enter a name for the new Smart
   Group.

3. Use the first pop-up menu from
   the selection lines to choose a
   contact attribute.

4. Use the second pop-up menu to
   set a comparison.

5. Enter the value to use in the comparison in the text field at the end
   of the selection line.

6. Use the + and − buttons to add
   or remove additional selection
   criteria.

7. Click OK when you're satisfied
   with your group definition.

8. The new group is added and
   automatically shows the contacts
   based on the criteria you defined.

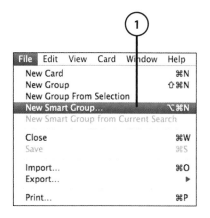

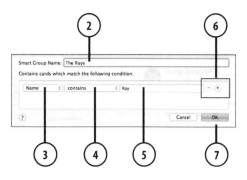

Adding Contacts

The bulk of what you'll do with Contacts is entering contacts. When it comes to people, one size contact does not fit all. For your family, you might want to store email addresses, instant messaging screen names, and birthdays. But for business contacts, you might only be interested in an address and a phone number. Contacts adapts to the information that you want to store.

Creating a New Contact

To create a new contact, gather all the information you have available for the person, then do the following:

1. With the groups visible, click the group name that the contact should be added to.

2. Click the + button below the member names column.

3. A new No Name contact is added, and the empty contact details display.

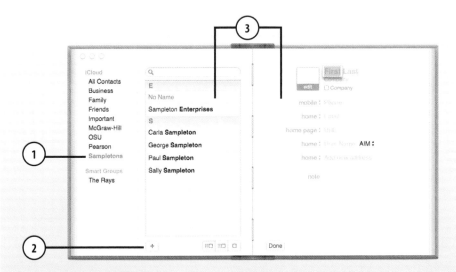

4. Use the fields in the detail view to enter information for the contact.

5. Click Company to classify the entry as a business rather than a personal contact.

6. Set the context for the card's fields (for example, choose home, work, or cell for a phone number) using the pop-up menu in front of each field.

7. If you'd like to store additional information for the contact, choose Card, Add Field from the menu, and choose the type of field to add.

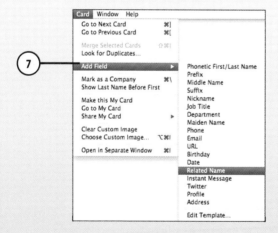

8. Click the Done button at the bottom of the contact details to save changes to the contact.

Moving and Editing Contacts

If you find that you've filed your contact in the wrong group, just drag and drop the contact name into another group. You can re-edit contact details at any time by selecting them and clicking the edit button below the details pane.

Setting a Contact Image

Contact images can help you visually identify individuals in your Contacts and are even displayed in Mail or shown on your iOS device if you sync Contacts. To set an image for a contact, complete these steps:

1. Find and select the contact that you want to associate with an image.

2. Double-click the picture within the card details.

3. Click the Camera label to take a new picture, or see step 4 to use an existing picture.

4. Alternatively, click Recents and drag an image file into the right half of the window.

5. Set cropping and size for the picture by dragging it within the image window and adjusting the zoom slider.

6. Apply effects, if desired, using the Effects button.

7. Click Done to finalize the contact's custom image.

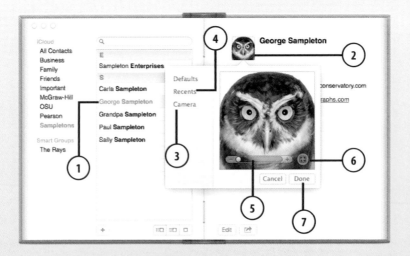

Creating "My" Card

Many system applications and utilities need to identify information about you. To tell Contacts who you are, enter a new contact for yourself, and then follow these steps:

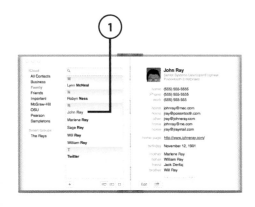

1. Find and select your name in the Contacts.

2. Choose Card, Make This My Card from the menu bar.

The Importance of Me

You need a functional "My" card to fully use Calendar, so be sure to set this if you have any intention of using Calendar.

Editing the Contact Template

If you find that you constantly need to add new fields to contacts, you might want to consider modifying the default contact template. Changing the default gives you a starting place for all future contacts.

1. Choose Contacts, Preferences from the menu bar.

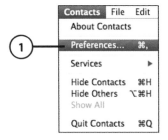

2. Click the Template icon in the Preferences toolbar.

3. Use the Add Field drop-down menu to add additional fields to the contact template.

4. Click the double arrows to open the pop-up menus in front of each field to set the context for fields displayed in the template.

5. Close the Contacts preference window when you're finished.

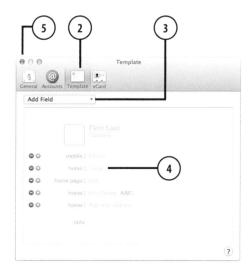

Searching Contacts

When you aren't sure of an exact name, or where you filed a contact, you can quickly search across all your groups and contact data.

1. With the Groups visible, click the name of the address group to search.

2. Type into the search field.

3. As you type, the contact list is filtered to show only matching contacts.

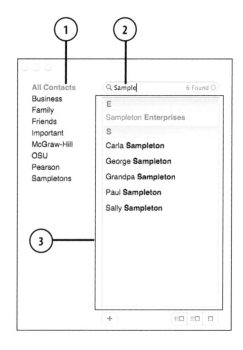

Detecting and Merging Duplicates

Over time you might find that you've created several Contacts entries for a single person. To identify and merge duplicate cards, follow these steps:

1. Choose Card, Look for Duplicates from the menu bar.

2. Contacts analyzes your contacts and presents you with the option to merge identified duplicates.

3. Click Merge to fix the duplicates.

Merging Cards

If you manually identify two or more cards that need to be merged, select the cards, and then choose Card, Merge Selected Cards from the Contacts menu bar.

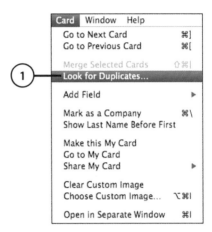

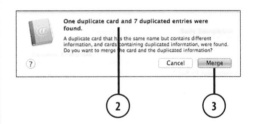

One duplicate card and 7 duplicated entries were found.

A duplicate card that has the same name but contains different information, and cards containing duplicated information, were found. Do you want to merge the card and the duplicated information?

Using iCloud and Server-Based Contacts

Contacts isn't just limited to keeping information on your iMac; it can also synchronize with Google, Yahoo! contacts, and connect to enterprise directory servers such as Exchange, standard LDAP servers, as well as Apple's iCloud service. In fact, if you've already configured iCloud (see Chapter 4), you're probably already storing your contacts "in the cloud."

Connecting to iCloud Contacts Syncing

To connect to iCloud, or verify that your Contacts app is using iCloud to store and sync contacts across your devices, follow these steps.

1. Open the iCloud System Preferences panel.

2. Check the box beside Contacts.

3. Close the System Preferences. Your Contacts application is now connected to iCloud.

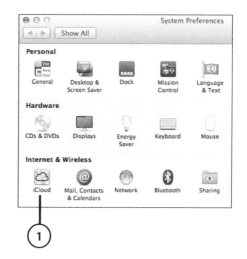

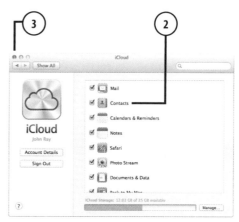

Connecting to Other Contact Servers

While iCloud is consumer-friendly, many organizations provide central enterprise contact directories that you can access via Contacts. Contacts supports several enterprise standards, including Google and Yahoo contacts as well as Exchange servers. Using a central server means that changes and updates are available immediately for everyone who is connected.

To configure server-based contacts, follow these steps:

1. Open the Mail, Contacts & Calendars panel.

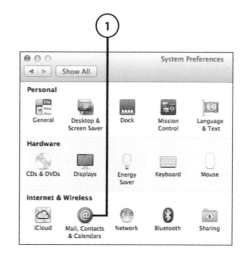

2. Choose the service providing contact information from the list on the right. Alternatively, click Add Other Account (at the bottom of the list) to add LDAP, CardDAV, or OS X Server accounts.

3. The account creation window appears. Use the fields in the window to configure your account information.

4. Click Set Up or Continue (the button name depends on your service provider) to walk through the account setup wizard.

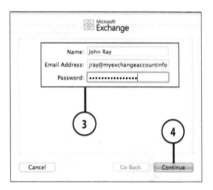

5. If you're setting up a service that provides more than just contacts (such as Exchange), you are prompted to automatically set up corresponding email accounts and calendars.

6. Click Add Account to configure your iMac to connect to the server.

7. Close the System Preferences.

Settings, Settings, Everywhere!

At the time of this writing, Apple is including the option of defining *some* contact servers directly within the Contacts apps preferences (the same goes for the Calendar app, which we'll cover next). If you happen to stumble upon these, you can use them (it's the same as using the Mail, Contacts, & Calendars preference panel), but I'd suggest using the central preferences to be consistent.

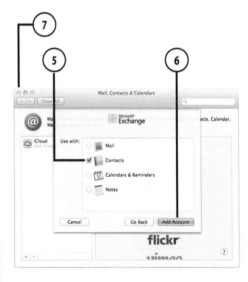

8. The new server appears in the Contacts group list. You can click to select groups within it, and from there, create new groups if desired.

Sharing Contacts via Email and Messages

To share a contact via email, messages, or airdrop, you can use a Mountain Lion Share Sheet. For detailed information on Share Sheets, refer to Chapter 7, "Sharing Devices, Files, and Services on a Network." For now, be aware that the basic process works like this:

1. Navigate to a contact that you want to share.

2. Click the Share Sheet button to show the sharing options.

3. Choose the method of sharing that you'd like to use.

4. Your choice launches the appropriate supporting application and attaches the note for sending.

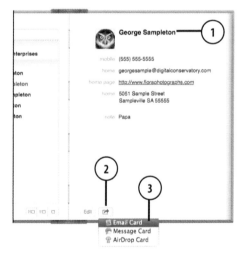

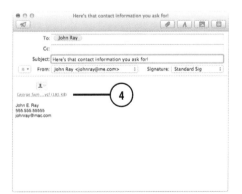

Exporting and Importing vCards

In addition to sharing contacts, you can also export the contact information directly to a vCard. These are small files that store all the information for one or more contact entries. Just highlight the entries in Contacts, and then drag them to your desktop. A vCard file is created with all of the contact data.

To import a vCard, reverse the process. Drag a received vCard into Contacts (or double-click it in the Finder), and it is imported automatically.

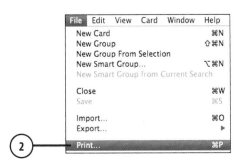

Printing Addresses

When you need to use actual paper for your communications, Contacts provides several useful print options for printing your contacts onto envelopes or labels.

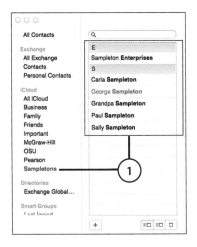

1. Select individual contacts or contact groups to print.

2. Choose File, Print from the menu bar.

3. Click the Hide/Show Details button so that the full print dialog window appears.

4. Use the Style pop-up menu to select an output format (Mailing Labels, Envelopes, and so on).

5. Set any of the additional configuration options for the style you've chosen.

6. Click Print to output the contact information in the selected style.

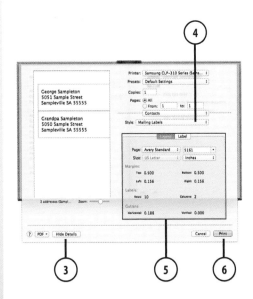

Working with Schedules in Calendar

Much of our lives, like it or not, revolve around adhering to a schedule. Calendars, in whatever form we use them, keep us informed of upcoming appointments, holidays, birthdays, and anniversaries. Your iMac can serve as your scheduling work center. Mountain Lion's Calendar application (found in the Applications folder) is a fast and well-connected way to keep your life in order.

Unlike applications such as Microsoft Outlook, Calendar is an unimposing application that shows you everything you need within a single window.

Calendar's general operation is similar to other Mountain Lion applications you've used. Clicking the Calendar button displays a list of calendars you have access to. Selecting a calendar in the calendar list displays the content of the calendar to the right. Double-clicking a calendar entry shows the details of the entry. The four buttons at the top (Day, Week, Month, Year) coupled with the View menu control the appearance of the calendars.

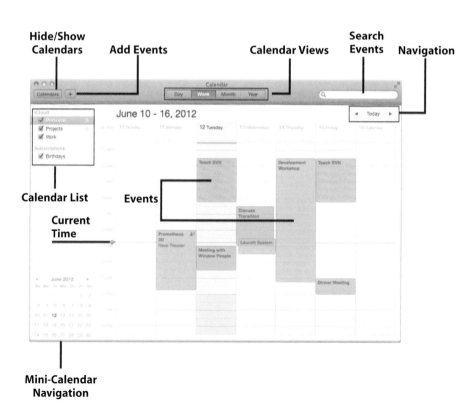

Despite its simple styling, Calendar works just as well for managing calendars located on your iMac as it can interacting with Exchange, iCloud, Google, and other standards-based enterprise calendaring systems.

Adding Calendars

The first step in using Calendar is to establish the calendars that you use to store your events. Calendar comes with two calendars already created: Home and Work. If you've established an iCloud account and turned on Calendar syncing, these will be iCloud-based calenders. If not, they'll be stored locally on your iMac. Use these default calendars or create new calendars depending on how you want to categorize your events.

Creating New Calendars

To create a new calendar (locally or on a server), follow these instructions:

1. Open the Calendar application from the Dock, Launchpad, or Applications folder.

2. Click the Calendars button to show the list of calendars (if they are hidden) on your iMac.

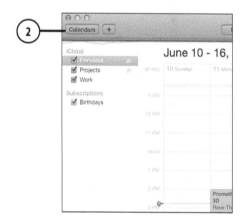

3. Pick File, New Calendar from the main menu bar. You may have to Choose iCloud (or another calendar provider if you've already set up a calendar account).

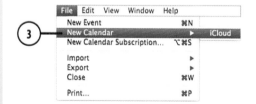

4. A new Untitled calendar is added at the bottom of the calendar list. Type to replace Untitled with whatever name you'd like.

5. Verify that the checkbox next to the calendar is selected so that the calendar entries are visible.

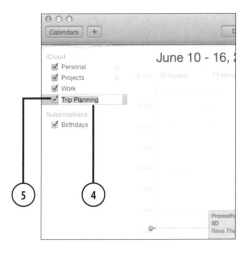

Local vs. Network Calendars

The Calendar application can work with calendars located directly on your iMac (local) as well as calendars located on a server, such as iCloud. Depending on how your iMac is set up, the menus in the Calendar application may change slightly. For example, if you are using calendars hosted on multiple network servers (iCloud and your office's Exchange calendar server, for instance), you'll notice that when you choose to create a new calendar, you are given the option of choosing which server should hold it. Only if no server accounts are visible will the On My Mac (locally) option be available.

Additionally, Calendar supports the notion of local calendar groups (go to File, New Calendar Group) when working with local calendars. Using calendar groups, you can organize clusters of calendars and enable or disable all of them at once. The bad news? As soon as you use iCloud or another network service, this option completely vanishes. Because Apple is obviously weaning us off this feature, we're omitting it from this edition.

Connecting to iCloud and Server-Based Calendars

Server-based calendars are stored on a central network location rather than on your iMac. Network calendars can be accessed and modified in Calendar on multiple computers. Many businesses use Exchange Server, for example, to provide shared calendars and scheduling. Apple's iCloud service provides free shared calendaring that can be used across your Mac and iOS devices. Another option, Google Calendar, is also free and can be used on virtually any desktop or mobile device.

Connecting to iCloud Calendar Syncing

iCloud is the easiest and fastest way to create shared network calendars on all your devices. To use iCloud to store your calendars, follow these steps:

1. Open the iCloud System Preferences panel.

2. Check the box beside Calendars & Reminders.

3. You may be prompted to merge any existing calendars with your iCloud calendars. Click Merge to move their information to iCloud.

4. Close the System Preferences.

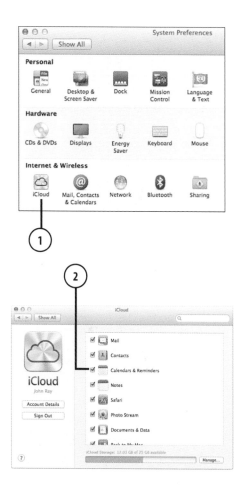

Connecting to Other Calendar Servers

Most server-hosted calendars are associated, in some way, with an email account. To configure a server-based calendar, you probably only need an email account and password. If you know, however, that your calendar is hosted somewhere else, you should collect the server name in addition to your username and password before proceeding. As you'd expect, calendar services are configured through the Mail, Contacts, and Calendars panel, as you've become accustomed.

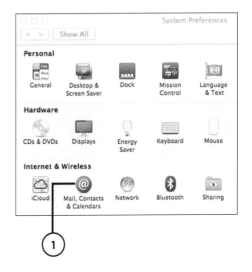

1. Open the Mail, Contacts & Calendars panel.

2. Choose the service providing the calendar information from the list on the right. Alternatively, click Add Other Account (at the bottom of the list) to manually add a CalDAV account. If you aren't sure, ask your ISP or network administrator.

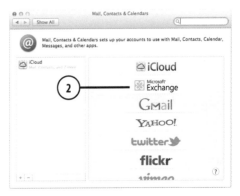

3. The account creation window appears. Use the fields in the window to configure your account information.

4. Click Set Up or Continue (the button name depends on your service provider) to walk through the account setup wizard.

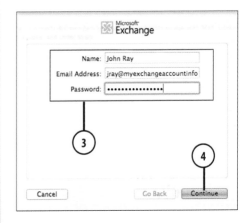

5. If you're setting up a service that provides more than just calendars (such as Exchange, Yahoo!, or Gmail), you are prompted to automatically set up corresponding email accounts and contact servers. Be sure to choose Calendars & Reminders.

6. Click Add Account.

7. Close the System Preferences when finished.

8. The calendar list displays a new section with any calendars that are located on the server.

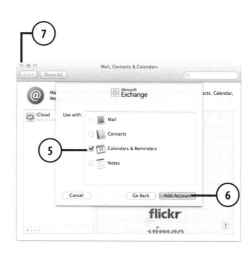

Subscribing to a Public Shared Calendar

Another calendar type is a shared calendar. These read-only Internet-published calendars are available for TV show schedules, holidays, sports team game dates, and other useful information. To subscribe to a shared calendar, copy the URL for the calendar and then follow these steps:

1. Choose File, New Calendar Subscription from the Calendar menu bar.

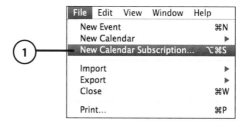

2. Enter the URL for the calendar you are subscribing to.

3. Click Subscribe. If prompted, enter a login name and password to access the calendar, and then click OK to continue.

4. Set a name, color, and storage location for the calendar.

5. If there are any embedded Alerts or Attachments in the calendar (this depends entirely on the person making the calendar available), you may want to strip them out. Click the Remove checkboxes to make sure you get only calendar data and no surprises!

6. To enable the calendar to automatically update, choose an Auto-refresh time.

7. Click OK.

8. The subscribed calendar appears in a new section within the calendar list.

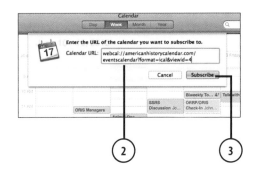

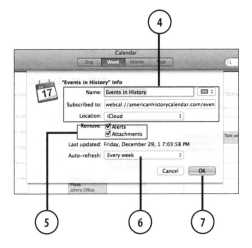

It's Your Birthday!

By default, Calendar shows one Subscription-based calendar, even if you haven't added any. This is the "Birthdays" calendar, which displays the birthdays for individuals in your address book (assuming you've added their birthdays!).

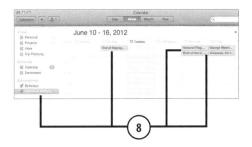

Viewing Calendars

After you've set up one or more calendars in Calendar, you can view their contents. To view a calendar in the calendar list, follow these steps.

1. Click the checkbox in front of the calendars you want to view.

2. Use the Day, Week, Month, and Year buttons to narrow or expand your calendar view.

3. Use the arrows to move forward or backward by day, week, month, or year, depending on the current view. You can always navigate by month using the arrows by the mini-calendar in the lower-left corner.

4. Click Today to jump to today's date.

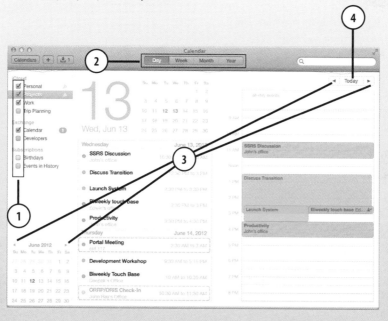
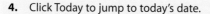

Working with Events

What good is a calendar if you don't have the ability to add events? In Calendar, events can be anything you'd like—birthdays, outings, reminders, anything—as long as they are associated with a date. If you'd like to include other people in the event, you can even send out invitations that are compatible with other calendaring systems, such as Exchange.

Creating a New Event

Events can hold a large number of attributes that describe what the events are, when they are, where they are located, and so on. All you need to know to create an event, though, is the date and a name for the event:

1. Navigate to the day on which the event takes place.

2. Switch to Day or Week view.

3. Click and drag from the start time to the end time to create the event. The default event name, New Event, is highlighted automatically.

4. Type a name for the event, and then click off of the event to save it.

5. Control-click the event box, and choose the calendar that the event should be added to.

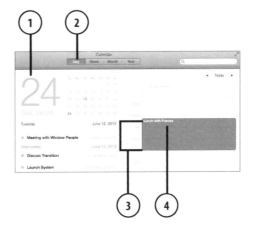

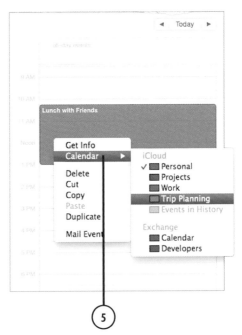

Double-Click to Add

You can add an event in the month view of the calendar by double-clicking a day. This method, however, does not let you define the start and end time of the event initially, so you need to edit it later to add that information.

Using the Quick Event Feature

Mountain Lion's Calendar application also supports a simple way of creating events without any calendar navigation at all. Quick Event provides simple, plain-text entry of new events directly from the Calendar toolbar. To use this feature, follow these steps:

1. Click and hold the + icon in the Calendar toolbar.

2. Choose the calendar that should hold the new event.

3. In the Create Quick Event field that appears, type a description of the event, such as "Dinner on November 12th at 6 pm," and press return.

4. A new event is added and opened for additional editing.

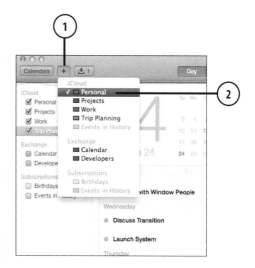

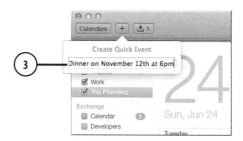

Editing Event Information

To edit the information for an event that you've created, first find the event on the calendar where you added it, and then follow these steps:

1. Find and double-click the event you want to edit.

2. Unless you've just added the event, an event summary window appears.

3. Click Edit.

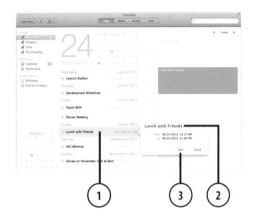

4. The event information window appears. Click any of the available fields to change values such as start or end times, location, alarms (notifications), and so on.

5. Click Done when you are finished editing the event.

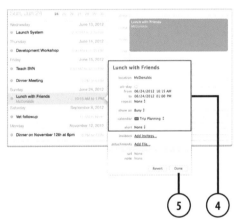

Sending Event Invitations

Calendar can work directly with Mail to send invitations for your events. When the invitees respond, their attendance status is updated directly in Calendar. Use the previous task to find and start editing an event, and then follow these steps to send invitations for that event:

1. Click the Add Invitees link.

2. Enter email addresses in the field that appears, just as you would in Mail. Add as many as you'd like.

3. Click Send to send the invitations.

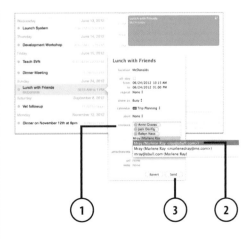

4. An icon appears in the upper-right corner of the event to show that invitations have been sent. A question mark indicates that responses haven't been received from all invitees.

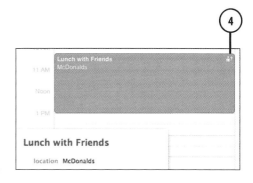

Setting Optional Attendees and Resending Invitations

After you've added an invitee to an event, you can click the name in the event summary or edit screen to show a drop-down menu that enables you to flag the person as an optional attendee or to re-send an invitation.

Checking Availability

If supported by your calendar server (such as Exchange), you can view an individual's availability for events by selecting an event, then choosing Window, Availability Panel from the menu bar.

Accepting Invitations

You can easily add to your calendar invitations that you receive. Even though invitations are sent through email, Mountain Lion's Mail program works with Calendar to automatically transfer the invitations to the Calendar Notifications area where you can act on them.

1. When a new invitation arrives, the Calendar application icon updates to show the count of invitations in the Dock.

2. The event is shown with a dotted outline in Calendar to indicate it has not yet been added.

3. Click the Notification button to show the notification panel in Calendar.

4. Use the Maybe, Decline, and Accept buttons to respond to the invitation.

5. Declined invitations are removed from your calendar; accepted and tentative invitations are added.

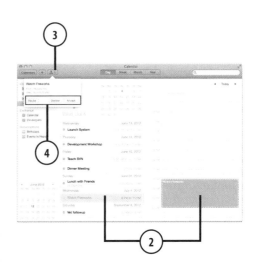

Changing Your Event Status

If you change your mind about an event, you can edit it in Calendar and change the My Status field to Accept, Maybe, or Decline.

Searching Events

If you're a heavy scheduler, or have dozens of enterprise calendars to manage, sometimes it's useful to be able to quickly search for events, which is a breeze in Calendar.

1. Make sure the checkboxes are selected for the calendars you want to search.

2. Enter your search terms in the Search field.

3. As you type, search options are displayed; pick the best option from the drop-down list.

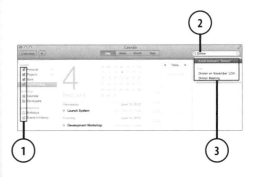

4. The results of the search are displayed in a pane at the right of the Calendar window. Click an entry to jump to that event.

5. Click the X in the search field to hide the search results.

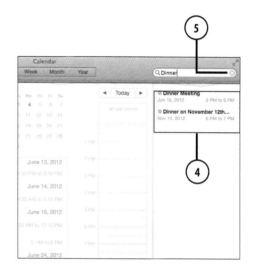

Printing Calendars

When you need your calendar information in paper form, Calendar does an amazing job of printing calendar and itinerary views.

1. Choose File, Print from the Calendar menu bar.

2. Set the view you want to print.

3. Set a time range for the calendar being printed.

4. Click the checkboxes beside each calendar to print.

5. Select which options should be added to the printed page.

6. Click Continue, which takes you to available printing options; after selecting options, you are ready to print.

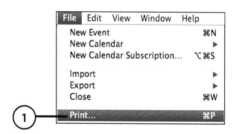

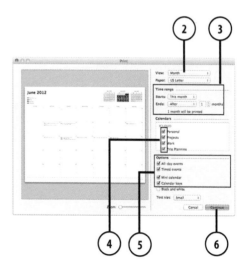

Remembering with Reminders

Beyond simple events that happen on a given date, day-to-day life often requires that you keep track of multiple to-do lists in your head—from home repairs that need to be done, to birthday shopping lists, and grocery store visits. Using Mountain Lion's Reminders app, you can create your own digital to-do lists and even make them contextually aware of your location—prompting you with reminders that apply only at home or the office.

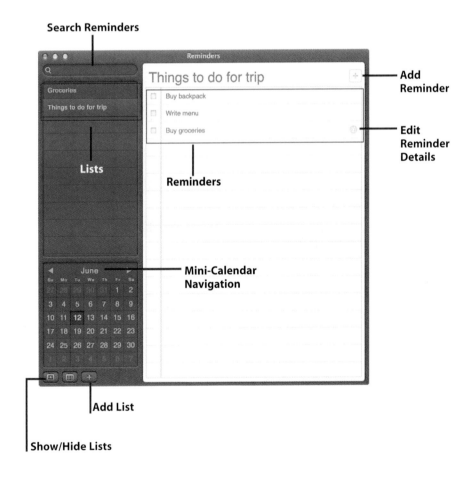

Creating a List

Reminders are organized into lists of related items. You can have as many lists as you want, but you need to have at least a single list to contain reminders at any given point in time. By default, you start with a single list called "Reminders," but you can add as many as you'd like. To create a new reminder list, follow these steps:

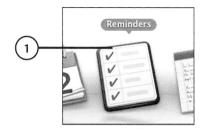

1. Open Reminders from the Dock, Launchpad, or Applications folder.

2. If the lists aren't visible, click the arrow in the lower-left corner of the window.

3. Click the + button near the bottom of the Reminders window.

4. A new list appears with the name selected. Type a new name and press return. The list is added and ready to be used.

Nothing Is Set in Stone

To rename a list, click its name in the left column in Reminders—it becomes immediately editable. Delete lists by clicking to select them and then pressing your Delete key.

Adding a Reminder

Once a list exists, you'll want to fill it with individual reminders. To create a new reminder within a list, complete the following actions:

1. Click to select the list you want to add a reminder to.

2. Click the "+" button in the upper-right corner of the Reminders window.

3. The cursor moves to a new line in the reminder list. Type the name for your reminder.

4. Press return to add additional reminders, or click on an empty line to end editing.

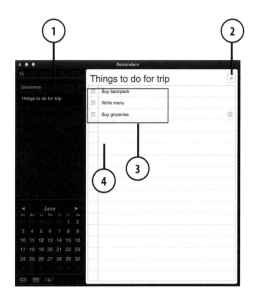

Setting Reminder Attributes, Including Location

A reminder can be more than just a title in a list—it can contain a date, a location, a repeating schedule, and more. Set the attributes for a reminder by doing the following:

1. Hover your pointer over a reminder item. An "i" icon appears near the right side of the reminder.

2. Click the "i" to show the reminder settings.

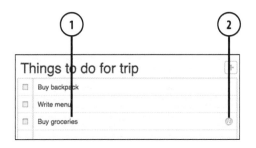

3. Use the title field to change the name of the reminder.

4. Click the On a Day checkbox to set a specific date/time for the reminder.

5. Use the date/time field to configure when the reminder is shown and set a repetition schedule.

6. Click the At a Location checkbox to receive the reminder when leaving or arriving at a given location.

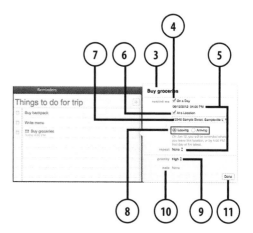

7. Use the drop-down list/field to choose a contact's address, or enter a new address to be used in conjunction with the location-aware reminders.

8. Set whether the reminder occurs when arriving or leaving.

9. Set a priority for the reminder using the priority pop-up menu.

10. Use the Note field to set any additional notes related to the reminder.

11. Click Done to save the reminder.

Location Reminders Require Your Location!

The first time you use reminders based on a location, you may be prompted to enable Location services. Click Open Privacy Preferences when prompted, or follow the instructions in Chapter 12, "Securing and Protecting Your iMac."

Completing Reminders

When you're done with a reminder, you'll want to indicate that it is completed. To set the completion status of a reminder, follow these steps:

1. Click the list that contains the reminder you want to complete.

2. Click the checkbox to the left of the reminder.

3. The reminder moves to a "Completed" list, accessible from the top of the current reminder list or by clicking the "Completed" heading in the column to the left.

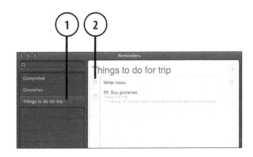

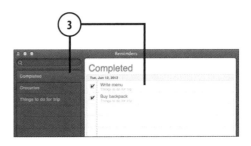

Don't Want to Do It? Just Delete It!

To delete a reminder or a reminder list (rather than having to actually follow through on it), just highlight it and press your Delete key.

Finding Reminders

Because reminders can be created across many different lists and many different dates, it's helpful to be able to quickly search your lists to figure out what you are supposed to be remembering, and when you should be remembering it. Thankfully, Reminders makes it easy to search all your lists and all your reminder dates very quickly.

Viewing Reminders by Date

If you've set dates for reminders, it's easy to see what reminders are associated with what dates (across all your lists) using the built-in mini-calendar in the Reminders application:

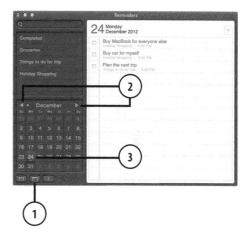

1. Show the mini-calendar (if hidden), by clicking the Calendar button in the lower-left corner of the application window. If the button isn't visible, you need to click the disclosure arrow button first.

2. Use the forward and backward arrows to navigate the calendar.

3. Click an individual date to show reminders associated with that day. Double-clicking a date opens it in a new window.

4. Choose View, Go to Today from the menu bar to quickly jump to the current date.

Searching Reminders

To search for reminders across all of your lists, follow these steps:

1. Click to position your text cursor inside the search field, and then type a search term.

2. The results are shown, organized by list, on the right side of the window.

3. Click the X in the search field to clear the results.

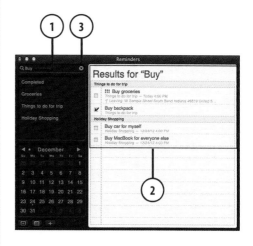

Using iCloud and Server-Based Reminders

As you may have noticed, reminders are very similar to Calendar entries. They're so similar, in fact, that they use the same server connections to manage their information. To learn how to configure Reminders to use an iCloud account, follow the instructions in "Connecting to iCloud Calendar Syncing" in the Calendar section of this chapter. Similarly, to connect to a different server for your reminders (Exchange or Google, for instance), follow the instructions in "Connecting to Other Calendar Servers."

Choosing Servers When Creating a New List

If you are connected to several different servers that each provide Reminder storage, you can choose which one a new reminder list is created on by clicking and holding the + icon in the bottom-right corner when you create a new list.

Keeping Track with Notes

Calendars and reminders capture much of our hectic schedules, but life can also be less structured—with new information and ideas coming at us from a dozen different directions. To keep us from losing our idea for "the next big thing," Mountain Lion includes a simple and effective note-taking application—Notes. Like the other apps in this chapter, Notes is also iCloud/server-connected, meaning that no matter where you take your notes, they'll be seamlessly accessible across all your devices.

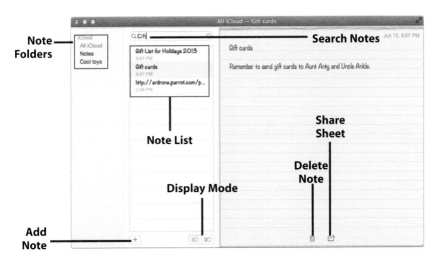

Note Folders

Search Notes

Note List

Share Sheet

Delete Note

Display Mode

Add Note

Managing Folders

Thoughts and ideas are rarely truly random. Chances are, you take notes about things you want to do at home, at work, with the kids, and so on. To create a sense of order, you'll want to start your OS X note-taking by setting up some folders for yourself.

Adding Folders

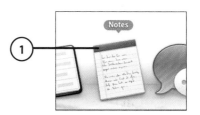

By default, notes are added to a default folder called Notes. To add a new folder of notes, do the following:

1. Open Notes using the icon in the Dock, Launchpad, or Applications folder.

2. Open the list of Note Folders by clicking the show folder list Display Mode icon near the bottom-center of the window.

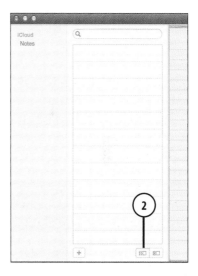

3. Choose File, New Folder from the menu bar, or Control-click in the folder list and choose New Folder.

4. A new folder appears with its name selected and editable. Type a new name for the folder and press return to save it.

Delete to Delete

Despite the different appearance, deleting a folder in Notes is the same as deleting a List in reminders. Click to select its name, and then press your delete key.

All On My Mac

The "All" folders (All On My Mac, All iCloud) can't be removed. They contain all the notes stored on that device.

Adding Notes

The most import aspect of using the notes application is also the easiest—adding notes. To add a new note, follow these steps:

1. Select the folder that should contain the note.

2. Click the "+" icon beneath the middle column in the application.

3. A New Note title appears at the top of the list, and the text entry cursor appears in the content area, ready to edit.

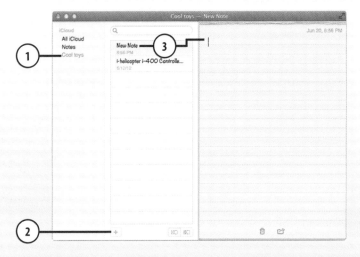

4. Type your note as you see fit.

5. The top line of the note automatically becomes the title for the note in the column to the right of the content.

6. If you decide you don't want a note, click the trash can icon to delete it.

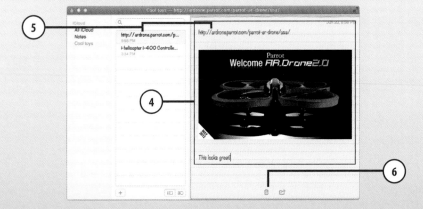

Prettify Your Most Mundane Notes
Your notes don't have to be plain text—you can drag or paste in pictures or other media. You can also use the Format menu to apply fonts, add lists, or indent your text.

Moving Notes Between Folders

If you've created notes in one folder that you later want to move to another, this is easily accomplished with a simple drag and drop. Do the following to move notes between folders:

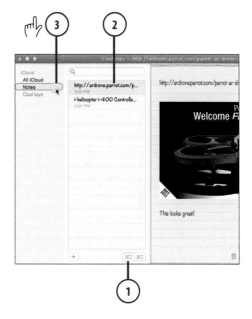

1. Make sure the folder names are visible using the Show Folder List icon at the bottom of the Notes window.

2. Click a note title to select it. Hold the Command key to select multiple notes at a time.

3. Click and drag from the selected note to a folder in the folder list. The notes are immediately transferred to the folder.

Searching and Displaying Notes

Notes can contain quite a bit of information, and after you've amassed a library of hundreds of notes, you may find yourself trying to track down a single tiny bit of information within a note. To search the available notes (in all note folders), just follow these steps:

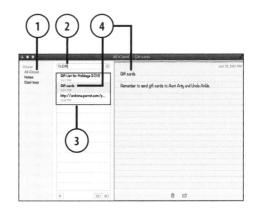

1. Choose a folder of notes to search or view, or All Notes to access all folders.

2. Type a search term in the search field to filter the notes being displayed (if desired).

3. The results are shown in the center column of the window.

4. Click a result to show that note's content to the right of the search results.

5. Double-click a note's title to show it in a new window.

Sharing Notes via Email and Messages

To share a note via email or messages, you can use a Mountain Lion Share Sheet. For detailed information on the process, refer to Chapter 7. The basic process works like this:

1. Navigate to a note you want to share.

2. Click the Share Sheet button to show the sharing options.

3. Choose the method of sharing that you'd like to use.

4. Your choice launches the appropriate supporting application and attaches the note for sending.

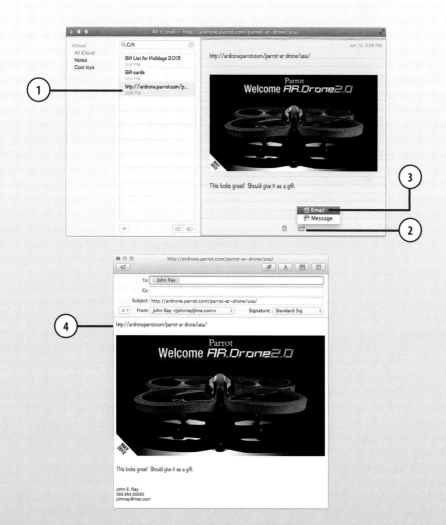

Using iCloud and Server-Based Notes

Notes, like the other utilities in this chapter, are stored, by default, on an available server account—probably iCloud, if configured. To set up or verify an existing server setup for your notes, you can use the instructions in the next two sections.

Connecting to iCloud Note Syncing

If you've already established an iCloud account, connecting Notes to iCloud is just a matter of clicking the right checkbox. If you do not have an iCloud account, you should review Chapter 4 for information on setting one up.

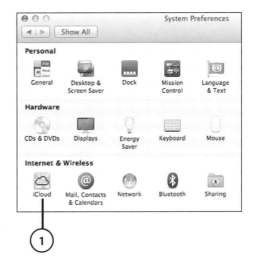

1. Open the iCloud System Preferences panel.

2. Check the box beside Notes.

3. Close the System Preferences. Your Notes application is now connected to iCloud.

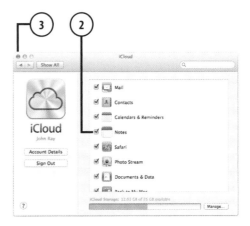

Connecting to Other Note Servers

As you've probably guessed, Exchange servers and Google accounts can also provide shared note storage. To use one of these servers to share notes between your computers or devices, follow these steps:

1. Open the Mail, Contacts & Calendars panel.

2. Choose the service providing Note storage from the list on the right.

3. The account creation window appears. Use the fields in the window to configure your account information.

4. Click Set Up or Continue to proceed.

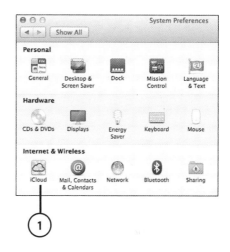

Choose a Folder to Set Your Server

If you have multiple servers set up, the process of creating a new folder is a bit ambiguous as to what server it will be created on. To force the folder to be created on a specific server, first make sure the Notes folder list is visible, and then click a folder name on the server you want to use. Subsequent *new* folders will be created on that server.

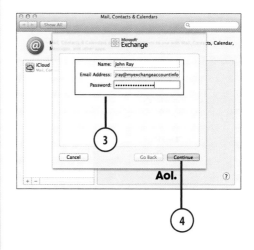

5. If you're setting up a service that provides more than just calendars (such as Exchange, Yahoo!, or Gmail), you are prompted to automatically set up corresponding email accounts and contact servers. Be sure to click the checkbox beside Notes.

6. Click Add Account.

7. Close the System Preferences when finished.

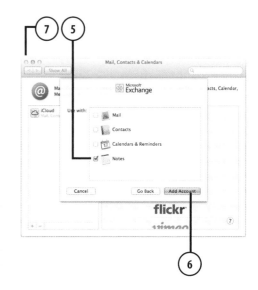

Your Utilities, Everywhere

Wish you had access to the suite of utilities described in this chapter wherever you may be? You do! You can access Calendars, Contacts, Notes, and Reminders using Apple's iCloud web service. Just sign in at http://www.icloud.com/ to use Apple's meticulously crafted and stunningly beautiful web versions of these useful tools.

It's Not All Good

GONE FOR GOOD. EVERYWHERE.

Even though the applications in this chapter are frequently configured to use servers (much like Mail), it doesn't mean that they work with information in the same way as Mail. In email, when you delete a message, it typically gets moved to your email's trash folder—where it can be recovered.

In Calendar, Reminders, and Notes, deleting an event, reminder, or note is permanent. You'll be asked to confirm the deletion, but once it's gone, it's gone.

Additionally, if you delete an iCloud reminder, event, or note using any of the applications in this chapter, it will be removed from all of your devices—virtually simultaneously.

Configure file, printer, scanner, screen, and Internet sharing in the Sharing System Preferences panel.

Point and click to browse available servers on your network.

Connect directly to a wide range of servers using their Internet addresses.

In this chapter, you learn how to use your iMac to share and access resources over a network, including:

→ Sharing files and folders with Macs Using AirDrop and File Sharing

→ File sharing with Windows 7 computers

→ Setting Share Permissions

→ Using Share Sheets to quickly share files online

→ Sharing and accessing network printers

→ Sharing and accessing flatbed scanners

→ Sharing your iMac screen and viewing remote systems

→ Turning your iMac into an Internet Access Point

Sharing Devices, Files, and Services on a Network

Your iMac is a self-contained workstation that packs all the power you need into a highly integrated package—and one that is fully capable of integrating with new or existing networks. An iMac with Mountain Lion can share and access a variety of resources with other computers on your network. Files and folders can be shared with other Macs and Windows PCs; printers and scanners can be shared with other Macs; even your screen can be made available to other computers on your network.

To make the most use of the information in this chapter, the assumption is that you've already established a network connection and have connected any printers or scanners to either your iMac or another Mountain Lion-based Macintosh on your network. You might want to refer to Chapter 3, "Connecting

Your iMac to a Network," and Chapter 11, "Connecting Devices to Your iMac," for more details on networking and peripherals, respectively.

File Sharing on Your iMac

The most common network activity (beyond email and Web surfing) is file sharing. Your iMac comes ready to share files using several popular protocols—AFP (Apple Filing Protocol) and SMB (Simple Message Block) are the most popular. AFP, as the name suggests, is for Mac-to-Mac file sharing, and SMB is used primarily in Windows environments. In addition to the protocols for sharing files, you also have different methods for *how* you share them. Traditional file sharing requires that you turn on file sharing, choose what you want to share, tell another person how to connect, and so on. With Mountain Lion, your iMac includes a zero-configuration version of file sharing called AirDrop. AirDrop lets you wirelessly share files with other Mac users who are in your vicinity—with no setup required!

Authenticate to Make Changes!
Many of the settings in this chapter require you to authenticate with Mountain Lion before the settings can be made. If you find yourself in a situation where a setting is grayed out, click the padlock icon in the lower-left corner of the window to authenticate and make the necessary change.

Using AirDrop to Wirelessly Share Files and Folders

AirDrop is a fast and easy file-sharing system that lets you send files to another Macintosh without any setup—no usernames, no passwords, nothing except a Wi-Fi adapter that is turned on! Unlike traditional file sharing, AirDrop's simplicity does present a few challenges that might make it less than ideal for your particular file-sharing situation. Specifically, AirDrop requires the following:

- All computers sharing files must be using Lion (or later) operating system.

- All systems must have recent wireless-N Wi-Fi hardware—2010 or later iMacs will work fine.

- Your iMac will not be able to browse the contents of other computers, only send files.

Sending Files with AirDrop

To use AirDrop, be sure that your Wi-Fi adapter is turned on (see Chapter 3 for details), identify the files that you want to share with another person, and then follow these steps:

1. Open a new Finder window and make sure the Favorites sidebar section is expanded.

2. Click the AirDrop icon to browse for other OS X computers.

3. Other computers are shown using the owner's avatar picture (set in Address Book) as their icon.

4. Drag the files you want to transfer to the icon of another computer.

5. Confirm the transfer by clicking Send when prompted.

6. You will be asked to wait while the remote system confirms the transfer.

7. The files are copied to the remote system. A blue circle around the receiving computer indicates progress.

8. Close the AirDrop window to stop being visible on the network. After you've closed the AirDrop window, you can go your merry way. You don't need to disconnect or change your network settings. You're done!

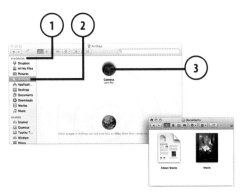

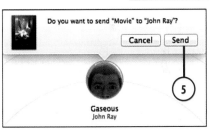

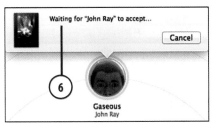

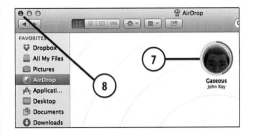

Receiving Files with AirDrop

Receiving files with AirDrop is even easier than sending them. When a nearby Mountain Lion user wants to send files to your iMac, follow these steps:

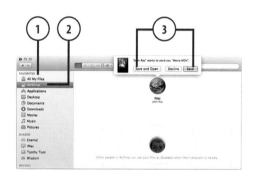

1. Open a new Finder window and make sure the Favorites sidebar section is expanded.

2. Click the AirDrop icon to become visible to other AirDrop users.

3. When prompted to receive files, click Save or Save and Open to accept the transfer, or Decline to cancel.

4. The files are transferred to your Download folder.

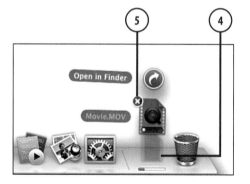

5. Click the X on the downloading file or folder to cancel the download.

6. Close the AirDrop window to stop being visible on the network. That's it! Your AirDrop session is automatically ended when the window closes.

Note

AirDrop uses peer-to-peer ad hoc wireless networking, which is only supported in recent iMacs and desktop Macs. Although this may seem limiting, this hardware is what makes it possible to communicate with zero configuration and without using a common Wi-Fi access point.

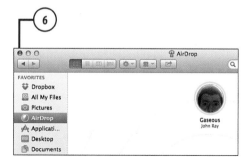

Using Share Sheets to Send via AirDrop

Share Sheets are a new UI element and feature in Mountain Lion that enable applications to share files and folders from almost anywhere—even file open and save dialog boxes, as you'll see here. To use a Share Sheet to send a file via AirDrop, complete these steps:

1. Select a file (or open a file) within an application.

2. Look for the Share Sheet button. Click to show the Sharing menu.

3. Select AirDrop from the list of sharing options.

4. A new window appears listing all nearby users with AirDrop open in the Finder.

5. Click the person you want to send the file to.

6. The copy begins as soon as the recipient accepts the transfer. On the receiving end, an AirDrop transfer sent via an application appears identical to one sent directly from the Finder; the process is the same as that discussed earlier.

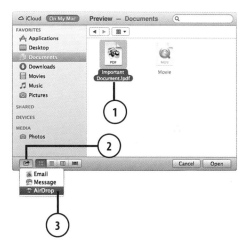

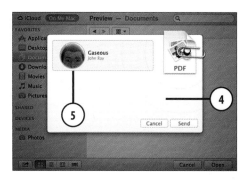

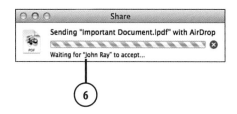

Beyond the 'Drop

Share Sheets are much more powerful than just sharing via AirDrop. We look at a few other sharing scenarios that use this feature later in this chapter.

Configuring Traditional File and Folder Sharing

When AirDrop won't do (you need to browse another computer's files or share with Windows/older Macs), you need to turn to the traditional file sharing features built into OS X. Mountain Lion provides consolidated controls for sharing files, regardless of what type of computer you want to share them with. You set up file sharing by first enabling sharing for your iMac and then choosing the protocols available for accessing the files. Finally, you decide which folders should be shared and who should see them.

Enabling File Sharing

Before your iMac can make any files or folders available over a network, file sharing must be enabled.

1. In the System Preferences, click the Sharing icon.

2. Click the checkbox in front of the service labeled File Sharing.

3. The details about your sharing configuration are displayed on the right side of the sharing window.

4. Close the Sharing Preferences panel, or continue configuring other sharing options.

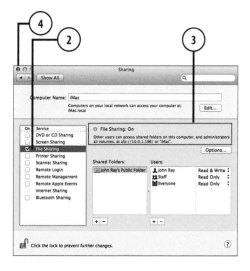

Choosing File Sharing Protocols

Files can be shared over AFP (Mac) or SMB (Windows). If you're working in a Mac-only environment, AFP will be perfect. Mixed environments should use SMB.

To choose which protocols can be used to access the files on your iMac, follow these steps:

1. In System Preferences, click the Sharing icon.

2. Click the File Sharing service label.

3. Click the Options button to display the available sharing protocols.

4. Check or uncheck the protocols that you want to use.

5. If you're configuring Windows file sharing (SMB), all accounts are disabled by default. Check the box in front of each user account that should be *allowed* to connect.

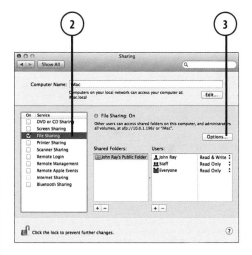

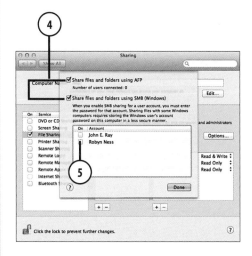

6. Enter the password for each account.

7. Click Done.

8. Close the Sharing Preferences, or continue configuring sharing options.

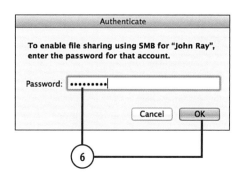

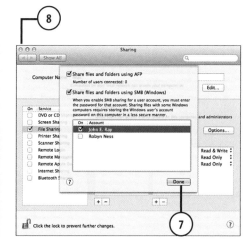

Selecting Folders and Permissions

After enabling file sharing and choosing the protocols that are used, your next step is to pick the folders that can be shared. By default, each user's Public folder is shared and accessible by anyone with an account on your computer. (See Chapter 12, "Securing and Protecting Your iMac," for configuring user accounts.)

1. In the System Preferences, click the Sharing icon.

2. Click the File Sharing service label.

3. Click the + button under Shared Folders to share a new folder.

4. Find the folder you want to make available and then click the Add button.

5. Close the System Preferences, or continue configuring sharing options.

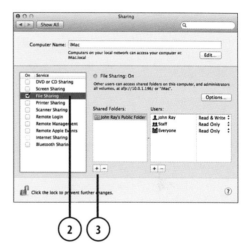

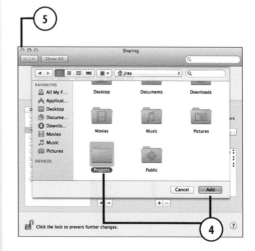

Setting Folder Access Permissions

By default, your user account has full access to anything that you share. The default user group named Staff, and everyone with an account on the computer, have read-only access.

To change who can access a file share, complete the following steps:

1. In the System Preferences window, click the Sharing icon.

2. Click the File Sharing service label.

3. Click the Shared Folder name that you want to modify.

4. Click the + button under the User's list to add a new user (or – to remove access for a selected user).

5. A window for selecting a user displays. Within the Users & Groups category, pick the user or group and click Select.

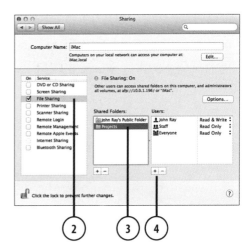

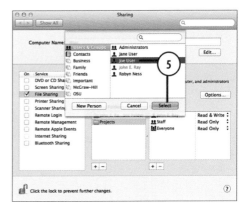

6. Use the pop-up menu to the right of each user in the Users list to choose what the user can do within the shared folder.

7. Close the System Preferences.

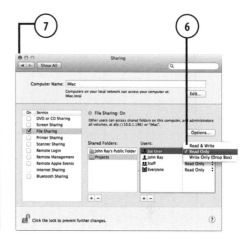

WHAT PERMISSIONS CAN BE APPLIED TO A SHARED FOLDER?

Shared folders can have the following permissions set on a per-user or per-group basis:

Read & Write—Grants full access to the folder and files within it. Users can add, edit, and delete items within the folder.

Read Only—Provides access to the files in the folder, but users cannot modify or delete them, nor can they create new files or folders.

Write Only (Drop Box)—Allows users to write to the folder, but not see its contents.

No Access—Available only for the Everyone group; disables access for all user accounts except those explicitly granted access in the permissions.

Accessing Shared Files

Shared files are only useful if you can access them! Your iMac provides two methods of connecting to shared folders: by browsing for them on your local network and by entering a URL to connect directly to the shared resource.

Browsing and Connecting to Network Shares

Browsing and connecting to a local network share is similar to browsing through the folders located on your iMac. To browse for available network shares, do the following:

1. Open a new Finder window and make sure the Shared sidebar section is expanded.

2. Click the computer that is sharing the folders and files that you want to access.

3. If you have not logged into the computer before and saved your password, a list of the publicly accessible file shares is displayed in the Finder window.

4. Click the Connect As button on the upper right of the Finder window.

5. Enter the username and password that you have established for accessing files on the server.

6. Click Remember This Password in My Keychain to enable browsing directly to the file shares in the future.

7. Click Connect.

8. The file share list updates to display all the shares that your user account can access. Double-click the share you want to use.

9. The share is mounted as a disk and can be used as if it were local to your iMac.

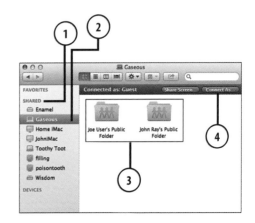

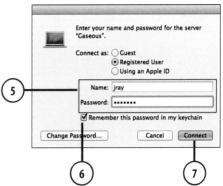

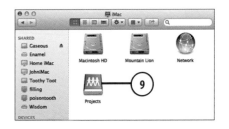

One Password to Rule Them All

You may notice when connecting to other Mountain Lion servers that you are given the option of connecting with your Apple ID. This will work if your account has had an Apple ID associated with it on the remote server. This association is made by selecting a user within the Users & Groups System Preferences panel and then clicking the Set button that is next to the Apple ID field.

Browsing Large Networks

If there are many different computers sharing files on your network, you can browse them in a Finder window rather than the Finder sidebar. To open a Finder window that browses your network, choose Go, Network from the menu bar, or click the All… icon within the Shared section of the Finder sidebar.

Connecting to Remote Shares

Sometimes file shares aren't directly browseable because they're hiding their available shares, or they are located on a different network from your iMac. To access remote shares by URL, follow these steps:

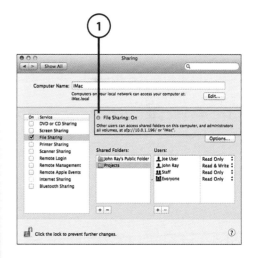

1. When you create a new file share on your iMac, Mountain Lion provides you with a list of URLs that can be used to access that file share (see step 3 of "Enabling File Sharing"). You can use these URLs to directly access a file share rather than browsing.

2. Choose Go, Connect to Server from the Finder menu.

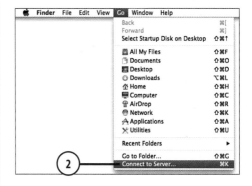

3. Enter the URL for the file share in the Server Address field.

4. Click + if you want to add the server to the list of favorite servers.

5. Click Connect to connect to the server and view the available shares.

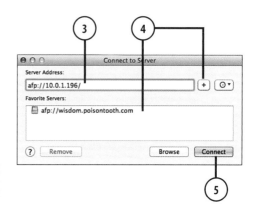

Tip

Your Windows friends might give you network shares to connect to in the format \\server-name\sharename. You can translate this into a "Mac-friendly" URL by adding the prefix smb: and reversing the direction of the slashes—that is, smb://servername/sharename.

Sharing Files via Share Sheets

Mountain Lion introduces a new way of sharing files from almost anywhere via Share Sheets. A Share Sheet menu (indicated by an icon of an arrow pointing out of a rectangle) can be used to quickly send a file through a variety of different means, including AirDrop (discussed earlier in this chapter), Mail, and other online services.

Sharing Files via Mail

A simple example of Share Sheets is using the sheet to share a file via email. To do this, either open the file or select it in the Finder, and then follow these instructions:

1. Click the Share Sheet button.

2. Choose Email from the drop-down menu.

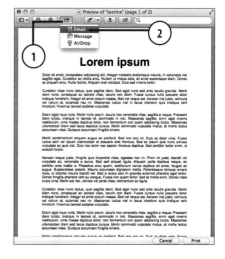

3. Mail starts, and the file is added as an attachment to a new message.

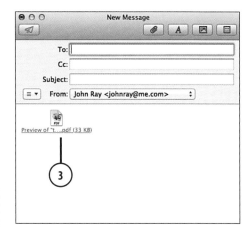

Sharing Media to iTunes

Mountain Lion makes it simple to transfer your media to iTunes for syncing with your iOS devices or playback on your Apple TV. While we might not consider making a file available to another application as "sharing", Mountain Lion places this option in a Share Sheet. Begin by finding the movie you want to open.

Find the movie file you want to transfer to iTunes and follow these steps:

1. Double-click to open the movie in QuickTime Player.

2. Click the Share Sheet button and choose iTunes from the pop-up menu that appears.

3. Pick which device you plan to view the movie on and click the Share button. The quality and file size increase on the devices at the right side of the list. Be aware that not all choices are always available.

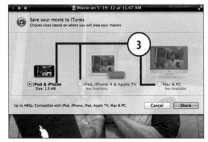

4. The Movie Export window appears and displays the status of the encoding process.

5. When finished, close QuickTime Player. Your movie is available in iTunes.

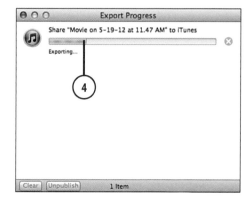

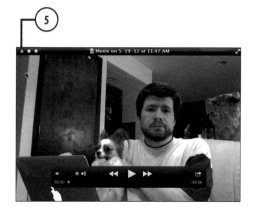

Uploading Files to an Online Service

Using Mountain Lion, you can now share your files with the world via a number of online services—such as YouTube, Facebook, Vimeo, and Flickr—without even needing to touch a web browser. YouTube is the most popular destination for videos on the Internet, so we'll use that as our example. To upload a video to the online service of your choice, follow these steps:

1. Locate the movie file you want to upload, and double-click to open it in QuickTime Player.

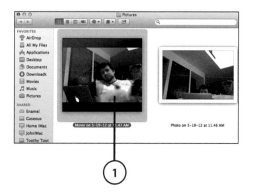

2. Click the Share Sheet to display sharing options and choose the online destination (in this case, YouTube) from the pop-up menu.

3. Enter your username and password when prompted.

4. Choose Remember This Password in My Keychain to streamline the process in the future.

5. Click Sign In to log into the YouTube service.

6. Set a category for the uploaded video file.

7. Enter a title, description, and a set of keywords (called Tags) to describe the video.

8. Use the Access setting to set the video as Personal, if desired. This limits viewing of the video to individuals who you share it with via the YouTube website. Please note that these settings may vary between the various online services supported in Mountain Lion.

9. Click Next.

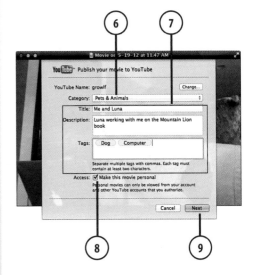

10. Review the YouTube Terms of Service, and then click Share.

11. The Movie Export window appears and displays the status of the encoding process.

12. When finished, a link to the video is displayed.

13. Close QuickTime Player. Your movie is available online.

Cutting It Down to Size

To trim a video before sharing it, click the Share Sheet button and choose Edit, Trim from the menu bar. You can move the start and end points of your video clip to wherever you'd like and then trim off the extra.

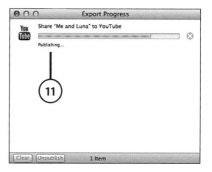

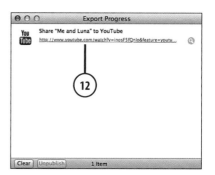

Sharing Printers

Sharing a printer is a convenient way to provide printing services to your iMac without having to connect any physical wires. With Mountain Lion, printer sharing just takes a few clicks and then your iMac can act as if it has a physical printer attached.

Enabling Network Printer Sharing

To share a printer, you must first have the printer connected and configured on another Macintosh (see Chapter 11 for details). After the printer is set up and working, follow these steps to make it available over a local network:

1. In the System Preferences window, click the Sharing icon.

2. Click the checkbox in front of the Printer Sharing service.

3. Within the Printers list, click the checkboxes in front of each printer you want to share. The printers are immediately made available to everyone on your network.

4. Close the System Preferences, or continue setting sharing preferences.

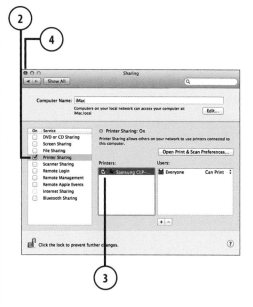

Setting Printer Sharing Permissions

Any shared printer is initially available to anyone with a computer connected to your network. To restrict access to specific user accounts on your computer, do the following:

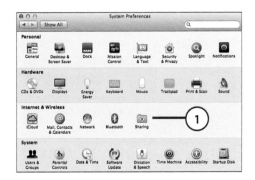

1. In the System Preferences window, click the Sharing icon.

2. Click the label for the Printer Sharing service.

3. Highlight the name of the shared printer that you want to configure.

4. Click the + button to select a user that can print to your printer. (Use – to remove access for a user you added previously.)

5. A window is displayed to select a user. Choose the user or group and click Select.

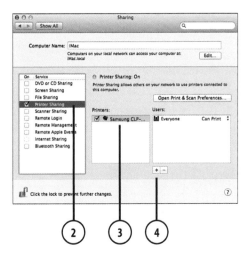

Tip

The Everyone group can't be removed from the Users list. To remove access for Everyone, the group must be toggled to No Access.

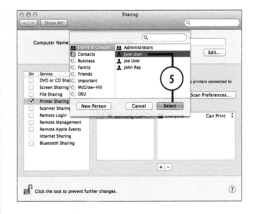

6. Toggle the pop-up menu beside the Everyone group to No Access to keep everyone except the listed individuals from being able to access the printer.

7. Close the System Preferences.

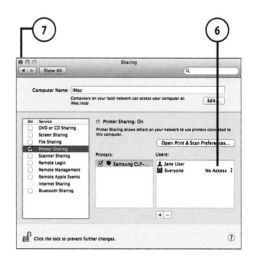

Accessing a Network Printer

To access a printer that is being shared by another Macintosh, first make sure that both computers are on and connected to the same network and then follow these steps:

1. Choose File, Print from the menu bar within an application of your choice.

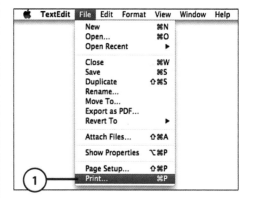

2. The Printer dialog box appears. Click the Printer drop-down menu to see the options.

3. If you haven't used the shared printer before, select the printer from the Nearby Printers section of the drop-down menu.

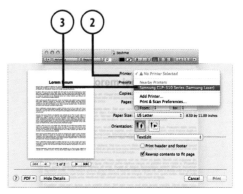

4. Mountain Lion automatically connects your iMac to the printer and configures it.

5. Choose the options for the document you are printing, then click Print. The printer behaves exactly as if it is connected directly to your computer. The next time you print, the printer will be available directly in your main printer list.

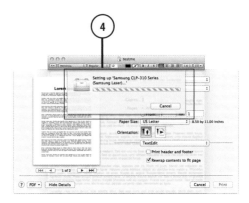

Printing to Protected Printers

If you set up specific user accounts that can access the printer, you are prompted for a username and password the first time you print. You can, at that time, choose to save the printer connection information to your keychain, which eliminates the need to authenticate for subsequent use.

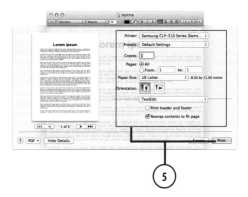

Sharing a Scanner

A unique (and little known) ability of OS X is sharing scanners! With scanner sharing, you can use a scanner that is connected to a desktop system as if it were connected directly to your iMac. Before proceeding, make sure that you've correctly installed a scanner on a Macintosh on your local network (see Chapter 10, "Making the Most of Your iMac Hardware," for details).

Tip

If you can start Image Capture or Preview (both are found in the Applications folder) on the Macintosh with the directly connected scanner and create a scan, you're ready to enable sharing.

Enabling Network Scanner Sharing

Scanner sharing is virtually configuration-free! To enable scanner sharing on your Macintosh, follow these steps:

1. In the System Preferences window, click the Sharing icon.

2. Click the checkbox in front of the Scanner Sharing service.

3. Review the list of available scanners and then click the checkboxes in front of each scanner that you want to share. The scanners can now be accessed in Image Capture or Preview from any Macintosh connected to the local network.

4. Close the System Preferences.

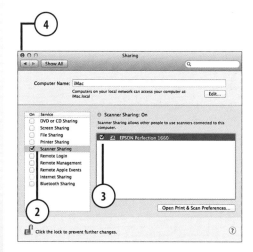

Accessing a Shared Scanner

Accessing a shared scanner is just like using a locally connected scanner. Make sure that both the computer sharing the scanner and the scanner are turned on, gather your materials to scan, and then follow along:

1. Open your preferred Mountain Lion scanning utility—Preview or Image Capture (Preview is used here).

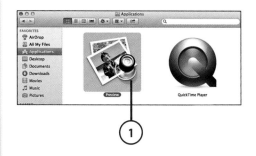

2. Choose Import from Scanner from the Preview application's File menu.

3. Proceed with scanning as if the scanner were connected directly to your iMac.

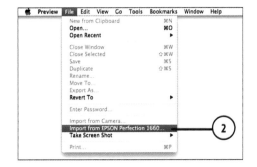

Sharing an Optical Drive

For those using a CD- or DVD-less iMac (the new 2012+ slim models), you can use another Macintosh on your network (including another iMac) to share a CD or DVD inserted into the other Macintosh's drive. This gives you the ability to install software and access files even if you don't have a physical drive connected.

Enabling DVD and CD Sharing

From a Macintosh with CD or DVD drives available, follow these steps to turn on optical drive sharing:

1. In the System Preferences window, click the Sharing icon.

2. Click the checkbox in front of the DVD or CD Sharing service.

3. Click the Ask Me Before Allowing Others to Use My DVD Drive checkbox to prompt you when other people attempt to access your optical drive.

4. Close the System Preferences.

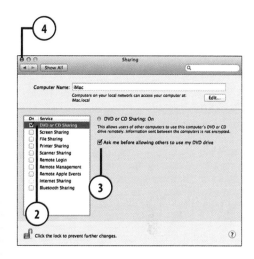

Accessing a Shared Optical Drive

To access a shared optical drive from your DVD-free Mac, do the following:

1. Open a new Finder window and make sure the Devices section in the Finder sidebar is expanded.

2. Click the Remote Disc item in the Devices sidebar area.

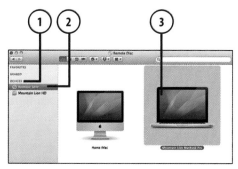

3. Double-click the computer that is sharing the DVD you want to use.

4. If the DVD is not immediately visible, click Ask to Use to prompt the host computer that you'd like to use its drive.

5. After access has been granted, the available DVD or CD is listed. Double-click the DVD or CD to begin using it.

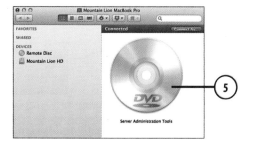

Can I Access a Shared Optical Drive Even If My iMac Has a DVD Drive?

Yes, but not without a few changes. You'll need to open the Terminal application (found in the Utilities folder in the Applications folder) and then type in the following two lines to enable optical drive sharing:

defaults write com.apple.NetworkBrowser EnableODiskBrowsing -bool true

defaults write com.apple.NetworkBrowser ODSSupported -bool true

Reboot your computer after entering these commands.

Sharing Your iMac Screen

Chapter 6, "Keeping Contacts, Appointments, Reminders, and Notes," includes instructions on how to share your Macintosh's screen using Messages, but there are many instances where you might want to access another Mac's display without having to start a chat.

Built into Mountain Lion is a standards-based screen-sharing system. Using screen sharing, you can access your Mac's display from anywhere on your local network or, in some cases, from anywhere in the world. New in Mountain Lion is the ability to share a computer's "screen" even if someone else is using the computer. The screen sharing software can now automatically create a virtual screen that you can see and use while the person sitting in front of the computer continues to see their own desktop!

Enabling Screen Sharing

To configure another Mac so that you can access its screen from your iMac, you initially need direct access to the computer:

1. In the System Preferences window, click the Sharing icon.

2. Click the checkbox in front of the Screen Sharing service.

3. A URL that you can use to connect to your computer is displayed on the right side of the sharing pane.

4. Close the System Preferences, or continue setting sharing preferences.

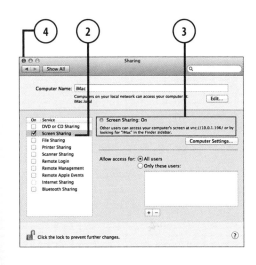

Setting Screen Sharing Permissions

After screen sharing is enabled, choose who can access the display. Initially, only administrative users can view your screen.

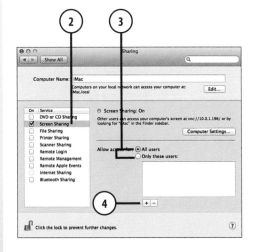

1. In the System Preferences window, click the Sharing icon.

2. Click the Screen Sharing service label.

3. Choose whether All Users on the computer can access its screen, or click Only These Users to restrict access to specific individuals or groups.

4. Use the + button to choose a user or group that should be granted access, or use − to remove a user or group that you had previously added.

5. A window for selecting a user displays. Choose the user or group and click Select.

6. For additional control, click the Computer Settings button.

7. In the dialog box that appears, click Anyone May Request Permission to Control Screen to allow anyone to access the display if the person sitting in front of the computer grants them access.

8. To provide access to your Mac's screen using a standard VNC (Virtual Network Computing) client, click the VNC Viewers May Control Screen with Password checkbox and provide a password that grants access to those users.

9. Click OK.

10. Close the System Preferences.

Tip

There are VNC clients available for Windows, Linux, and even platform-independent Java. If you want to access your Mac's screen from another operating system, check out TightVNC (www.tightvnc.com).

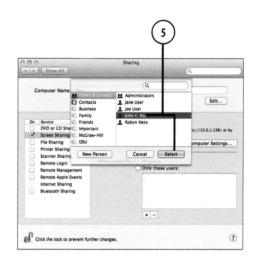

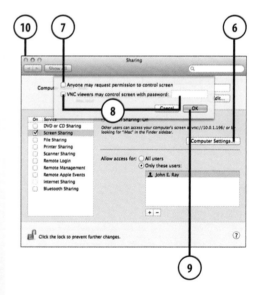

Accessing the Screen of a Local Mac

To access the shared screen of a Mac on your local network, make sure that your iMac is connected to the network and then follow these steps:

1. Open a new Finder window and make sure the Shared sidebar section heading is expanded.

2. Click the computer whose screen you want to access.

3. Click Share Screen in the upper-right corner of the Finder window.

4. Enter your username and password on the remote system, if prompted.

5. Click Remember This Password in My Keychain to store the password and enable password-less connections in the future.

6. Click Connect to begin using the remote display.

7. If another person is using the computer, you can ask to share the display with them, or connect to a new virtual display. Click whichever approach you prefer.

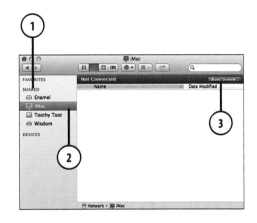

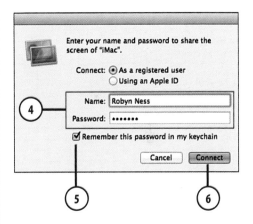

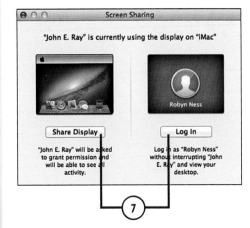

8. The remote display is shown in a window on your iMac.

9. Toggle between controlling and observing with the Control Mode icon in the toolbar.

10. Use the Scaling Mode icon to view the screen fullsize or shrink it to fit your window.

11. Click the Capture Screen item to save a screenshot of the current screen.

12. Use Get Clipboard to transfer the contents of the remote computer's clipboard into your local clipboard, and Send Clipboard to transfer your clipboard to the remote system.

13. Click Shared Clipboard to share a single clipboard between the two systems.

14. Close the window when you're finished using the remote system.

Tip

You can connect to multiple shared screens simultaneously with your iMac; each appears in a separate window. Additionally, you can use the fullscreen button in the upper-right corner of the Screen Sharing window to view the remote desktop in fullscreen mode or select Switch to Virtual Display from the View menu to create your own virtual desktop on the remote computer.

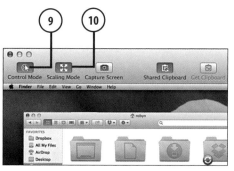

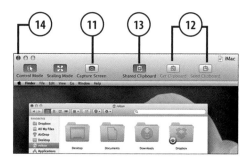

Accessing Remote Computers and Non-Macs

If you can't browse to a computer to access its screen, or you need to connect to a non-Macintosh computer, you can do so using almost the same process as you used to connect to a remote file share:

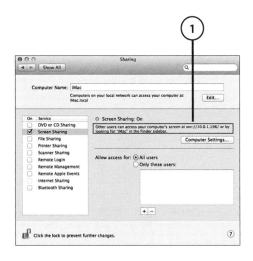

1. When you're sharing a screen on your iMac, Mountain Lion provides you with a URL that can be used to access your screen, even if you can't browse to it on the network.

2. Choose Go, Connect to Server from the Finder menu bar.

3. Enter the screen-sharing URL in the Server Address field. Alternatively, if you only have an IP address (such as 192.168.1.100), prefix the IP address with vnc:// to create a properly formed URL (for example, vnc://192.168.1.100).

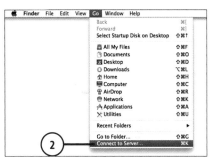

4. Click + if you want to add the server to the list of favorite servers.

5. Click Connect to connect to the remote server's screen.

6. Enter a username (and/or password), if prompted, and click Connect.

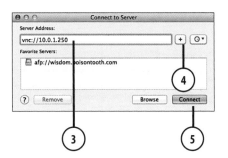

7. The remote display is shown in a window on your iMac.

Tip

To connect to a Windows or Linux computer, you need to first install a VNC server (Virtual Network Computing) on the computer whose display you want to share. TightVNC (www.tightvnc.com) is an entirely free Open Source option that will work on both Windows and Linux platforms.

>>> Go Further

THERE ARE A LOT OF PLACES LIKE HOME

The Shared portion of the sidebar shows you the computers on your local network. This is great for accessing things around you, but what about accessing your computer at home or from work? You could use the address of your home computer to access it remotely, but you'd need to remember the address and have your home network configured correctly. Instead, you can simply enable the iCloud service "Back To My Mac" (see Chapter 4, "Accessing iCloud, Email, and the Web," for details). Once enabled, this free service makes all your computers visible to one another wherever you have an Internet connection. You won't be able to tell the difference (network-wise) from being at home or being on a remote (well-connected) island.

Sharing Your Internet Connection

Your iMac is a perfect Internet-sharing platform because it includes both Ethernet and wireless network connections. You can, in a matter of minutes, create a wireless network using just your iMac and a cable or DSL modem.

Sharing Your Connection

1. In the System Preferences window, click the Sharing icon.

2. Click the Internet Sharing service label. (Note: The checkbox is initially disabled!)

3. Use the Share Your Connection From drop-down menu to choose how you are connected to the Internet (Ethernet, Airport, iPhone, and so on).

4. Within the To Computers Using list, click the checkboxes in front of each of the interfaces where the connection should be shared.

5. If you're sharing a connection over your Wi-Fi card, a Wi-Fi Options button appears. Click this button to configure how your computer presents itself wirelessly.

6. Set the name of the wireless network you are creating.

7. Leave the channel set to the default.

8. If you want to enable password protection for the network, choose WPA2 Personal from the Security drop-down, and then provide a password.

9. Click OK to save your settings.

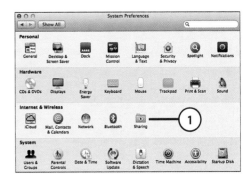

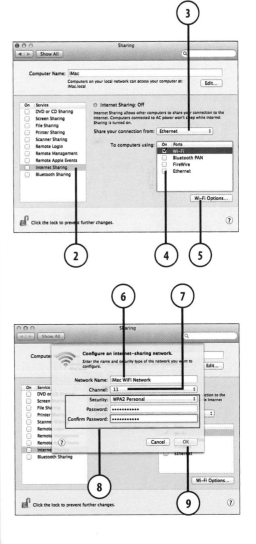

10. Click the checkbox in front of the Internet Sharing service.

11. Close the System Preferences.

12. Connect to the new wireless network from other computers as described in Chapter 3. You should set the other computers to configure themselves automatically rather than manually configuring the network (not shown).

Tip

If you're sharing your connection over Ethernet, you need to connect a switch to your iMac's Ethernet port and then connect the other computer systems/devices to the switch.

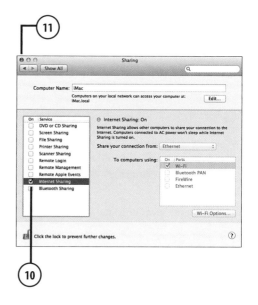

Download movies, music, and more in iTunes.

Use Plex to create a media center.

Watch DVDs with your iMac using DVD Player.

In this chapter, you learn how to use digital music and video to turn your iMac into a big-screen entertainment center, including:

→ Watching DVD video

→ Viewing video files online

→ Adding support for Windows Media and other video

→ Using iTunes to play audio CDs

→ Copying audio CDs into iTunes

→ Buying digital media using iTunes

→ Syncing your iOS device with iTunes

→ Keeping your computers in sync with Home Sharing

→ Setting up Plex for the ultimate media center experience

8

Entertainment on the (iMac's) Big Screen

In case you hadn't noticed, your iMac has a gorgeous screen. The LED IPS display provides excellent color reproduction and amazing depth—at HDTV resolutions or higher. Why bother sitting in front of the TV when your iMac does so much more? Using iTunes, you can build a library of thousands of songs, TV shows, and movies.

In addition to iTunes, your iMac also includes software to play your existing DVD library and thousands of online streaming videos. If you want to take things a step further, you can install full-featured media center software that plays back virtually any video format you might encounter.

Using DVD Player

DVD Player is an application bundled with OS X that enables you to watch DVDs on your iMac. Of course, you need an iMac with a DVD drive (all models before 2012) or an external USB DVD drive. DVD Player launches automatically when you insert a video DVD in your optical drive.

OPENING DVD PLAYER

Your iMac should automatically open DVD Player when you insert a video DVD, but if it doesn't you can launch the application manually from your Applications folder. If DVD Player does not automatically open, you can enable this behavior under the System Preferences, CDs & DVDs settings. Simply set Open DVD Player as your preference for when you insert a video DVD. From this preference window, you can also choose behaviors for inserting blank CDs, blank DVDs, music CDs, and picture CDs.

Playing a DVD

If you've used a standalone DVD player and remote, you should have no trouble applying your experience to navigating menus and playback controls on your iMac. To begin playing a DVD, follow these steps:

1. Insert a disc in your optical disc drive. The content opens fullscreen, and a controller appears at the bottom to allow you to navigate DVD menus and control playback.

2. Navigate the DVD menu. You can use either your trackpad or the arrow keys on your keyboard.

3. Press the Return (enter) key on your keyboard, or use your cursor to click the onscreen Enter (center) button to select an item, such as an episode, scene, or special features.

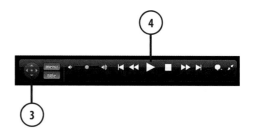

4. To toggle playing and pausing the video, click the Play/Pause button or press the spacebar. To stop playback, click the Stop button.

5. Press Escape to exit fullscreen mode, if desired. When in windowed mode, a slightly different (but equally functional) controller is displayed.

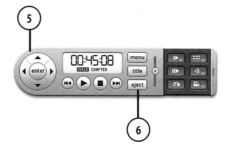

6. To eject the DVD, press the Eject key on your keyboard, or use the Eject button on the windowed mode controller.

Note

The first time you play a DVD in DVD Player, the drive region is set to match the code of that DVD. If you later insert a disc from another region, you have the option to change; however, you can only change your region code settings five times (including the initial setting).

Setting Bookmarks

If you want to mark your favorite parts of a DVD, DVD Player allows you to set bookmarks. Bookmarks are stored on your computer, not the DVD itself, so they are only available when you watch the DVD from your iMac.

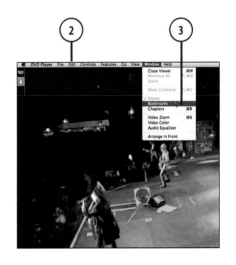

Setting Bookmarks

To set a bookmark, follow these steps:

1. Use the DVD controls (shown in the previous task) to rewind or fast-forward playback to the point you want to bookmark.

2. If you're watching a DVD in full-screen mode, move your cursor to the top of the screen to reveal the DVD Player menu.

3. Choose Window, Bookmarks. The Bookmarks window opens.

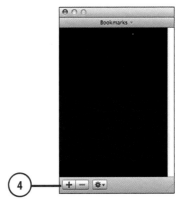

4. Click the + (also known as Add Bookmark) button at the bottom of the Bookmarks window. Playback pauses at the moment to show which frame will be marked.

5. Choose Make Default Bookmark to have video playback automatically start at this point in the future.

6. Name your bookmark and click Add to set it.

7. The frame, name, and timecode appear in the Bookmarks window.

Starting Playback at a Bookmark

To start playback at a bookmark you've set, follow these steps:

1. Insert the DVD you have bookmarked and begin playback.

2. While in full-screen mode, move your cursor to the top of the screen to reveal a black panel with tabs for Chapters and Bookmarks.

3. Click the Bookmarks icon to reveal bookmarks for the current DVD.

4. Select a bookmark to jump to that location.

Tip
You can also jump between Chapters without leaving playback or full-screen mode by moving your cursor to the top of the window and choosing the Chapters icon from the shaded panel.

Viewing Browser Video or Downloaded Video Files

Your iMac's native application for playing media, both within a web browser and from your desktop, is QuickTime. QuickTime, like DVD Player, has fairly standard buttons for controlling playback.

QuickTime supports common digital formats, including MPEG-4 and H.264 video, WAV sound files, and images.

STREAMING MEDIA BASICS

>> Go Further

QuickTime is perhaps most useful for playing streaming media, which means the file isn't downloaded outright to your computer, but is played incrementally as the data is "streamed" from the server to your machine.

For longer videos, streaming decreases your wait time because you can start watching the video before transferring the entire file. Typically, there is a short wait time before the video begins, known as buffering, to keep the video playback from being choppy while additional frames and audio are transferred.

Playing QuickTime Files in Your Web Browser

To view a QuickTime movie in your web browser, follow these steps.

1. Open your web browser and navigate to a page containing QuickTime compatible content. (For example, visit Apple's movie trailers web page at www.apple.com/trailers/ to enjoy QuickTime previews of upcoming releases.)

2. Select an item.

3. If you're asked, choose your preferred options on video size, such as automatic or high-definition options (HD). These options affect the wait time for viewing— because larger, higher quality video requires transfer of more data to your iMac.

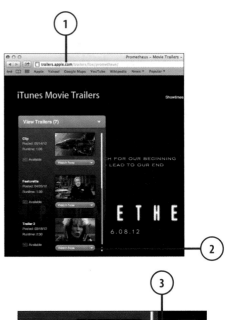

4. The QuickTime panel opens and, after a few seconds, begins to play.

5. You can pause playback, change volume, rewind and fast-forward, or go fullscreen using the controls at the bottom of the panel.

Playing QuickTime Files from Your Desktop

In addition to playing files within a web page, you can also use QuickTime to play files on your iMac. Native QuickTime files end with the file extension .mov. (Applications such as Apple's iMovie and Final Cut Pro export video in this format.)

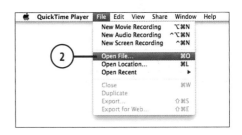

To play a .mov file, follow these steps:

1. Open QuickTime Player (found in Launchpad or the Applications folder).

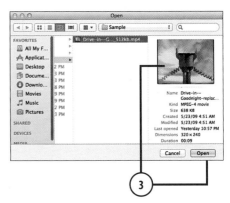

2. Choose File, Open File from the menu.

3. Navigate to the file you want to play and click the Open button.

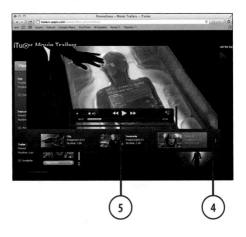

4. Click the Play button to begin playback.

5. Click the rewind and fast-forward buttons to skim backward and forward through the video.

6. You can also drag the "scrubber" back and forth to skip through the video.

7. Click the double arrows to view the video in fullscreen mode.

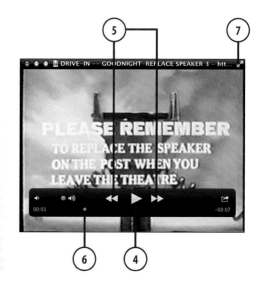

EXTENDING QUICKTIME WITH ADDITIONAL COMPONENTS

Although QuickTime is a reasonably flexible media player without any additions, you can increase the range of media it supports by installing support for additional video formats.

To add seamless support for Windows Media Player files (files ending with .wma and .wmv), install the Flip4Mac component available from http://www.telestream.net/flip4mac/overview.htm.

To play other popular formats (such as Flash video, DivX, MKV, and AVI), download and install Perian, a free addition for QuickTime that adds support for a range of file types. Perian is available from http://www.perian.org/ and works with Mountain Lion (despite being recently discontinued by the developers).

After these components have been installed, QuickTime will be able to play these file formats without any additional help—just open the file and watch the show!

Refer to Chapter 9, "Installing and Managing Software on Your iMac," for additional instructions on adding software to your system.

Creating a Media Library in iTunes

Apple's iTunes enables you to manage and play digital media files, including song tracks you import from CD, content you purchase from the iTunes Store, or podcasts you subscribe to online.

You can also create and sync playlists with your iDevices or share them with other iTunes users on your local network.

Running iTunes for the First Time

The first time you launch iTunes, you won't have anything in your music library. Follow these steps to complete the setup process:

1. Open iTunes from the Dock, Launchpad, or by locating its application icon in the Applications folder.

2. Click Agree after reviewing the iTunes Software License Agreement.

3. The Welcome window, with video tutorials for various tasks, appears. Click Watch Tutorials if you'd like to see video demonstrations of iTunes in action.

4. If you're okay with iTunes sharing information about your library in order to see artist information, album covers, and other niceties, click Agree; otherwise click No Thanks.

5. Click Scan for Music to search your account for any music files you might already have. These are copied to the iTunes folder, inside your Music folder. (This option might not appear if you have a previous version of iTunes already installed.)

6. To immediately start searching the iTunes Store, click Go to the iTunes Store.

Finding Your Way Around iTunes

First, here is a quick tour of the iTunes controls to acquaint you with the basics. The default view in iTunes is the Library view.

Let's discuss a few of the Library view elements in greater detail:

1. The Library menu enables you to choose between Music, Movies, TV Shows, and Home Sharing (other computers sharing their iTunes libraries with you).

2. The organization buttons in the center top of the window enable you to choose how your library is displayed (by song, album, artist, genre, and so on). The options change depending on the type of library you have selected.

3. The iTunes Store button jumps you into the iTunes Store. This view takes over the full screen. In this view, you can click a Library button when you are ready return to your media library.

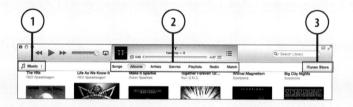

After choosing a Library and a viewing organization, your screen shifts to one of many different displays of your media library. The interface encourages exploration. The album view for music, for example, has these features:

1. Double-clicking an item (song, album, and so on) begins playback.

2. Clicking an album opens an expanded view of the contents.

3. Positioning your cursor over an item displays a disclosure arrow that opens a menu that enables you to jump between different media organizations, add the item to your playback list, or show the iTunes Store for the artist.

4. Clicking In the Store shows additional items you can purchase related to the chosen media. If iTunes cannot find related content within the store, you do not see this option.

Not In the Store

You can always toggle whether or not iTunes shares information about your library using the Store settings within the iTunes preferences. Be aware that if you choose not to share, certain iTunes features will not be available to you— such as In the Store links that help you locate additional music by your favorite artist.

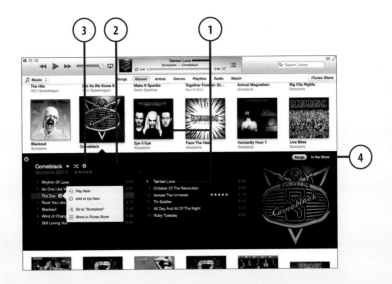

Along the top of the window are controls for all your playback needs:

1. Move back, forward, play, and pause your media playback.

2. Adjust your speaker volume.

3. Choose a device, such as an Apple TV or Airport Express, to output your sound. If you don't have an Airplay-compatible device, you won't see this icon at all.

4. View the playback progress.

5. Set playback to loop repeatedly.

6. Set playback to shuffle.

7. View the next song that will be played or the songs that already have been played.

8. Search all your media or the iTunes Store.

9. Switch to a small version of the iTunes player that can sit in the corner of your screen.

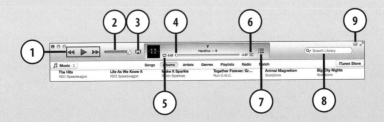

Building Your Media Library

The two most common ways to fill your iTunes Library with media are to import CDs you already own and get new content from the iTunes Store.

Tip

Open the iTunes Preferences (iTunes, Preferences) and Click Import Setting in the General panel if you want to change the format of import from the standard AAC (common for most iTunes content) to other common formats such as MP3, AIFF, or WAV. You can also change the quality (and, subsequently, the file size) of the tracks by switching the Setting drop-down from iTunes Plus to Higher Quality (256 kbps).

Adding Audio CDs (Optical Drive Only)

To import audio tracks from a CD, follow these steps:

1. Insert a CD into the computer's optical disc drive. Your iMac is automatically set to open iTunes when you insert a music CD.

Note

If iTunes does not automatically open when you insert an audio CD, you can enable this behavior under the System Preferences, CDs & DVDs settings.

---

2. Click Yes after iTunes launches and displays a dialog box that asks if you would like to import the CD to your library.

3. iTunes displays the status of the import by showing which tracks have been imported and which are in progress.

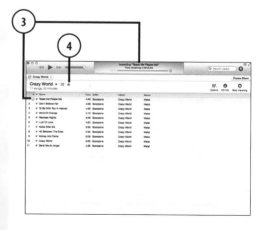

4. Eject your CD by clicking the Eject button.

SETTING TRACK INFO

Go Further

When you insert an audio CD, iTunes connects to a music database, identifies your disc, and applies information such as title, artist, and genre to each track. Album artwork might also be available if the album is part of the iTunes Store.

If iTunes doesn't find your CD in the database, you can edit the track information yourself by selecting it and choosing File, Get Info. Select several tracks at a time to update all the shared information and save yourself some typing.

Purchasing Digital Media on the iTunes Store

To purchase media from the iTunes Store, follow these steps:

1. Click iTunes Store in the upper-right corner (or use the In the Store link when viewing media) to connect to the iTunes Store.

2. Click Sign In. If Sign In doesn't appear, skip to step 5.

3. Enter your Apple ID and password in the Sign In dialog box.

4. Click Sign In.

5. When you're logged in, your Apple ID appears in place of the Sign In button.

Note

You can authorize up to five computers to play songs purchased on a single account. To do this, choose Store, Authorize Computer and enter your Apple ID. (Remember to deauthorize computers that no longer need access, which frees openings for new computers to be added.)

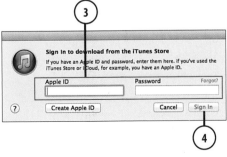

6. Use the links and scrolling content views to browse available media—just as you would a web page.

7. Click the Play button that appears as you move your cursor over a song to play a preview.

8. To make a purchase, click the Price button that appears beside items. In the case of music, you can buy individual songs or albums.

9. When you're asked to confirm that you want to buy the selection, click the Buy button. Your selection is downloaded and added to your library under the Purchased playlist.

10. Click the download button (down arrow) to view all the current downloads taking place.

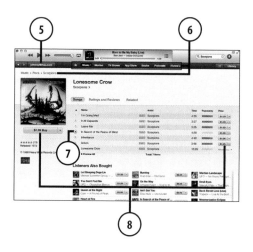

Tip

If you have an iTunes gift card to redeem, click the button with your Apple ID (visible after signing into the iTunes Store), then choose Redeem from the menu that appears. On the subsequent screen you can type in your gift card number or click Use Camera to scan the card with your FaceTime HD camera.

Tip

When you choose to rent a movie, you have 30 days to watch it and 24 hours from the time you start watching it to finish it. Rented movies appear in your library just as other files do.

It's Not All Good

BUY HERE, READ ELSEWHERE

One of the types of media available in iTunes is books. You can currently download books, but no provision is available for reading them in Mountain Lion! You need an iOS device to read your book purchases!

Using Genius Recommendations

Genius Recommendations attempt to predict what new and existing media you might enjoy based on the current items in your library. Follow these steps to enable and peruse Genius Recommendations:

1. Choose Store, Turn on Genius from the menu bar.

2. Click the Turn On Genius button on the screen that appears. (If you're already signed in with your Apple ID, you won't see this or the next step.)

3. Enter your Apple ID and password in the Sign In dialog box and click Continue.

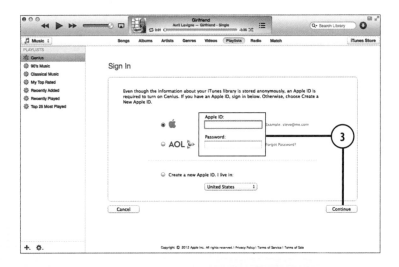

4. Check the box to agree to the terms of service and click Agree.

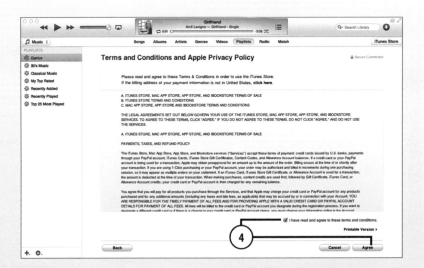

5. A screen announcing Turning on Genius appears while the contents of your library are analyzed and personalized results are prepared. Three stages are displayed while this occurs: gathering information, sending information, and delivering Genius results.

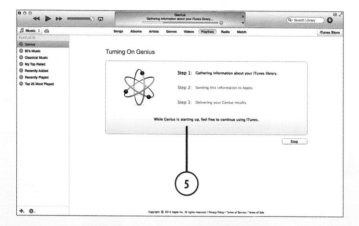

6. Select a song in your library.

7. When viewing In the Store items, new song recommendations are shown on the right.

8. Click the disclosure arrow beside a song or album to view recommendations in your existing library.

9. Choose Start Genius to begin playing a playlist of songs similar to the currently selected song.

10. Pick Create Genius Playlist to create and save a new playlist based on the current song. The new playlist is saved and visible within the Playlists view category.

11. Click Genius Suggestions to list the songs that Genius thinks are similar to the chosen song.

12. Pick from the genius recommendation list to jump to any song.

Downloading Podcasts

Podcasts are series of digital files, either audio or video, that you can subscribe to for regular updates. You can locate and subscribe to a variety of podcasts (most of them free) in the iTunes Store by following these steps:

1. Click iTunes Store to open the store.

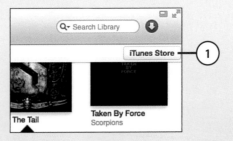

2. Click the Podcasts button categories list at top center of the screen.

3. Click an item to see details and a list of available episodes.

4. Click the Subscribe button to download the most recent episode and all future episodes of this podcast. The podcasts are downloaded to your iTunes library.

5. Click Subscribe when you're asked to confirm that you want to subscribe.

6. Exit the store and select the Podcasts item in the Library menu.

7. Choose the podcast from the list on the left.

8. Select an episode and click the Play control button to listen.

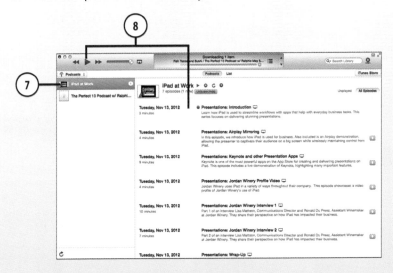

Tip

Episodes produced prior to your subscription appear with a gray download arrow to the right—in case you want to download them as well.

Tip

iTunes checks for updates as long as you are subscribed; if you change your mind about following a podcast, select it in the list and click the Unsubscribe button displayed at the top of the list of individual podcasts.

Go Further

FREE EDUCATION WITH iTUNES U

If you're looking for educational materials, iTunes U is the place to go. Here, dozens of schools publish free course material that is yours for the downloading. Audio, video—it's all here, and subjects from business management to programming are available. iTunes U lessons work identically to podcasts, but are downloaded from the iTunes U section of the iTunes Store and are managed in the iTunes U category of your library.

Searching the Library

Your iTunes library can grow large quite quickly with so many sources from which to draw. Fortunately, it's easy to search your library to find just what you're looking for.

Quick Searches

If you know the title of a song or album or the name of an artist, follow these steps to search for it:

1. Click inside the Search box at the upper right of the iTunes window and begin typing a search term. As you type, a popover appears showing potential matches.

2. Choose an item to jump to it within your library.

Setting a Search Filter

To filter your search results further, do the following:

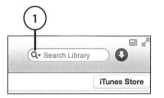

1. Click beside the magnifying glass in the search field.

2. Uncheck the Search Entire Library item to search only the type of media you are currently viewing.

3. Choose the filter option you wish to apply (Song, Album, Artist, Composer, and so on).

4. Perform the search as described in the section "Quick Searches."

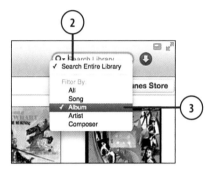

Using Playlists

Playlists help you organize your music and media into themes to suit your mood. You can define your own playlists, set search criteria to automatically cluster certain artists or genres, or have iTunes use the Genius profile it created from your library to generate lists for you.

Creating Playlists

To define a playlist of songs you choose, follow these steps:

1. Within the Music library section, click the Playlists category.

2. Click the plus button at the bottom of the list of playlists on the left. (There are several playlists provided by default.)

3. Choose New Playlist.

4. The screen refreshes with a playlist column on the right and the playlist name highlighted. Enter a name for the new playlist and then press Enter.

5. Browse your music library as you normally would.

6. Drag songs, albums, or artists to the playlist column on the right.

7. When finished adding songs, click Done.

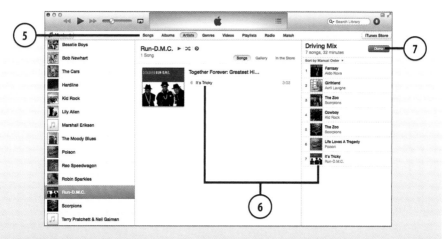

Tip

If you add so many playlists that you feel the need to put them in folders to keep track of them, choose New Playlist Folder when clicking the same plus button you used to add a playlist.

Defining Smart Playlists

To set criteria that iTunes can use to make a playlist for you, follow these steps:

1. Within the Music library section, click the Playlists category.

2. Click the plus button at the bottom of the list of playlists on the left. (There are several playlists provided by default.)

3. Choose New Smart Playlist.

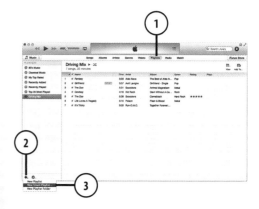

4. In the Smart Playlist window, set your search criteria. Options include obvious choices, such as artist, album, or rating, as well as more obscure settings, such as bit rate (which relates to sound quality) and skip count (which tells how often you choose not to listen to it). You can also set a limit on the number of songs and allow live updates, which creates a list that changes as your library changes.

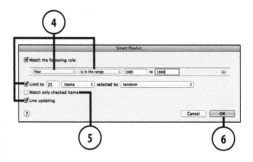

5. One option that might not make immediate sense is Match Only Checked Items. This only matches songs that have checkmarks. If you view your library as a list, you can check/uncheck beside each song. This refers to that checkmark.

6. Click OK when you're done setting search criteria. Your Smart Playlist appears under the Playlists.

7. Enter a Name for the new Smart Playlist, and then press Return.

Tip

Refer back to "Using Genius Recommendations" to have iTunes generate a playlist for you based on a song, album, or artist of your choice.

Accessing Playlists

To access, edit, or play back the media in your playlist, follow these steps:

1. Within the Music library section, click the Playlists category.

2. Click the playlist you want to use from the list on the left.

3. Click the View button to switch between song, artist, and album views.

4. Click Add To to modify the playlist (or Edit for Smart Playlists).

5. Click Play to begin playback.

6. Click Shuffle to randomize the playback order.

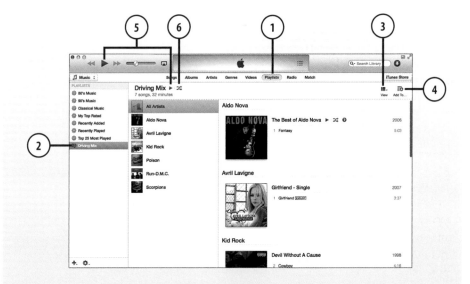

Playing Internet Radio

To listen to Internet radio through iTunes, follow these steps:

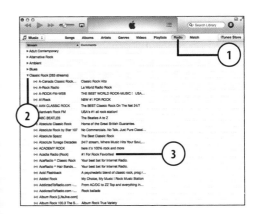

1. Choose the Radio category under the Library's Music section.

2. Click the disclosure arrow in front of a genre in the Streams list.

3. Double-click an item to connect to the stream and begin playback.

You Can't Take It with You

Internet radio differs from other sources in the iTunes library because it is streamed, not downloaded. You can't burn it to a disc or listen to it when you're not online.

Using the Mini Player

After you've set up your media library and decided on the songs you want to play, chances are you don't want to keep the huge iTunes window around. To use the mini player, follow these steps:

1. Click the Mini Player button in the upper right of the iTunes window.

2. The mini player appears and displays the currently playing song.

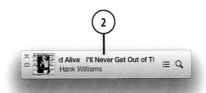

3. Move your cursor over the window to show standard playback controls.

4. Click the list icon to show upcoming songs or your playback history.

5. Use the magnifying glass to search for songs directly from the mini player.

6. Click the tiny rectangle on the left to exit the mini player.

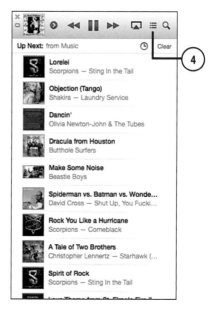

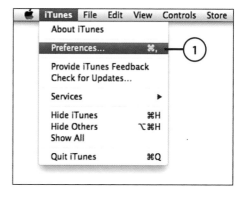

Keeping Media in Sync

iTunes is more than a virtual filing cabinet for storing music and media files. It also syncs with iPods, iPhones, and other computers on your network so you never have to be without those items, even when you're away from your iMac.

Syncing Purchases

By enabling syncing of purchases in iTunes, you ensure that your purchases are downloaded to other copies of iTunes that are signed in with your Apple ID.

Follow these steps to turn on purchase syncing:

1. Open the Preferences from the iTunes menu.

2. Click the Store button at the top of the Preferences window.

3. Click the checkboxes in front of Music, Apps, and Books (or any combination of these) to download any purchase made on another Mac (or even your iOS device) to your iTunes library automatically.

4. Click OK to close Preferences.

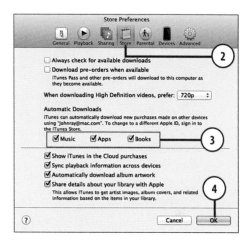

Syncing Your Media with Your iPod, iPad, or iPhone

iTunes was designed to be used with iPods, iPhones, and iPads, which makes syncing your Library between devices a cinch.

Follow these steps to transfer content from your iMac to your iPod, iPhone, or iPad:

1. Connect your iOS device to your iMac using the supplied USB cable. iTunes detects the device and begins synchronizing. (If it has not been connected before, iTunes guides you through a short registration process.) Click the device button to open information about the connected device.

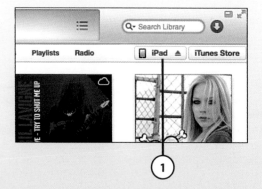

2. View the Summary screen, which shows the name, capacity, software version, serial number, and any updates available to your device.

3. Choose Sync over Wi-Fi to sync without your USB cable in the future!

Note

If your device was previously synced with another Mac, you have the option to Erase and Sync or transfer purchases to your new Mac.

---

4. To conserve space on your device, open the different Media categories, and, on each, select which items to sync.

5. Click Sync to apply your selection and sync your device. The status of the sync appears at the top of the window. Do not disconnect your device until syncing is completed.

6. When the sync completes, click Eject and unplug your device and cable.

Cable-Free Bliss

After you've enabled Wi-Fi syncing, you can start a sync any time your iPhone, iPad, or iPod is on the same network as your iTunes library. Just open the Settings app on your iOS device and navigate to General, iTunes Wi-Fi Sync.

Wait... What About the iCloud Syncing I've Enabled on My iOS Device?

If you've chosen to automatically download media purchases to your iOS device, chances are you will rarely even need to sync directly with iTunes because iCloud will keep everything up-to-date on its own!

Sharing Media Between Home Computers

Home Sharing allows you to browse up to five computers on your local network and import music to your own library. In addition, it will allow you to stream media to your iOS device when it is connected to your home network.

Follow these steps to activate Home Sharing:

1. Using the Library menu, choose Home Sharing. This item only appears when Home Sharing is turned off or iTunes has detected available shared libraries on your network.

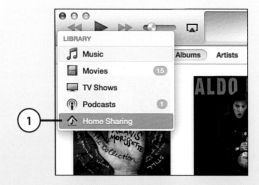

2. Sign in with your Apple ID by entering your username and password.

3. Click Turn On Home Sharing.

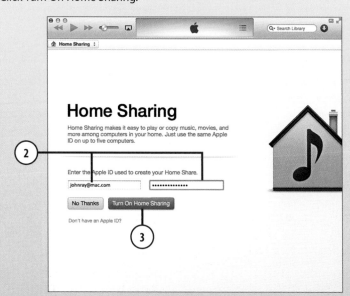

4. Click Done when the confirmation page appears.

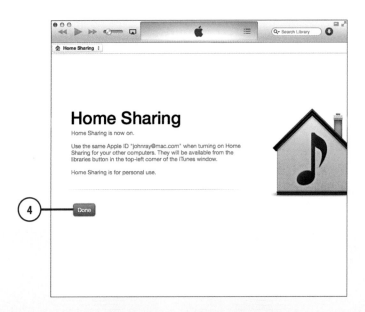

5. Repeat the previous steps for all the other computers in your home, connecting with the same Apple ID.

6. Use the Library menu to choose the shared library you wish to peruse.

7. Select items you want to copy to your local library.

8. Click Import.

Automate Your Imports!

To automatically copy purchases between systems with Home Sharing acti-vated, select the shared library you want to use, and then click the Settings but-ton in the lower-right portion of the window. You'll be given the option of automatically transferring any (and all) purchases from the remote library to your local library.

Keeping an iCloud Music Library with iTunes Match

All songs that you purchase through iTunes are available on any of your computers, as long as you're signed into iTunes with your Apple ID. These songs are referred to as being "stored in iCloud." While this is fine and dandy, what about all the songs you have that *weren't* purchased through iTunes?

For that, we have Music Match. Music Match keeps your entire iTunes music library in Apple's iCloud service and makes it available to all your devices, including the Apple TV. What's more, it replaces poorer quality recordings that you may have in your library with the best Apple has to offer.

It's Not All Good

PAY TO PLAY

iTunes Match isn't free. It costs $25 per year and matches up to 25,000 songs that you didn't purchase from iTunes. Any song purchased through iTunes doesn't count toward the total song limit.

Activating iTunes Match

To sign up for iTunes Match, follow these simple steps:

1. Choose Turn On iTunes Match from the Store menu.

2. Click the Subscribe button to join the iTunes Match service.

3. Enter your Apple ID and password.

4. Click Subscribe.

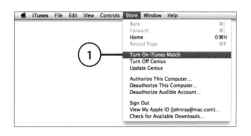

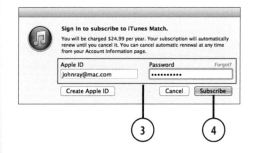

Adding Your Existing Library to iCloud with iTunes Match

After signing up for iTunes Match, you can connect your iMac's iTunes library to the service and begin uploading your songs. If you have multiple computers, each can connect and upload its songs individually.

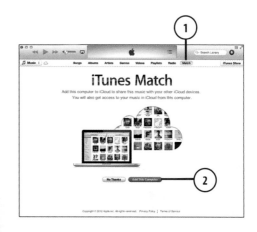

1. Within the Music library, choose Match from the category list at the top center of the screen.

2. Click Add This Computer.

3. Enter your Apple ID and password when prompted.

4. Click Add This Computer.

5. The iTunes Match process runs, analyzing your library and adding your music to iTunes Match in iCloud. You can continue to use iTunes during this process.

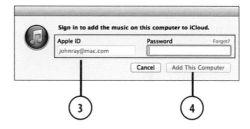

Accessing Music in iCloud

After you've activated iTunes Match on a computer or iOS device, all your songs appear—whether they're located in iCloud or stored locally. To access your music, simply follow these steps:

1. Choose Music from the Library menu—there will now be a cloud icon next to the popup menu.

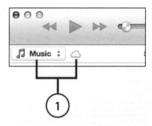

2. Browse your library. Songs and albums available for download from iCloud (but not stored locally) are shown with a cloud and a download arrow. Songs that are stored locally have no cloud icon.

3. You can select and play any song or album. As long as you are connected to the network, iTunes Match songs are instantly streamed.

4. Click the cloud/arrow icon to download a local copy of the song.

Music and More

In addition to your music being stored in the cloud, any TV shows and movies are also available through iTunes on machines that are signed in with your Apple ID. Note that this is only for purchased shows and movies—there is no "video matching" within iTunes Match.

Building the Ultimate Media Center

Prior to OS X Lion, Apple included a home theater/media center package called FrontRow with OS X. Although relatively simplistic, it made it easy to transform an iMac into a media center—all controlled through Apple's tiny infrared remote. Today, OS X Mountain Lion ships without a media center experience. iTunes is great, but it's hardly an application that you can easily control across the room from your bed or couch.

To round out this chapter, I'd like to introduce you to Plex: a media center application that costs you nothing yet creates a user experience far beyond what FrontRow or even Microsoft's Media Center ever offered. Plex automatically catalogs all your media and plays back any modern file format you can find. In short, Plex is the perfect complement to your big-screen iMac.

Installing Plex

Plex consists of two separate components—a media server and a client. The Plex media server catalogs and presents your media files to the client. You can also use your Playstation 3 or Xbox 360 as a client or even download a Plex client app for your iPhone or iPad.

The first step to using Plex on your iMac is downloading and installing both the OS X server and the client.

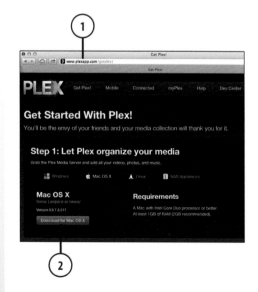

1. Visit http://www.plexapp.com/getplex and navigate to the server download page.

2. Click Download for OS X.

3. While the download is in progress, navigate to the client download page: http://www.plexapp.com/download/plex-media-center.php.

4. Download the OS X version of the Plex Media Center Client.

5. After the downloads complete, locate the Plex Media Server file within your Downloads folder. (If it is a disk image, open the image.)

6. Drag the Plex Media Server icon to the Applications folder.

7. Repeat steps 5–6 for the Plex client application (not pictured).

Need Help Installing?

Refer to Chapter 9 for additional instructions on adding software to your system.

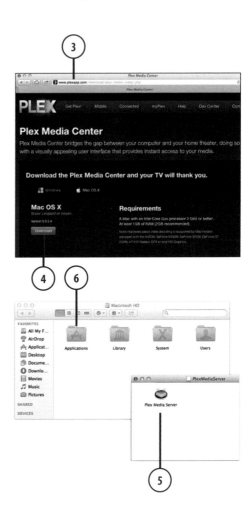

Configuring the Plex Server

Believe it or not, Plex only takes a minute or two to get up and running. The first time you start Plex Media, you are guided through the process of configuring the media server.

1. Launch the Plex Media Server application in your Applications folder or via Launchpad. After it is started the first time, it sets itself to automatically start when you log into your account.

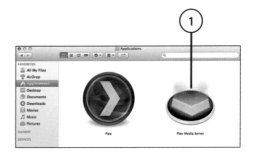

2. The first time you start Plex Media Server, it opens your web browser with a quick-start wizard. Begin by agreeing to the license.

3. Choose a name for the server. This isn't really important unless you have multiple servers on your network.

4. Click Next.

5. On the Create Your Media Library screen, click Add a Section.

6. Choose the type of media you want to add by clicking one of the icons.

7. Name the section—this will be shown in the user interface.

8. Click Add a Folder.

9. On the screen that appears, either type a path to the folder or just click Browse Folders to pick a folder of your choosing.

10. Click Add Folder to set your folder selection.

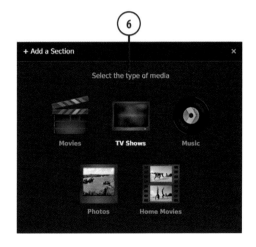

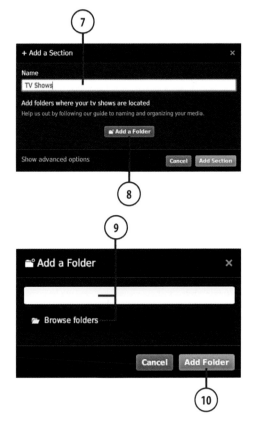

11. Click Add Section to finish configuring the section.

12. Repeat steps 5–11 for each type of media you want to add. Each section will be shown differently in the Plex user interface.

13. Click Next to continue the setup process.

14. You are now asked to choose Channels to install. Channels provide you with quick access to online streaming video but have some prerequisites. Click the Silverlight and Soundflower icons to download and install these packages.

15. Click the channels you want to install, if any. Plex automatically adds channels to access your local iTunes media.

16. Click Next to continue (not pictured).

17. Enter account information to sign up for My Plex. Although not required, you can enter this information in the iOS Plex client to enable streaming to your iPhone or iPad without any additional configuration.

18. Click Next.

19. You're finished! On the final setup screen, Plex presents you with a bookmark that you can drag to your browser's bookmark bar for marking online videos and an email address where you can email video links. Videos you identify with either of these methods show up within the Plex client interface for you to watch.

20. Click Done.

21. Plex displays a summary of all the media items you've configured.

22. Close your browser.

Manage Your Media with Ease

You can access the media management screen at any time by visiting the URL http://<*your iMac's IP address*>:32400/web/ from your local network, or just http://127.0.0.1:32400/web/ on the iMac itself.

Using the Plex Media Server Menu Item

When the Plex Media Server is running, you'll notice a new icon in your menu bar. This can be used to quickly access common features of Plex:

1. Click the Plex Media Server Menu icon to show the server options.

2. Check Open at Login to have the server start when you log in.

3. Select Media Manager to open a window for configuring new media sections and managing existing sections.

4. Choose Update Library to force Plex Media Server to scan your library for changes.

5. Select Quit to Exit Plex Media Server.

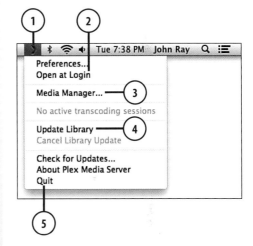

What Is Plex Media Server Doing?

When you aren't watching videos or listening to music in a Plex client, Plex Media Server is watching for changes in your media libraries. When it finds a change, the server queries a number of online databases for information about the media. It caches artwork and descriptions for TV shows, movies, music, and so on.

Using Plex

Plex Media Server runs quietly in the background. After it is set up, you can forget that it's even there; you're ready to enjoy your media center! To use Plex, follow these steps.

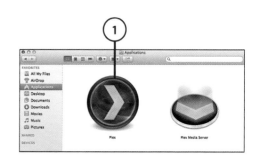

1. Open the Plex application from the applications folder or Launchpad.

2. After a few seconds, Plex opens and displays your media library.

3. Each section is presented in a vertical scrolling list.

4. Use your cursor keys or Apple remote to navigate up and down, left and right to select media.

5. Press Return (or the Select button on the remote) to play back a piece of media or navigate to a lower menu.

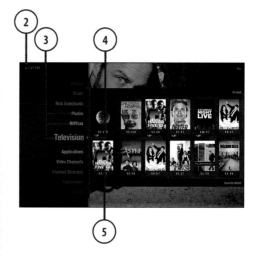

Simply Complex

While Plex is extremely easy to get started with, it is also a very configurable piece of software with many options. I highly recommend you visit http://www.plexapp.com/help/ for a full guide in using Plex and customizing it to your liking.

Download, install,
and update
applications using
the Mac App Store.

Manage your
Mountain Lion
system updates using
Software Update.

In this chapter, you learn how to install applications on your iMac and keep Mountain Lion up-to-date, including:

→ Browsing the Mac App Store

→ Downloading and maintaining App Store applications

→ Downloading and installing non–App Store software

→ Working with OS X software distribution formats

→ Configuring system software updates and auto downloads

Installing and Managing Software on Your iMac

Up to this point in the book, you've been looking at software that came as part of Mountain Lion. That's a bit limiting, don't you think? There is a wide world of software waiting to enhance your computing experience—including upgrades to Mountain Lion itself.

Through the use of the Mac App Store and the Software Update mechanism, you can install new applications, keep them up-to-date, and keep your Mac running smoothly and securely. When that isn't enough, you can turn to thousands of other non-App Store apps that run natively on your iMac.

Mac App Store

Applications make a Mac a Mac. As intangible as it is, a certain "something" about using a Mac application is rarely replicated on a Windows computer.

When you've become accustomed to the day-to-day operation of your iMac, you'll likely want to begin installing third-party software. The easiest place to do this is through the Mac App Store. Like the popular App Store for iOS devices, the Mac App Store is a one-stop shop for thousands of apps that you can install with point-and-click ease.

Logging into the App Store

To use the Mac App Store, you need a registered Apple ID—the same account you used to access iCloud in Chapter 4, "Accessing iCloud, Email, and the Web," will work just fine. If you don't have an ID, you can create one directly in the App Store. To log into the store, follow these steps:

1. Open the App Store application from the Dock or from the Applications folder.

2. The App Store window opens.

3. Click Sign In from the Quick Links on the right side of the page.

4. Provide your Apple ID and password in the form that appears.

5. Click Sign In.

Creating an ID

If you do not have an ID, click Create Apple ID and follow the onscreen prompts.

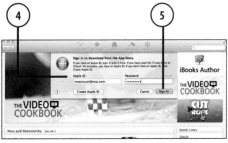

6. Your Login Status and links to your account information are shown in the Quick Links section.

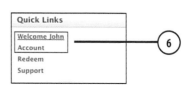

Browsing for Apps

Part of the joy of using the App Store is that browsing is simple and fun—and it works very much like a web browser. As you encounter links (such as See All), click them to view more information. You can browse within a variety of categories that cover the gamut of what you can do on your iMac:

1. Follow steps 1–6 of the previous task, "Logging into the App Store."

2. Click the Featured icon to browse apps tagged by Apple as New and Noteworthy or Hot.

3. Click Top Charts to see the apps that are currently selling the best or being downloaded the most.

4. Click Categories to browse by the different types of apps (games, business, developer, and so on).

5. When you see an app you are interested in, click the icon or name.

6. A full page of information, including reviews, opens.

7. Use the Forward and Back buttons to move back and forth between pages, just like a web browser.

Quick Links for Faster Browsing

The featured page actually contains more than the new/hot apps. In the column on the right side of the page, you can quickly jump to specific app categories to see Top Paid apps, Top Free apps, and more without leaving the page.

Searching for Apps

Sometimes you might know the app you want but do not know where it is located. In these cases, you can simply search the App Store:

1. Follow steps 1–6 of the earlier task, "Logging into the App Store."

2. Type a search term or terms into the field in the upper-right corner. You can use application names, categories (type **news**, for instance), and even author/publisher names.

3. As you type, a list of possible searches appears. Click one if you want to use it; otherwise, press Return to use the search term you've typed.

4. The Search results are displayed.

5. Use the Sort By menu to choose how the results are sorted within the window.

6. Click App Icons or Names to view more information.

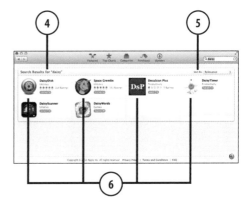

Purchasing an App

When you've decided to purchase an app, the process couldn't be simpler. Follow these instructions to download an app and install it on your iMac:

1. Browse or search for an app, as described in the previous tasks, "Browsing for Apps" and "Searching for Apps."

2. From within the search/browse results or the larger application information page, click the App Price button.

3. The Price button changes to read Buy App. If the app is free, it reads Install App. Click the Buy App (or Install App) button.

4. Provide your App Store Apple ID and password, if prompted, and then click Sign In.

5. The application immediately downloads to your Applications folder and is visible in Launchpad.

Remember It on Payday!

The right side of the Price button for an app has a downward-pointing arrow. This is actually a separate button that opens a pop-up menu. Use this menu to copy a link to the app or to send an email message to someone (maybe yourself) about the app.

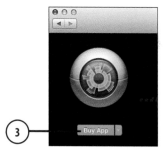

I Don't Want It—Make It Go Away!

If the App Store makes it so easy to install things, it certainly makes it easy to delete them, right? Yes and no. The App Store is used for installing, but Launchpad is used to uninstall the apps. Learn about Launchpad in Chapter 2, "Making the Most of Your iMac's Screen Space."

Reinstalling Apps and Installing Purchases on Other Macs

One of the best things about buying applications through the App Store is that you can install them on other Macs you own. No licensing hassles—just download and go. You can also reinstall apps that you may have deleted in the past but want to start using again.

To download an app you've purchased but that isn't installed, follow steps 1–6 of the "Logging into the App Store" task and then complete these steps:

1. Click the Purchases icon at the top of the App Store window.

2. The Purchases list is displayed, along with a button/label showing the status of each app.

3. Apps labeled as Installed are currently installed and up-to-date.

4. Click the Install button to install (or reinstall) an app that you already own.

5. Click the Update button to update a piece of software that is currently installed. (This functions identically to updating the software through the Updates view.)

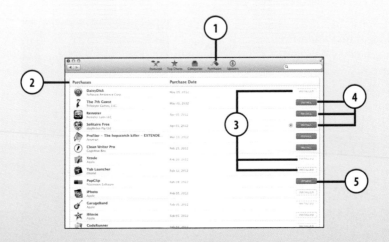

Auto-Install Your Apps!

Mountain Lion will prompt you to turn on automatic downloading of Apps that you download on other machines. If you activate this feature, any software you download on one Mac will automatically be downloaded on any other Mac that is logged into the Mac App Store with your account. This can also be controlled via the Software Update preference pane.

Hiding Apps You No Longer Want

I've downloaded a lot of apps; you probably will, too. Unfortunately, these won't all be apps you want to keep updating (or even remember that you purchased). To hide an app from the update list, follow these steps after logging into the App Store.

1. Click the Purchased icon at the top of the App Store window.

2. Click the X icon beside the Install or Update buttons to hide the application in the list.

Find What's Missing

To show the items that you've hidden, choose the Account quick link from the right side of the Mac App Store after following the instructions in the section "Logging into the App Store." Use the View Hidden Purchases button to show the hidden apps.

Installing Non–App Store Applications

The App Store is great, but it doesn't mean that it defines the limits of what you can do on your iMac. There are certain restrictions in place on the App Store that make some pieces of software impossible to distribute through that site. There are also thousands of developers who want to sell and market their applications through their own websites.

By default, Mountain Lion enables you to install and run any software you want—but this can be disabled by an administrator. Read the section "Limiting Application Execution," in Chapter 12, "Securing and Protecting Your iMac," to learn how to adjust the controls to enable (or disable) software installations on your iMac.

Installing software from non–App Store sources is frequently a matter of browsing the web in Safari, clicking a download link, and copying the application to your Applications folder.

Getting the Lowdown on the Download

Recall that Mountain Lion has a Downloads folder that is available in your Dock. Software archives that you download in Safari or most other Mac applications are stored in this location.

Unarchiving Zip Files

A decade ago, almost all Mac applications were distributed in a compressed archive format called SIT (StuffIt). Today the Mac has adopted a standard used on Windows and other platforms called zip files. A zip file can contain one or more compressed files.

To unarchive a zip file and access the contents, follow these steps:

1. Find the file that you want to unarchive.

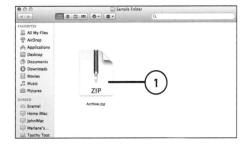

2. Double-click the file. Unarchiving can be virtually instantaneous or can take several seconds, depending on the archive size.

3. The contents of the archive are made available in the same folder where the zip file was located.

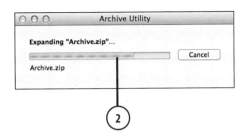

Just StuffIt

If you find that you need to deal with a StuffIt file, you can download StuffIt from http://www.stuffit.com. Despite decreasing use of the format, it has been actively maintained over the years.

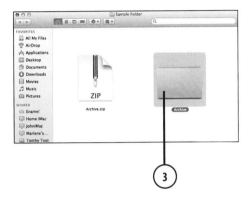

Accessing Disk Images

Sometimes applications are distributed on a disk image, or DMG file. When mounted on your system, DMGs act like a virtual disk drive. Files in a DMG must be copied off the disk image by way of an installer or a simple drag-and-drop process.

To mount and access the contents of a disk image, follow this process:

1. Find the Disk Image you want to access.

2. Double-click the DMG file. The disk image mounts and appears as a disk in the Finder.

3. Access the files in the disk as you would any other storage device.

4. To eject the disk image, click the Eject icon beside the mounted disk in the Finder sidebar or drag it to the trash.

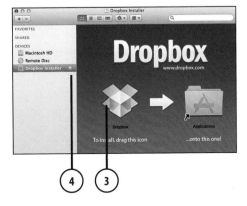

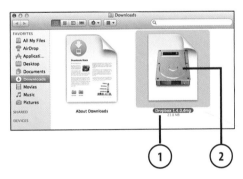

Useful Apps for Your iMac

Apple writes great applications for maintaining a mobile lifestyle, but third-party publishers have created utilities that meet or exceed Apple's own efforts. To get you started, I recommend a handful of non–App Store software packages that can make your iMac experience even more enjoyable and productive.

>>> Go Further

WHERE CAN I FIND SOFTWARE FOR MY iMAC?

Many websites track Macintosh applications, but two of the best are MacUpdate (http://www.macupdate.com/) and VersionTracker (http://www.versiontracker.com/).

Adium (http://adium.im/)—We all have friends (frenemies?) who use chat services other than what iChat supports. Adium supports more than a dozen different instant messaging protocols, including MSN, Yahoo!, and Facebook.

AppCleaner (http://freemacsoft.net/AppCleaner/)—This finds the files associated with an application and removes them from your system. Mountain Lion lacks a global uninstaller that works across *all* apps, so one of the first things you should install is an uninstaller such as AppCleaner.

Curio (http://www.zengobi.com/products/curio/)—This is an amazingly flexible project management and brainstorming software. No matter your line of work, Curio can be a valuable partner in exploring new ideas and creating plans.

Coda (http://www.panic.com/coda/)—This integrated web application development environment fits perfectly on your iMac's screen. If you're ready to graduate from Apple's iWeb software, Coda is a great next step.

CrossOver (http://www.codeweavers.com/products/cxmac/)—Run Windows applications (including Outlook!) and games within Mountain Lion without the overhead of a virtual machine. CrossOver enables you to run many Windows applications directly from your iMac.

Dropbox (http://www.dropbox.com/)—Get 2GB of free online storage that you can sync across OS X, Windows, and Mountain Lion platforms. This service offers the capability to track multiple versions of files wherever you are.

Hazel (http://www.noodlesoft.com/hazel.php)—Hazel offers automated file organization for your desktop. It can automatically discard incomplete uploads, empty your trash when it gets too full, and help keep your system nice and clean.

Microsoft Remote Desktop (http://www.microsoft.com/mac/)—If you need to use a Windows desktop, you can do so from the comfort of your iMac. Download Microsoft's Remote Desktop to remotely access your Windows system as if you were sitting directly in front of it.

Crashplan (http://www.crashplan.com/)—If you need true offsite continuous backups, Crashplan fits the bill. Crashplan works in the background to upload any files you choose (or your entire filesystem) to a remote storage location for quick disaster recovery.

Dolly Drive (http://www.dollydrive.com/)—Like the idea of Time Machine, but don't want to leave a drive connected? Dolly Drive brings Time Machine to the cloud. $5 a month gets you 50GB of backup space that works with Time Machine over your Internet connection, wherever you are.

1Password (http://agilewebsolutions.com/products/1Password)—Manage your password and other sensitive information, like the keychain, but in a much more functional and usable way. 1Password can autofill web pages and also syncs across computers and with the iPhone.

VirtualBox (https://www.virtualbox.org)—This is full Windows emulation, entirely for free! You'll need a copy of Windows to install, but that's all. VirtualBox is an open source project that can quickly turn your iMac into a full Windows system without having to reboot.

Keeping Your Applications and Operating System Up-To-Date

Keeping your operating system and applications up-to-date is important both from the standpoint of maintaining your system security and providing the best possible user experience.

With Mountain Lion, you can activate an automatic update process that periodically checks and prompts you with available updates. You can even set all your Macs to automatically download applications that you've purchased through the App Store—ensuring a seamless computing experience moving from system to system.

How Will I Be Notified of an Update?

All Mountain Lion software update notifications appear in the Notification Center. To learn more about the Notification Center, refer to Chapter 1, "Managing Your iMac Desktop."

Configuring Software Updates and Auto Downloads

To configure how iMac handles software updates and new downloads from Apple, follow these steps:

1. Open the Software Update System Preferences panel.

2. Select the Automatically Check for Updates check box to have your system periodically look for new software downloads.

3. Check Download Newly Available Updates in Background to have your system download the update packages while it is idle so that they are available to install when you are ready.

4. Choose Install System Data Files and Security Updates to keep many of the critical OS files automatically updated without any interaction required.

5. If you'd like all your App Store purchases to be downloaded automatically to your iMac, check Automatically Download Apps Purchased on Other Macs.

6. Close the System Preferences.

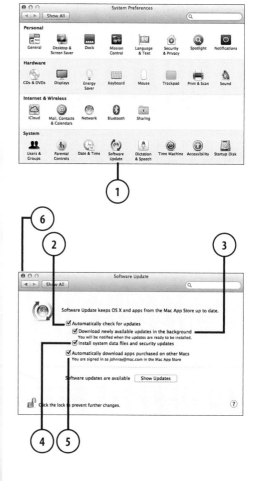

Checking for and Applying Software Updates

If you're like many people (myself included), you install updates only when you have to—or when you get so many notifications in the Notification Center that you just give in. With the Mac App Store, checking for updates is painless: Mountain Lion manages your applications and system updates in a single location.

To check and install application and OS updates, do the following:

1. The App Store icon displays a counter badge listing the number of updates available to you. Update notifications also appear in the Notification Center.

2. Open the App Store.

3. Click the Updates button in the App Store toolbar.

4. All your available app updates are listed.

5. Click the Update All button to update all software at once.

6. Click an individual Update button to update just a single app.

7. Update progress appears in the App Store window, but you don't have to wait to continue using your computer. The updates are automatically installed in the background.

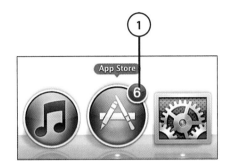

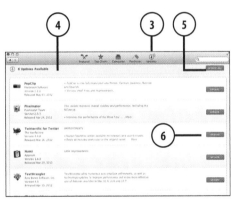

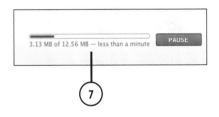

System Update? Your Assistance May Be Required!

Depending on the type of update, you might be asked to give your password and accept any applicable software license agreements before an update is installed. You might also be required to quit running applications or even reboot your Mac for low-level OS updates.

Optimize your iMac's built-in
hardware in System Preferences.

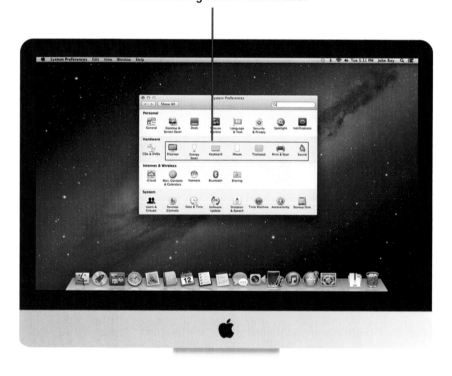

In this chapter, you learn how to make your iMac hardware work at its best for your particular needs, including:

→ Balancing performance and battery efficiency
→ Fine-tuning the keyboard settings
→ Adjusting trackpad and mouse gestures
→ Setting sound input and output
→ Configuring the monitor resolution and color
→ Recording audio
→ Recording video and screen actions

Making the Most of Your iMac Hardware

When you purchased your iMac, you bought more than just a "computer"—you bought a power system, monitor, keyboard, trackpad (or mouse), video camera, microphone, and speakers! On a traditional desktop system, these might all be separate components, but on your iMac, they're part of a tightly integrated package.

To help personalize your iMac, you can adjust many of the settings available for these hardware devices, such as enabling trackpad gestures, setting a system boot and shutdown schedule, setting your microphone up for dictation, and much more. Mountain Lion even includes a few new out-of-the-box tricks such as video, audio, and screen recording that let you take advantage of the built-in FaceTime HD camera without needing any additional software.

Going Green with Energy Saver

A decade ago, computers were appliances—much like microwaves. When you wanted something, you booted them up, performed your task, and shut them down. Today, computers that are actually turned *off* are harder and harder to find. Our expectation is that we can walk up to a computer, access it instantly, and move on.

Your iMac makes this scenario possible, and possible in an energy efficient way. You can always put your computer to sleep or shut it down from the Apple menu, but you can also have it take care of energy-saving tasks for you.

Configuring Display, Computer, and Hard Disk Sleep

To help improve energy efficiency, Mountain Lion includes the Energy Saver System Preferences panel.

1. Open the System Preferences window and click the Energy Saver icon.

2. Drag the sliders, Computer Sleep and Display Sleep, to set the period of inactivity after which your iMac puts itself or its display into sleep mode.

3. Select Put Hard Disks to Sleep When Possible to spin down your hard drive when it's not in use. This helps save power but sacrifices some speed. If you have a machine with a solid state drive, this option is not be available.

4. If you'd like to let your computer wake up if you attempt to access it over a network, click Wake for Network Access.

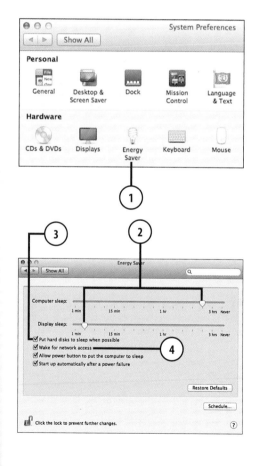

5. To set the system to sleep when you push the power button in back, click Allow Power Button to Put the Computer to Sleep.

6. Finally, if you want your system to boot back up after a power failure, click Start up Automatically After a Power Failure.

7. Close the System Preferences.

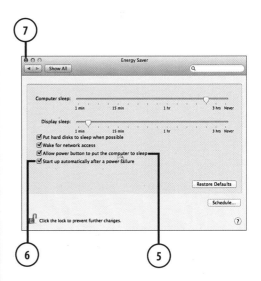

Creating a Sleep/Wake Schedule

If you have a daily schedule and want your iMac to follow it, you can configure wake-up and sleep/shutdown times for the iMac. Follow these steps to set a power schedule for your system.

1. Open the System Preferences window and click the Energy Saver icon.

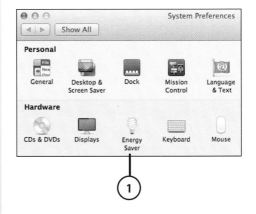

2. Click the Schedule button at the bottom of the window.

3. To have your computer start up on a schedule, click the checkbox beside Start Up or Wake.

4. Use the Every Day pop-up menu to set when (weekdays, weekends, and so on) the startup should occur.

5. Set the time for the computer to start up.

6. To configure your computer to go to sleep, shutdown, or restart, click the checkbox in front of the Sleep pop-up menu.

7. Use the Sleep pop-up menu to choose whether your iMac should sleep, shutdown, or restart.

8. Configure the day and time for the shutdown to occur, just as you did with the start options in steps 4 and 5.

9. Click OK.

10. Close the System Preference>s.

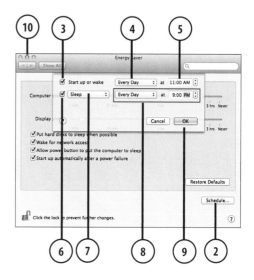

Updating Keyboard and Dictation Settings

Having trouble using the Apple wireless keyboard that came with your iMac? Never fear! Using the built-in keyboard settings, you can adjust the keyboard repeat rate, key delay, and even set system-wide shortcuts for trackpad and mouse-free operation.

If you prefer to talk rather than type, Mountain Lion includes built-in dictation, accessed from anywhere with a single keystroke.

Setting Keyboard Repeat Rate

To choose how frequently the keys on your keyboard repeat, and how long it takes to start repeating, follow these simple steps:

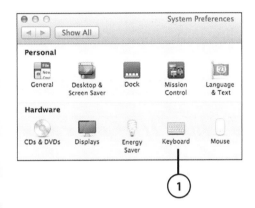

1. Open the System Preferences window and click the Keyboard icon.

2. Click the Keyboard button at the top of the panel.

3. Use the Key Repeat slider to set how quickly letters appear when you hold down a key on your keyboard. Move the slider all the way to the left to turn off repeating.

4. Move the Delay Until Repeat slider to choose how long you must hold down a key before it starts repeating.

5. Close the System Preferences.

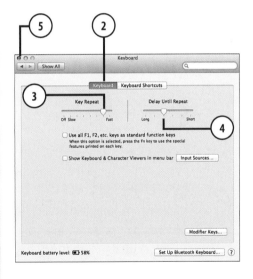

Using Function Keys

You've probably noticed that the top row of keys on your Apple wireless keyboard have special functions, such as dimming the display, changing the volume, and so on. These keys, however, are also function keys that your applications might need. To set the keys to always work as function keys without having to hold down the fn key, click the Use all F1, F2, etc. Keys as Standard Function Keys checkbox.

Creating Keyboard Shortcuts

There are times you might find your-self working with your iMac and thinking, "Geez, I wish I could just push a key for that rather than hav-ing to mouse around." Using key-board shortcuts, you can create key commands for almost anything.

Setting Shortcuts for Existing Mountain Lion Actions

To set the shortcut for an existing system feature, follow these steps:

1. Open the System Preferences win-dow and click the Keyboard icon.

2. Click the Keyboard Shortcuts button.

3. Choose one of the Mountain Lion system features from the left pane.

4. Scroll through the list of available actions in the right pane.

5. Click the checkbox in front of an action to enable it.

6. Double-click to the far right of an action name to edit its shortcut field.

7. Press the keys that you want to assign to the shortcut.

8. Close the System Preferences after making all of your changes.

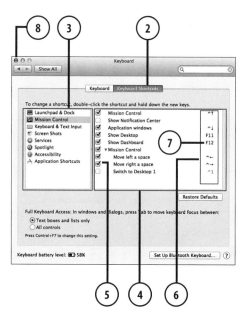

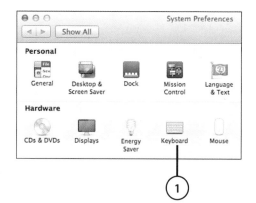

Setting Shortcuts for Arbitrary Applications

To configure a shortcut that works with an arbitrary application, not a built-in feature, do the following:

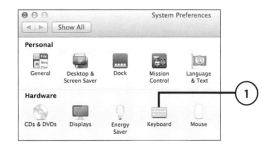

1. Open the System Preferences window and click the Keyboard icon.

2. Click the Keyboard Shortcuts button.

3. Click the Application Shortcuts entry in the list on the left side of the window.

4. Click the + button at the bottom of the shortcut list.

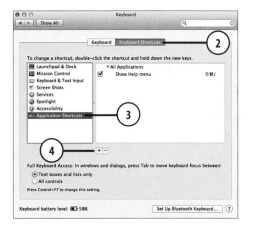

5. In the dialog box that opens, use the Application pop-up menu to choose an application to which you want to assign a shortcut.

6. Enter into the Menu Title field the exact wording of the menu item that you want the keyboard shortcut to invoke.

7. Click into the Keyboard Shortcut field and then press the keys you want to set as the shortcut.

8. Click Add when you're satisfied with your settings.

9. Close the System Preferences.

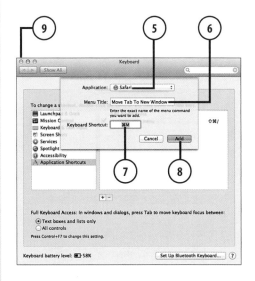

Activating Dictation

If you find that your iMac's keyboard is tiring your fingers, you may want to switch to using the Mountain Lion dictation feature. This enables you to input text *anywhere* using your voice. The only requirements are that you have an Internet connection available and work in a noise-controlled environment (or have a high-quality headset). The voice recognition itself is actually performed by Apple's cloud servers.

Enabling Dictation

To enable dictation support and configure how it is triggered, follow these steps:

1. Open the System Preferences window, and click the Dictation & Speech icon.

2. Click the Dictation button at the top of the panel.

3. Click the On radio button to turn on dictation support.

4. Use the Shortcut drop-down menu to configure what key combination will start dictation.

5. Set the language you will be speaking using the Language drop-down menu.

6. Close the System Preferences when finished.

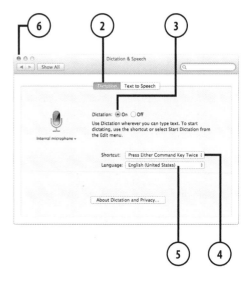

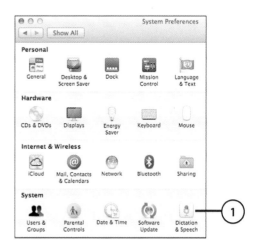

Your Mac Can Talk Back

Your iMac can talk back to you using a variety of different voices. To configure speech feedback, click the Text to Speech button at the top of the Dictation & Speech preference panel. This will let you test and choose your favorite speech synthesizer and the rate of speech.

Using Dictation

To use dictation, you must have it enabled (see the preceding task) and have an active Internet connection. If you meet those qualifications, just complete these steps to type with your voice:

1. Position your cursor where you want to dictate.

2. Press the key combination you configured when enabling dictation (not shown).

3. The dictation microphone appears. Begin speaking now—be sure to speak the name of the punctuation symbols you want to insert, such as "period," "comma," and so on.

4. Press any key or click Done to end dictation. After a short pause, the spoken text is inserted into the document.

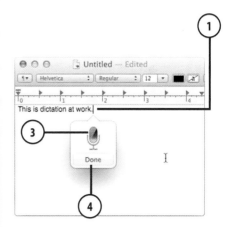

Changing Trackpad and Mouse Options

When you purchased your iMac, it came with either a Magic Trackpad or a Magic Mouse. While these devices are intuitive for beginners, they can be customized to provide advanced features within Mountain Lion. Using the Trackpad and Mouse preferences, you can fine-tune the operation of your input device and set up different multifinger gestures in popular applications.

Perfect Pairing

Your iMac arrived with its input device already "paired" with the system. If you have problems connecting a new mouse or trackpad to your computer, skip ahead to Chapter 11, "Connecting Devices to Your iMac," for details on Bluetooth pairing.

Setting the Trackpad Speed

To choose how quickly your trackpad follows your input, follow these steps:

1. Open the System Preferences window and click the Trackpad icon.

2. Click the Point & Click button at the top of the window.

3. Choose how quickly the cursor moves by dragging the Tracking Speed slider.

4. Close the System Preferences.

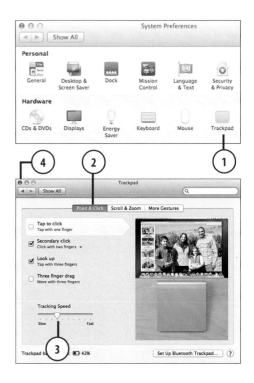

Controlling Trackpad Gestures

If you have an iMac with a Magic Trackpad you can take advantage of a wide range of different two-, three-, and even four-finger motions to control your applications.

1. Open the System Preferences window and click the Trackpad icon.

2. Use the Point & Click settings to configure click and drag options.

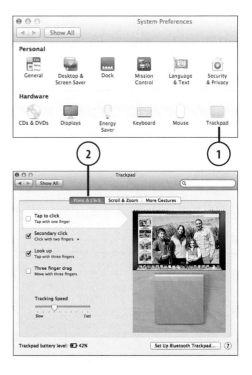

3. Use the Scroll & Zoom settings section to control scrolling, rotation, and pinching gestures.

4. The More Gestures settings control advanced features, such as whether swiping to the left or right moves forward or backward in Safari and how Mission Control is activated.

5. Many settings contain a drop-down menu to fine-tune the gesture.

6. As you mouse over a particular setting, a video demonstrating the action appears in the right side of the window.

7. Close the System Preferences.

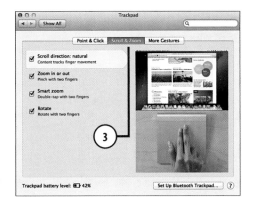

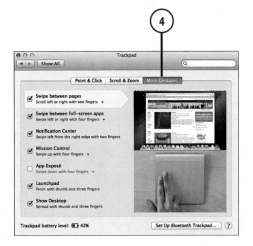

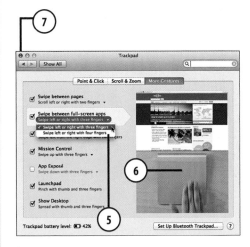

Configuring the Magic Mouse Speed

The Apple Magic Mouse is a multi-touch trackpad and mouse in one. Although it doesn't support nearly as many gestures as the Magic Trackpad, it's still a capable device. To configure the Magic Mouse tracking speed, follow these steps:

1. Open the System Preferences window and click the Mouse icon.

2. Click the Point & Click button at the top of the window.

3. Choose how quickly the cursor moves by dragging the Tracking Speed slider.

4. Close the System Preferences.

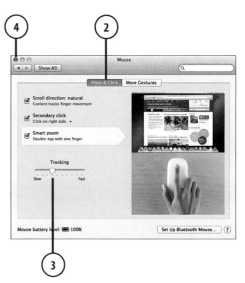

Configuring Magic Mouse Gestures

To set up the different single and two-finger gestures supported on the Magic Mouse, complete the following:

1. Open the System Preferences window and click the Mouse icon.

2. Use the Point & Click settings to configure click, scrolling, and zooming.

3. The More Gestures settings control advanced features, such as whether swiping to the left or right moves forward or backward in Safari and how Mission Control is activated.

4. Some settings contain a drop-down menu to fine-tune the gesture.

5. As you mouse over a particular setting, a video demonstrating the action appears in the right side of the window.

6. Close the System Preferences.

If you have to choose...

Choose the Magic Trackpad. Even if you are a life-long mouser, you'll find that the Magic Trackpad's gesture support integrates perfectly into Mountain Lion and makes performing common tasks similar to using an iPad.

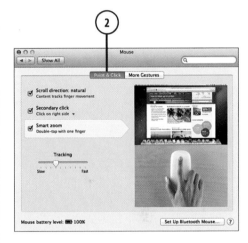

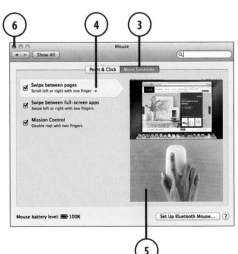

Adjusting the iMac Display

Your iMac's IPS display is your window into your computer, so it's important that you configure your display to best suit your needs. For detailed CAD or drawing, you might want to use the full resolution. Games or late-night typing might call for a larger (lower resolution) option. Using Mountain Lion's Display settings, you can control the image so that it is right for the task at hand.

Setting Display Resolution

The display resolution is the number of pixels that are viewable on the screen at any time. The smallest iMac display (21.5") is capable of 1920×1080 pixels—the highest HD standard available! To control the screen resolution on your system, follow these steps:

1. Open the System Preferences window and click the Displays icon.

2. Click the Display button at the top of the panel.

3. Click the Scaled radio button. Alternatively, the default radio button (Best for Built-In Display) chooses the best option for your iMac.

4. Scroll through the list of available resolutions (smaller numbers result in a larger, less crisp onscreen image).

5. Click a resolution to switch immediately.

6. Close the System Preferences.

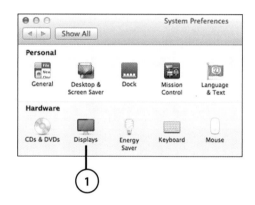

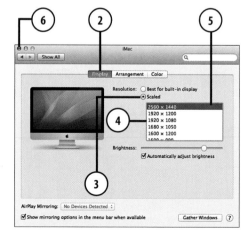

What Are Mirroring Options?

When setting your display resolution, you'll notice a checkbox for showing Mirroring Options in your menu bar. This is for working with external displays that can mirror your iMac's screen. You learn more about this feature in Chapter 11.

Controlling Display Brightness

Display brightness is a personal setting; some individuals like muted, dimmed displays and others like colors offered by full-brightness settings. To set the brightness of your display, follow these steps:

1. Open the System Preferences window and click the Displays icon.

2. Click the Display button at the top of the panel.

3. Drag the Brightness slider left or right to dim or brighten the display.

4. Click Automatically Adjust Brightness to have your iMac dim or brighten your screen depending on the room's ambient lighting.

5. Close the System Preferences.

Adjusting Brightness From Your Keyboard

You can also adjust display brightness using the dim/bright keys (shared with F1 and F2) on your keyboard.

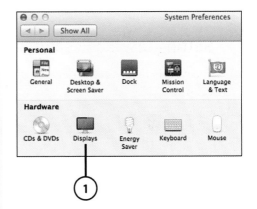

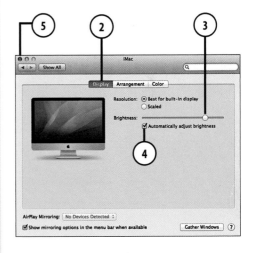

Choosing a Color Profile

Color profiles help keep colors consistent between computers with different monitors. By choosing a color profile that is calibrated for your display, you're ensured that colors you see on one machine match a similarly calibrated display on another machine. To choose a calibration profile, follow these steps:

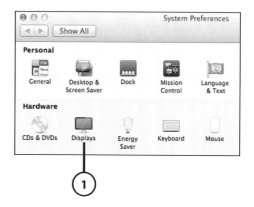

1. Open the System Preferences window and click the Displays icon.

2. Click the Color button at the top of the panel.

3. Click the preferred profile in the Display Profile list. The changes are immediately applied.

4. Close the System Preferences.

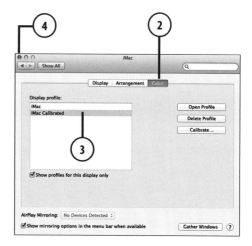

Where Do These Profiles Come From?

You can add profiles to your system by installing software or by running the calibration procedure, which creates your own personalized color profile.

Calibrating the iMac Display

If you'd like to calibrate your display manually, Mountain Lion provides a wizard-like interface for choosing the best display settings for your iMac.

1. Open the System Preferences window and click the Displays icon.

2. Click the Color button at the top of the panel.

3. Click Calibrate.

4. The Display Calibrator Assistant starts.

5. Click the Expert Mode checkbox to get the best results.

6. Click Continue to proceed through the assistant.

7. Follow the onscreen instructions to test the output of your display and click Continue to move on to the next screen.

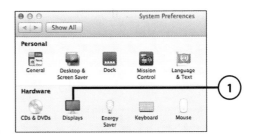

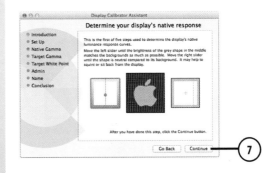

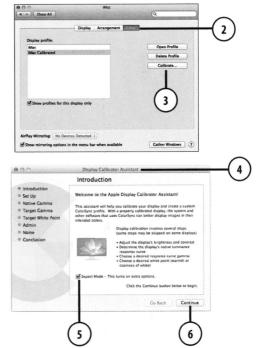

Chapter 10

8. When finished, enter a name for the new calibrated profile.

9. Click Continue to save the profile.

10. The new profile is added to the color profile list.

11. Close the System Preferences.

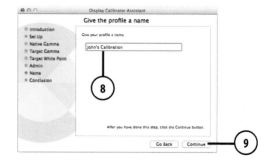

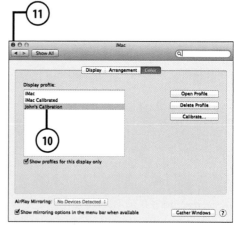

Setting Sound Input and Output

Sound has never been an afterthought on Macintosh systems, and your iMac is no different. Your system is equipped with a stereo sound system, headphone jack, microphone jack (shared with the headphone jack in recent models), and even digital audio out. You can configure these input and output options to reflect your listening needs.

Setting the Output Volume

Volume, as you might expect, is one control that is needed system-wide. To control the output volume of your system, follow these steps:

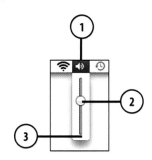

1. Click the speaker icon in the menu bar.

2. Drag the slider up to increase the volume, or slide it down to decrease the volume.

3. Drag the slider all the way to the bottom to mute all output sounds.

Keyboard Volume Controls

You can also use the special controls located on the F9, F10, and F11 keys to mute, decrease, and increase the system volume.

Adding the Volume Control to the Menu Bar

If sound control is not visible in your menu bar, it has been manually removed. You can re-add it to the menu using the Show volume in the menu bar option in the Sound System Preferences panel.

Configuring Alert Sounds

Your iMac generates alert sounds when it needs to get your attention. To configure the sounds, and how loud they play, follow these steps:

1. Open the System Preferences window and click the Sound icon.

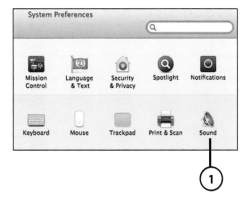

2. Click the Sound Effects button at the top of the panel.

3. Scroll through the alert sound list to see all of the available alert sounds.

4. Click a sound to select it as your alert sound and hear a preview.

5. Choose which sound output device (usually your internal speakers) should play the alert sound.

6. Use the alert volume slider to adjust the volume of alerts that your system plays. This is independent of the system output volume.

7. Check Play User Interface Sound Effects to play sounds when special events occur—such as emptying the trash.

8. Close the System Preferences when finished configuring the sound effects.

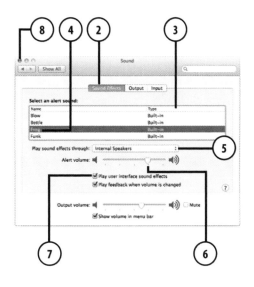

Choosing and Adjusting an Output Device

To configure your sound output options with a bit more flexibility than just changing the volume, you need to adjust the output settings for the device that is being used for playback—typically your speaker.

1. Open the System Preferences window and click the Sound icon.

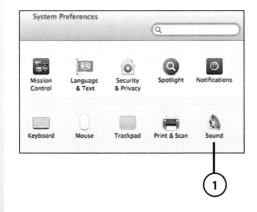

2. Click the Output button at the top of the panel.

3. Choose the output device to configure (probably your speakers).

4. Use the balance setting to adjust audio to the left or right speaker.

5. Set or mute the output volume.

6. Close the System Preferences when finished.

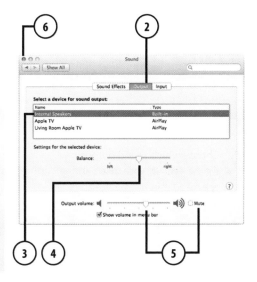

HOW DO I USE HEADPHONES OR DIGITAL AUDIO ON MY iMAC?

When headphones are plugged into your iMac, the sound output settings alter to reflect the change. All sound is directed to the headphones rather than the internal speakers.

Your iMac also sports a home-theater-worthy digital optical output, disguised as the headphone jack. To use the digital output, you need a mini TOSLINK adapter, which provides a standard TOSLINK plug for connecting to stereo equipment. These cables from Amazon.com easily get the job done: www.amazon.com/6ft-Toslink-Mini-Cable/dp/B000FMXKC8.

Picking and Calibrating an Input Device

In addition to sound output, you can also input sound on your iMac using either the built-in microphone or the line-in jack on the back. To configure your input device, follow these steps:

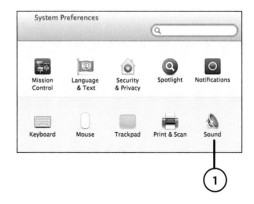

1. Open the System Preferences window and click the Sound icon.

2. Click the Input button at the top of the panel.

3. Choose the device to use for input.

4. Use the Input Volume slider to adjust the gain on the microphone—this is how much amplification is applied to the signal.

5. Click the Use Ambient Noise Reduction checkbox if you're working in an environment with background noise.

6. Speak at the level you want your computer to record. The Input level graph should register near the middle when you use a normal speaking level. If it doesn't, readjust the input volume slider.

7. Close the System Preferences.

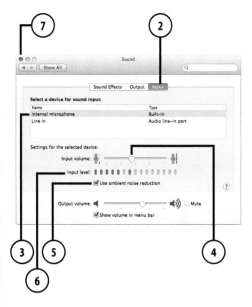

Keeping the Input Volume Under Control

It might be tempting to turn the input volume up as high as it goes so that the microphone detects even little noises. Keep in mind, however, that the higher the input volume for wanted sounds, the higher the volume for unwanted sounds as well!

Recording Audio, Video, and Screen Actions

It has always been possible to record audio and video "out of the box" with a new Macintosh, but not without jumping through a bunch of seemingly unnecessary hoops or trudging through unwieldy software. With Mountain Lion, Apple has made it easy to take advantage of your iMac's built-in capabilities to record audio, video, and even screen actions.

Recording Audio

To create and save a new audio recording, first make sure that you've configured your sound input settings correctly (including ambient noise reduction, if needed) then follow these steps:

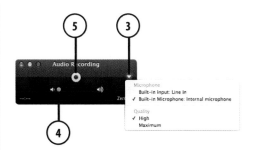

1. Open the QuickTime Player application (find it in the Launchpad or the Applications folder).

2. Choose File, New Audio Recording.

3. Use the drop-down menu on the right of the Audio Recording window to choose an input source, recording quality, and destination.

4. If you want to hear audio through the speakers as it is recorded, drag the volume slider to the right.

5. Click the Record button to begin recording.

6. Click the Stop button to stop recording.

7. Use the playback controls to listen to your creation.

8. Choose File, Export to save the audio, if desired.

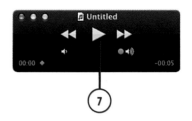

Recording with the FaceTime HD Video Camera

Although FaceTime allows you to see video of yourself on your computer, it doesn't give you the option to record. If you want to take a recording of what the built-in camera sees, follow these steps:

1. Open the QuickTime Player application (find it in the Launchpad or the Applications folder).

2. Choose File, New Movie Recording.

3. Use the drop-down menu on the right side of the recording controls to choose a camera (if you have more than one), input microphone, recording quality, and destination.

4. If you want to hear audio through the speakers as it is recorded, drag the volume slider to the right.

5. Click the double arrows to expand the video to full screen.

6. Click the Record button to begin recording.

7. Click the Stop button to stop recording.

8. Use the playback controls to view the video you've recorded.

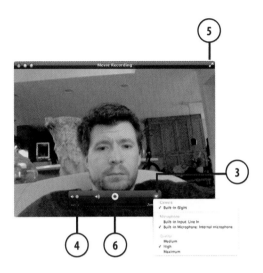

9. Choose File, Export to save the movie, if desired.

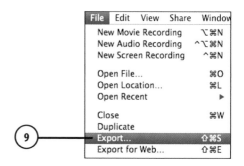

Recording Screen Actions

If you've ever been in a situation where you tried to explain to someone *how* to do something on a computer, chances are you've gotten a bit frustrated. By using Mountain Lion's screen recording capabilities, however, you can quickly create a movie that shows all your onscreen actions and then send that movie to your confused acquaintance to provide a better-than-words tutorial.

1. Open the QuickTime Player application (find it in the Launchpad or the Applications folder).

2. Choose File, New Screen Recording.

3. Use the drop-down menu on the right side of the recording controls to choose an input microphone, recording quality, whether or not to show mouse clicks, and, finally, destination.

4. Click the Record button to prepare to record actions.

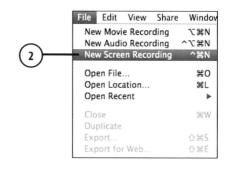

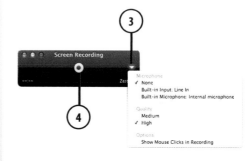

5. Click anywhere on your screen to record the whole screen, or click and drag to define a rectangular area to record.

6. If you've defined a recording area, click Start Recording, and then perform the actions that you want to record.

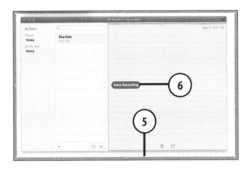

7. Click the Stop button in the recording controls to stop.

8. Use the playback controls to view the screen recording you've created.

9. Choose File, Export to save the movie, if desired.

Video and Photo Fun!

If you want to record and share videos and photos, or you want to just play around with your iMac's HD camera, try Photo Booth—located in the Mountain Lion Dock (or Launchpad or the Applications folder). Photo Booth provides a simple interface for taking pictures and video, applying effects, and sharing the results.

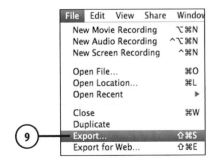

Connect your iMac to external displays and
peripherals using System Preferences.

In this chapter, you learn how to connect devices to your iMac and immediately expand your system's capabilities, including:

→ Adding a keyboard and mouse
→ Pairing Bluetooth devices
→ Connecting and configuring external displays
→ Sending video and audio to an Apple TV
→ Adding and using printers
→ Accessing and using popular scanners

Connecting Devices to Your iMac

The iMac comes with everything you need to get started using the system, but that doesn't mean that you can't expand it. Your iMac can interface with many different devices—frequently without requiring any additional software to be installed.

In this chapter we look at the different types of peripherals that work with your iMac out-of-the-box.

Connecting USB Input Devices

The iMac can connect to a variety of devices using the standard USB (Universal Serial Bus) ports located on the back. This section walks you through connecting a generic keyboard and mouse. Keep in mind, though, that there are *hundreds* of different input devices.

You should always refer to the documentation that came with your device. If the manual doesn't mention the Macintosh (such as for a Windows-specific keyboard), try plugging in the device to see what happens!

USB Device Compatibility

The USB standard includes a variety of different profiles that define how a device can be used (input, audio output/input, and so on). These standards are supported on both Macintosh and Windows platforms. Just because a device does not specifically say it supports the Mac, doesn't mean that it won't work anyway.

Configuring a USB Keyboard

Your iMac comes with a perfectly usable keyboard, but if you've got a favorite *wired* keyboard, you can plug it in and start using it almost immediately. To use a standard USB keyboard with your iMac, follow these steps:

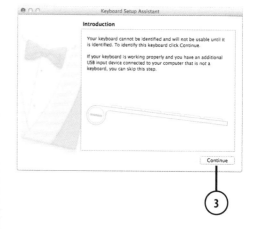

1. Plug the keyboard into a free port on your iMac (not pictured).

2. If the keyboard is an Apple or Mac-specific keyboard, it is recognized and immediately usable (not pictured).

3. If you are using a generic USB keyboard, the Keyboard Setup Assistant launches and you are asked to identify the keyboard. Click Continue.

4. Walk through the steps presented by the setup assistant, pressing the keyboard keys when requested. If the assistant can't identify the keyboard, you are asked to manually identify it.

5. Click Done at the conclusion of the setup assistant. The keyboard setup is complete and ready to be used.

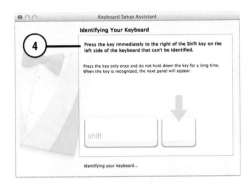

Manually Configuring the Keyboard Type

If the setup assistant does not start automatically when you plug in a USB keyboard, you can start it by opening the System Preferences window and clicking the Keyboard icon. In the Keyboard panel, click Change Keyboard Type.

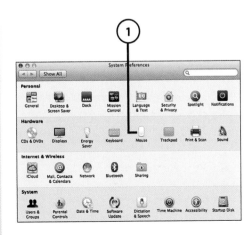

Configuring a USB Mouse

The Apple mouse is nice, but some of us like options! Want to use a shiny USB mouse with a zillion buttons? No problem. Like keyboards, USB mice plug right in and start working in a matter of seconds.

1. Open the System Preferences and click the Mouse icon.

2. Plug a USB mouse into your iMac (not pictured).

3. After a few seconds the Mouse panel updates to show the available options for your device.

4. Uncheck Scroll Direction: Natural if you prefer a scroll wheel that behaves in a traditional manner (down to go up, and vice versa).

5. Adjust the tracking speed, scrolling speed (if the mouse includes a scroll wheel), and double-click speed by dragging the sliders left or right.

6. Choose which button acts as the primary button.

7. Close the System Preferences panel when you've finished your configuration.

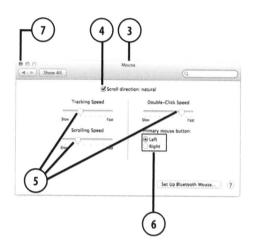

Using Bluetooth Devices

The iMac's built-in Bluetooth enables it to wirelessly connect to a variety of peripheral devices, including keyboards, mice, headsets, and so on. As with USB peripherals, your first step toward installing a device is to read the manufacturer's instructions and install any drivers that it came with.

After installing the software that came with the peripheral, you use the Apple Bluetooth System Preferences panel to choose and *pair* your device.

WHAT IS PAIRING?

When you're working with Bluetooth peripherals, you'll notice many references to pairing. Pairing is the process of making two devices (your Mac and the peripheral) aware of one another so they can communicate.

In order to pair with your computer, your device needs to be in pairing mode, which should be described in the device's manual.

Pairing a Bluetooth Mouse or Trackpad

To pair a Bluetooth device with your iMac, you follow the same basic steps, regardless of the type of peripheral. This task's screenshots show an Apple Magic Trackpad being paired with the iMac.

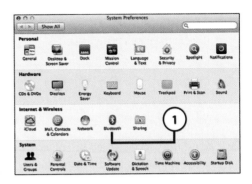

1. Open the Bluetooth System Preferences panel.

2. Click On to ensure that your iMac's Bluetooth system is enabled.

3. Click Set Up New Device, or click + below the list of devices you added previously to start the Bluetooth Setup Assistant.

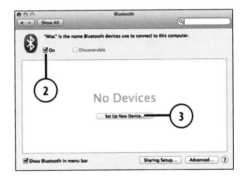

4. After a few seconds of searching, nearby devices are listed. Click to choose your device from the detected options.

5. Click Continue.

6. The device is configured and paired to your system. Click Quit to exit the Assistant.

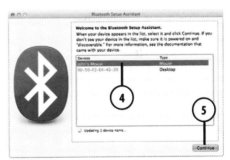

Setting Up Bluetooth Devices from Almost Anywhere

You may notice that there is a Set Up Bluetooth [Keyboard, Mouse, Trackpad] option within the keyboard, mouse, and trackpad system preference panels. You can use these as shortcuts to immediately start searching for a Bluetooth device of that type. The Bluetooth System Preferences panel, however, is the central point for pairing all devices.

7. Your new device is listed in the Bluetooth System Preferences panel.

8. Use the corresponding (Mouse/Trackpad) Preferences panel to configure your device.

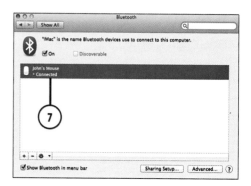

Monitoring Your Battery

When you're using an Apple Bluetooth device or keyboard, the corresponding preference panels display battery status for the devices. You can also monitor battery status by adding the Bluetooth status to your menu bar by selecting Show Bluetooth Status in Menu Bar in the Bluetooth System Preferences panel.

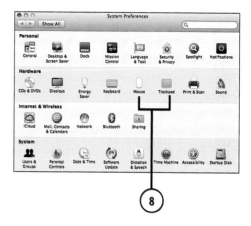

Pairing a Bluetooth Keyboard

Some Bluetooth devices, such as keyboards, require an additional step while pairing: the entry of a passkey on the device you are pairing with. To pair a keyboard with your system, follow these steps:

1. Follow steps 1–5 of the "Pairing a Bluetooth Mouse or Trackpad" task, selecting the keyboard device from the list of detected devices, then clicking Continue.

2. The Bluetooth Setup Assistant prompts you to enter a passkey on your device. Type the characters exactly as displayed on screen, including pressing Return, if shown.

3. If the passkey was successfully entered, the device is configured and paired.

4. Click Quit to exit the Setup Assistant.

5. Open the Keyboard Preferences panel and configure the device as described in Chapter 10's section "Updating Keyboard and Dictation Settings."

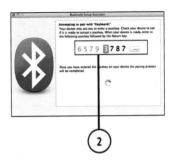

Dealing with Troublesome Passcodes

If, for some reason, you enter the passkey and get an error, look for a Passcode Options button in the lower-left corner of the Setup Assistant. Clicking this button *might* allow you to bypass the passkey or choose one that is easier to enter on your device.

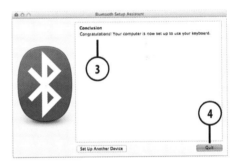

Connecting a Bluetooth Headset

Wireless headphones and headsets can help untether us from our computers when conferencing or listening to music. Your iMac with Mountain Lion supports high-quality audio over Bluetooth connections, and setup is a cinch:

1. Follow steps 1–5 of the "Pairing a Bluetooth Mouse or Trackpad" task, selecting the headset device from the list of detected devices, then clicking Continue.

2. The headset is added to your system. You might need to cycle the power on and off the headset before it will work, however.

3. Click Quit to exit the Setup Assistant.

4. To set the headset for audio input or output, use the Sound System Preferences panel, as described in the Chapter 10 section, "Setting Sound Input and Output."

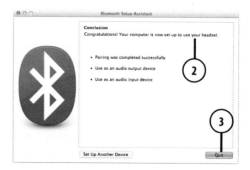

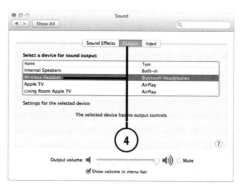

Adding and Using the Bluetooth Status Menu

Apple Bluetooth devices report their status directly to your computer, giving you a heads up on battery issues and other status problems. To use the Bluetooth status menu, follow these steps.

1. Open the System Preferences window and click the Bluetooth icon.

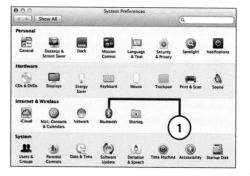

2. Click the Show Bluetooth in Menu Bar checkbox.

3. Close the System Preferences.

4. The Bluetooth menu is added to your display.

5. Each paired device has an entry in the menu for quick control of its features.

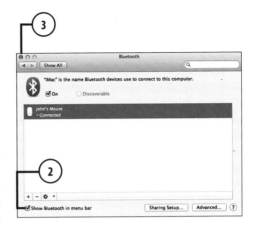

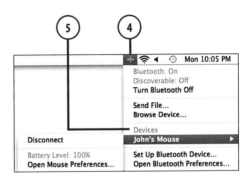

Using External Displays and Projectors

The iMac screens currently ship in 21.5" and 27" sizes—plenty of room for most applications. There are times, though, when using an external monitor or a projector is helpful. As long as you have the right cables, running an external monitor is plug-and-play—no rebooting required.

What Kind of External Displays Can I Run?

All modern iMacs have Thunderbolt or a Mini DisplayPort video output, which can be adapted to VGA or DVI output with a plug-in dongle from Apple. Earlier models used a miniDVI port, which, similarly, could be output to VGA or DVI monitors with the appropriate adapter.

Extending Your Desktop to Another Monitor

To use another monitor to extend your desktop, follow these steps:

1. Plug the monitor into your iMac using the appropriate adapter cable (not shown).

2. The monitor is initialized and displays your desktop at the highest resolution (not shown).

3. Open the Displays System Preferences panel.

4. A unique window is shown on each connected monitor, enabling you to customize its characteristics.

5. Close the System Preferences when finished.

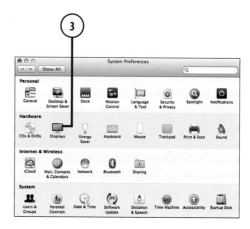

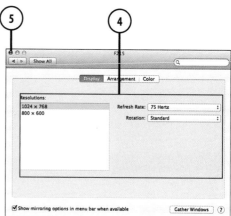

Setting Monitor Arrangements

Once a monitor has been connected to your system, you can choose how it is arranged in relationship to your iMac display and whether or not it displays the menu bar.

1. Open the Displays System Preferences Panel.

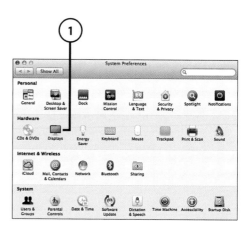

2. Click the Arrangement button at the top of the window.

3. Drag the visual representation of the monitors so that it best represents your physical setup (that is, external monitor on the left, right, above, and so on).

4. If you want, change your primary display by dragging the small white line representing the menu bar from one display to the other.

5. Close the System Preferences.

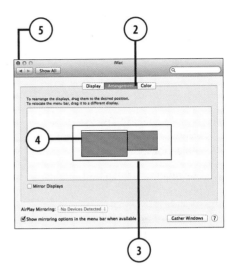

MANAGING MULTIPLE MONITORS

When the Displays System Preferences panel is opened with two or more monitors connected, a unique copy of the preference panel is shown on each monitor, representing that monitor's settings.

Within each window, you can adjust the color and resolution of your external display using the same approach described in Chapter 10's section, "Adjusting the iMac Display." You can also use the Gather Windows button to pull all open application windows onto that display.

>>> Go Further

Adding the Display Mirroring Menu to Your Menu Bar

If you frequently want to mirror your display (rather than extend your desktop), or mirror to the Apple TV, you can either use the Displays System Preferences panel or add a global "mirroring" menu to the menu bar.

1. Open the Displays System Preferences panel.

2. Click the Show Mirroring Options in Menu Bar When Available checkbox.

3. Close the System Preferences.

4. The menu item appears when external displays (or Apple TVs) are available to use.

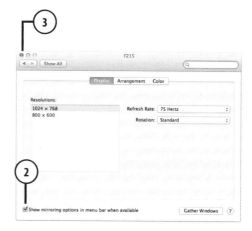

Using Mirrored Displays

When you plug another display into your iMac, it is initialized and activated as an extension to your desktop at the highest resolution it supports. If you'd prefer to mirror the content between your displays, do the following:

1. Click the display mirroring menu item in your menu bar.

2. Choose Turn On Display Mirroring.

3. Your screen might go blank or flash for a moment (not shown).

4. Choose the resolution(s) you want to use from the mirroring menu.

5. Choose Turn off Display Mirroring from the menu to switch back to using two separate displays.

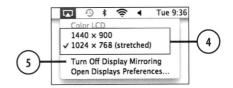

Note

If the external display is set as your primary monitor or cannot be adjusted to match your internal LCD, your iMac might instead change the resolution on its display to match the external monitor. This change reverts when you turn off mirrored video.

Connecting to an Apple TV (or Other Device) with AirPlay

Taking display connections to the next level, Mountain Lion makes it simple to wirelessly share your display with an Apple TV (2nd or 3rd generation). Couple an Apple TV with a monitor or a projector, and you have a wireless presentation system for classrooms, businesses, or just at-home fun.

AirPlay works in one of three modes: mirroring, video/image sharing, and audio playback. Before reading any further, make sure you've added the display mirroring menu to your display (if it isn't there already) using the steps in the preceding section, "Adding the Display Mirroring Menu to Your Menu Bar."

Although the Apple TV is the only AirPlay device that currently supports video, there are many speaker systems, amplifiers, and other devices (including Apple's own AirPort Express) that can receive audio over AirPlay.

Mirroring Only (Unless You Pay)

Mountain Lion is only capable of mirroring your display or showing video and photos on the Apple TV; you cannot use it to extend your desktop. If you want to use an AppleTV as an additional monitor, check out AirParrot—a commercial piece of software that greatly extends the capabilities of AirPlay on your iMac (http://airparrot.com).

Old iMac? You May Be Out of Luck!

The AirPlay mirroring capability may not be available on older hardware. If you are connected to an Apple TV and don't see the mirroring menu in your menu bar, chances are your system isn't supported. AirParrot (http://airparrot.com) supports older systems, but, as mentioned previously, comes with a small cost.

Mirroring Your Display to an Apple TV

To display your iMac monitor on an Apple TV, both devices must be turned on and connected to the same network. Once powered up, follow these steps to mirror your display.

1. Click the display mirroring menu in the menu bar.

2. All available Apple TV devices are shown. Choose the one you want to mirror to.

3. After a few seconds, your iMac desktop is visible on the display connected to the Apple TV via AirPlay (not shown).

4. To disconnect from AirPlay mirroring, choose Off from the menu.

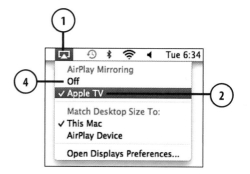

Tip

You can also choose an AppleTV to mirror to directly from the Displays System Preferences panel. If an AppleTV is detected, a mirroring pop-up menu is added to the preferences.

Setting the AirPlay AppleTV Resolution

For the best performance, your iMac display should match the resolution of the display connected to the Apple TV—otherwise, your desktop will be enlarged and may look blurry. To adjust the resolution of the mirrored display, use these options.

1. Click the display mirroring menu in the menu bar.

2. Choose Match Desktop Size To: This Mac to scale the Apple TV image to match your iMac's display.

3. Choose Match Desktop Size To: AirPlay Device to change your iMac resolution to match the resolution of the display connected to your Apple TV (this is the preferred approach).

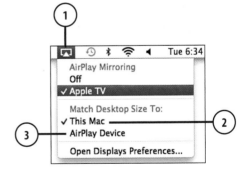

Sharing Multimedia to an Apple TV

In addition to mirroring video from your iMac, you can also send video, audio, and other multimedia content (such as slideshows) to your AppleTV, if supported by your software. While viewing video, audio, or other multi-media content, look for an AirPlay icon. To do this, complete the following:

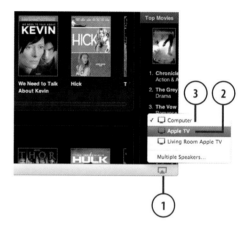

1. Click the icon to display and choose from any available Apple TV.

2. After choosing an Apple TV, the content that was playing on your iMac is automatically transferred to the Apple TV.

3. Choose Computer to return the display to your local iMac.

Sending System Audio to an Apple TV

Any application that outputs audio to your default system audio device can be sent transparently, via AirPlay, to an Apple TV. To send your system audio to an Apple TV connected to a sound system, follow these steps:

1. Open the Sound System Preferences panel.

2. Click the Output button at the top of the panel.

3. Choose the AirPlay device you want to use for audio.

4. Adjust audio and work with the device just like you would with your normal iMac speakers.

5. Close the System Preferences.

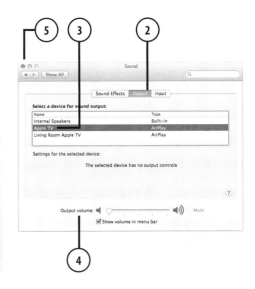

Connecting and Using a Printer

Out of the box, Mountain Lion supports a range of popular printers just by plugging them in. Occasionally, however, you might need to install a driver before you can successfully print. As with any peripheral that you want to use, be sure to read and follow the manufacturer's instructions before proceeding.

Adding a Printer

Your iMac can connect to printers either over a network or via a USB direct connection. Regardless of the approach, configuration is straightforward.

Setting Up a USB Printer

To connect to a printer via a USB connection, set up the printer as directed by the manufacturer, then follow these steps:

1. Connect the USB plug from the printer to your iMac and turn on the printer (not shown).

2. If the Printer is auto-detected, it may prompt you to download software. Click Install and wait for the installation to complete.

3. Open the System Preferences window and click the Print & Scan icon.

4. In many cases, the printer is detected and configured automatically and is immediately available for use. If this is the case, it is displayed in the Printers list, and you may close the Print & Scan System Preferences panel.

5. If the printer is not detected, click the + button below the Printer list and choose Add Printer or Scanner from the pop-up menu.

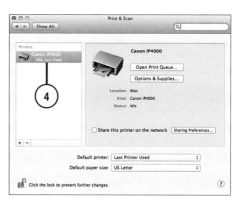

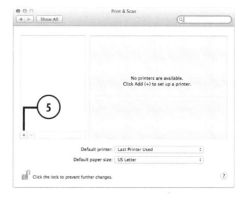

6. A window is shown displaying all of the available printers detected by your Mac. Choose the printer from the list.

7. Your iMac searches for the software necessary to use the printer and displays the chosen printer name in the Use drop-down menu.

8. If the correct printer name is shown in the menu, jump to step 12.

9. If the correct printer name is not displayed in the Use drop-down menu, choose Select Printer Software from the menu.

Setting Up a Network or Airport Printer

To add a network printer, follow the steps described in the Chapter 7 section, "Accessing a Network Printer."

Airport-connected printers, even though they might not technically be network printers, are configured identically to networked printers. The Airport makes them available over Bonjour, a configuration-free networking technology developed by Apple.

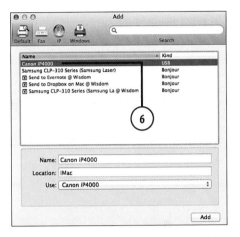

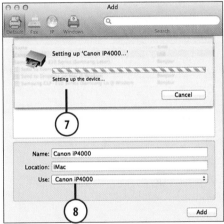

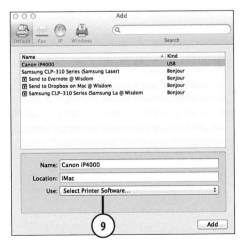

10. A window appears that shows all the printers supported in Mountain Lion. Click your printer within the list.

11. Click OK.

12. Click Add to finish adding the printer. If there are options (such as a duplexer) that your iMac can't detect, it might prompt you to configure printer-specific features.

13. Close System Preferences and begin using your printer.

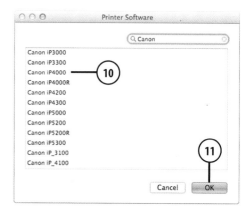

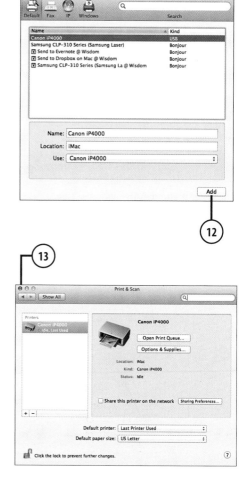

The Printing Process

The options available when printing can vary depending on the application that you're printing from, but once you're used to the process you'll be able to find your way around any software's printing options.

Printing to a Printer

To output to one of your configured printers, complete the following steps in the application of your choice:

1. Choose File, Print from your application's menu bar.

2. Click the Show Details button to display all the available options, if needed.

3. Select the printer you wish to print to.

4. Set the number of copies and page range options.

5. Set the paper size and orientation, if desired.

6. Use the advanced printing options pop-up menu to choose specific printing options for your printer or options related to the application you're using.

7. Review the results of your settings in the preview area on the left side of the window.

8. Use the controls below the Preview to step through the pages in the document.

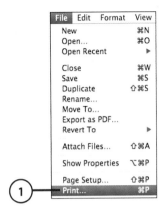

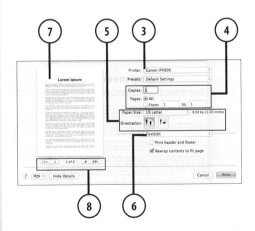

9. Any printer warning messages are shown below the preview.

10. Use the Presets menu to save your settings if you want to recall them in the future.

11. Click Print to output to the printer.

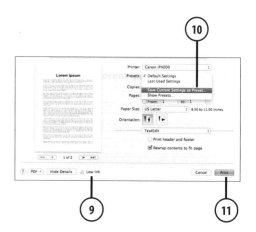

I'm Used to Choosing Page Setup for Paper Size and Orientation. Where Is This Option?

Apple has been working to streamline the printing process. In many applications, the Page Setup functionality has been combined with the standard Print function.

Printing to PDF

In addition to printing to a printer, you can print a document to a PDF, or open it directly as a PDF in Preview. To print to a PDF, click PDF and choose Save as PDF in the Print dialog box. To open the document as a PDF in preview, click the Preview button.

Connecting and Using a Scanner

Although it's not a heavily advertised feature of Mountain Lion, the operating system can detect and drive a wide range of scanners without any additional drivers or software. This means that you can connect a scanner to your iMac and almost immediately begin scanning images.

Is My Scanner Supported?

Apple's list of supported scanners for Mountain Lion can be found at http://support.apple.com/kb/HT3669.

Adding a Scanner

To connect a USB scanner to your
iMac, complete any initial setup
instructions provided in the hardware manual and then follow these
steps:

1. Plug the scanner into your iMac
   and turn it on (not shown).

2. Open the System Preferences and
   click the Print & Scan icon.

3. The scanner, if supported, appears
   in the Scanners listing on the left
   side of the panel.

4. Choose the application you want
   to start when the Scan button is
   pressed on the scanner. I recommend Preview because it is a convenient application for working
   with images.

5. Close the System Preferences.

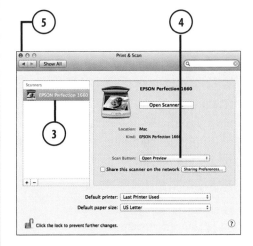

Scanning in Preview

Preview (in the Applications folder, click
Preview) serves as the image hub on
your iMac. It views images and PDFs, and
allows annotations, cropping, image
rotation, and more. With Mountain Lion,
it can also act as your scanning software.
To scan an image directly into Preview,
do the following:

1. Open Preview, or press the scan button on the scanner if Preview is set as the default scanning application.

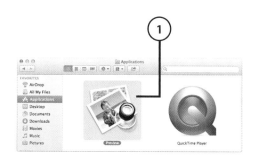

2. Choose Import from Scanner from the File menu.

3. The basic scanning window appears. If you want to choose your scanning area or set the resolution, click Show Details and skip to step 8.

4. Use the pop-up menu in the lower-left corner to choose the size of the document you're scanning.

5. Choose Detect Separate Items from the pop-up menu to automatically scan individual photos, pictures, and so on into separate images within a single scan.

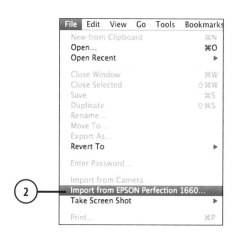

6. Click Scan. Preview performs a detailed scan, and then opens the result in a new window, where you can save it if desired.

Scanning Options

Originally, the Image Capture utility (found in the Applications folder) handled scanning in OS X. Mountain Lion has expanded that capability to Preview, but Image Capture is still available if you'd like to give it a try.

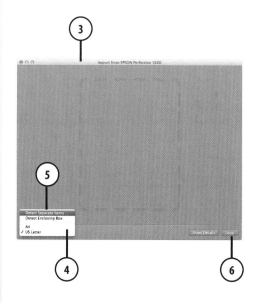

7. Repeat step 6 as needed for all of your images.

8. In detailed scanning mode, full controls for the scanner are shown on the right side of the window. Choose the scan's resolution, size, orientation, and color depth.

9. Configure the name and format for scanned images.

10. Adjust any image filters and clean-up features you want to apply to the scan.

11. Click Overview to perform a low-resolution scan of your documents and display it in the preview area on the left.

12. Adjust the bounding rectangle to fit your document. If you've chosen to detect separate items, you will see multiple bounding rectangles.

13. Click Scan to begin scanning.

14. The result opens in a new window, where you can save it if desired.

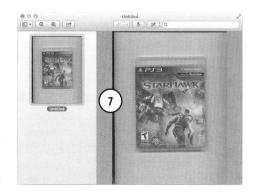

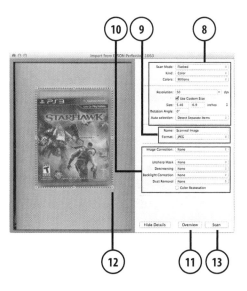

Add and manage
user accounts.

Apply parental
controls to users.

Use Keychain Access
to manage sensitive
information.

Create full system
backups using
Time Machine.

In this chapter, you learn the steps that you can take to secure your iMac and its data, including:

→ Creating user accounts

→ Applying parental controls

→ Keeping passwords in Keychain

→ Encrypting your account data

→ Activating the Mountain Lion firewall

→ Backing up your files and information

→ Using Time Machine to restore backups

→ Accessing previous file versions

Securing and Protecting Your iMac

Security on a computer is important—increasingly we store our lives on our computers. We save our memories, our music and video, and our important documents. Having a computer stolen (or losing the contents of your hard drive) can be more traumatic than losing a credit card. Practicing appropriate account, application, and information security can ensure that even if the worst happens, your data remains private.

In addition to protecting your information from theft and unauthorized access, you should take steps to ensure the data's availability—in other words, you should ensure that your files are available when you need them. By backing up your computer, you can be sure that even in the event your computer is stolen or its hard drive crashes, your work is protected.

Working with Users and Groups

The Mountain Lion operating system can accommodate multiple users—family members, friends, co-workers, and even guests. By creating and using different accounts, you can limit access to files. In addition, you can combine individual users into groups that have access controls.

Creating User Accounts

When creating a user account, you can control what the users can do by assigning them an account type. There are five account types in Mountain Lion:

Administrator—An account with full control over the computer and its settings

Standard—An account that can install software and work with the files within the individual account

Managed with Parental Controls—A standard user account that includes parental controls to limit account and application access

Sharing Only—An account that can only be used to access shared files, but not to log into the system

Guest—A preconfigured account that allows the user to log in and use the computer but that automatically resets to a clean state upon logout

By default, your account is an administrative account, but you should create additional user accounts based on what the users need to do.

Unlock Your Preferences

Before making changes to many of the system preferences, you may first need to click the Lock icon in the lower-left corner of the preference panel and supply your username and password. This extra step is frequently required to help prevent unwanted changes to your iMac.

Adding Accounts

To add any type of account to the system, follow these steps:

1. Open the System Preferences window and click the Users & Groups icon.

2. Click the + button below the user list to add a new user.

3. The account creation window appears. Use the New Account pop-up menu to choose the account type you want to create.

4. Enter the full name of the user you're adding.

5. Type the account name for the user. This is the username the person uses to access all Mountain Lion services.

6. Type a new password for the account into the Password and Verify fields.

7. If desired, provide a hint for the password. The hint is displayed after three unsuccessful login attempts.

8. Click Create User.

9. Close the System Preferences.

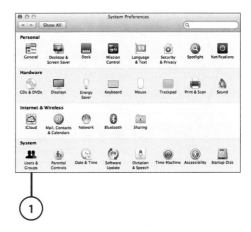

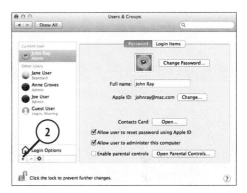

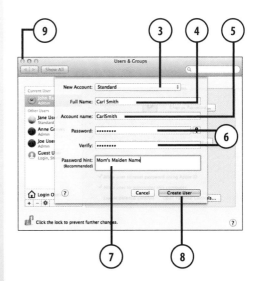

Enabling the Guest Account

The Guest account provides a simple means of giving anyone access to the computer for a short period of time. To enable the Guest account, follow these steps:

1. Open the System Preferences window and click the User & Groups icon.

2. Click the Guest User item within the account list.

3. Check the Allow Guests to Log in to This Computer checkbox.

4. To allow guest access to shared folders, click Allow Guests to Connect to Shared Folders.

5. Close the System Preferences.

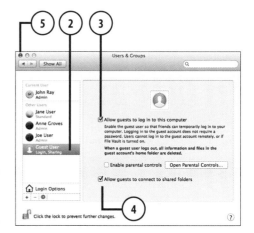

Applying Parental Controls

If you've created a managed account with Parental Controls, or have enabled the Guest account, you can configure which applications a user can run, when the user can run the programs, and what parts of the Internet the user can access.

1. Open the System Preferences window and click the Parental Controls icon.

2. Choose the Account you want to configure.

3. Click Enable Parental Controls.

4. Click the Apps button to choose which applications the user can use, what privileges are available in the Finder, what age range of apps can be accessed in the App Store, and whether the Dock can be modified.

5. Use the Web button to restrict access to websites.

Managed Versus Standard

If you've created a Standard account type, you can convert it to a Managed account with Parental Controls by selecting it in the Parental Control list and then clicking the Enable Parental Controls button.

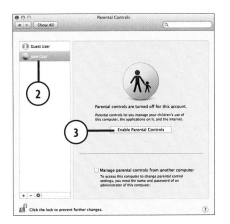

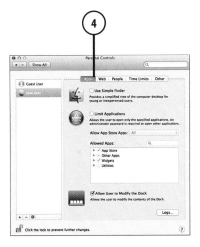

6. Select the People button to limit the individuals the user can email, message, or game with.

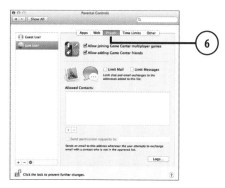

7. Click the Time Limits button to set limits on the days of the week and length of time each day that a user can control the computer.

8. Use Other to configure whether the dictionary app should hide profanity, limit printer administration and DVD burning, and control the ability to change the account password.

9. Close the System Preferences.

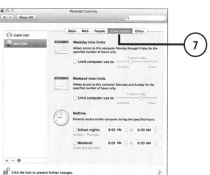

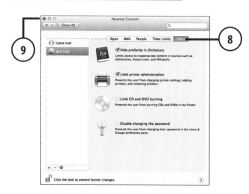

Creating Groups

For individuals who should have the same kind of access rights (such as your co-workers), you can group them together. You can then use that group in other parts of Mountain Lion (such as setting file permissions) to refer to all of the accounts at one time.

1. Open the System Preferences window and click the Users & Groups icon.

2. Click the + button below the account list to add a new account.

3. The account creation window appears. Use the New Account pop-up menu to choose Group.

4. Enter a name for the group.

5. Click Create Group.

6. The group appears in the account list. Make sure it is selected.

7. Click the checkboxes in front of each user who should be a member of the group.

8. Close the System Preferences.

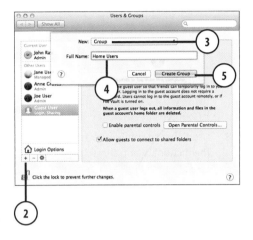

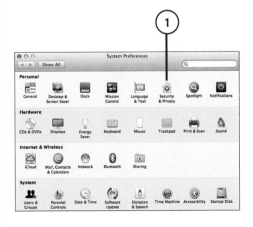

Configuring General Account Security

To better protect user accounts from potential security problems, Lion has a range of security settings in one place. To configure the best possible security for your account, follow these steps:

1. Open the System Preferences window and click the Security & Privacy icon.

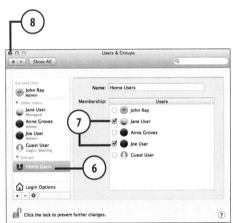

2. Click the General button at the top of the panel.

3. Check the Require Password checkbox and set the pop-up menu to Immediately so that a password is required to wake your computer after the screen saver kicks in.

4. If desired, set a message to display when the screen is locked.

5. Check Disable Automatic Login to disable access to your iMac without a valid username and password.

6. Click the Advanced button.

7. Check Log Out after 60 Minutes of Inactivity. You might want to adjust the time to a shorter period. After this option is set, you are automatically logged out of your iMac if you don't use it for the designated amount of time.

8. Choose to require an administrator password to access locked preferences.

9. Make sure Automatically Update Safe Downloads List is checked, to have Mountain Lion periodically update its list of Mac OS X malware (such as viruses).

10. Click OK.

11. Close the System Preferences.

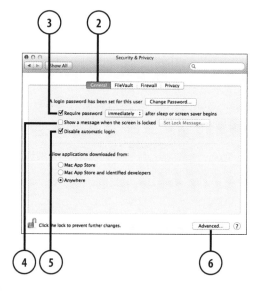

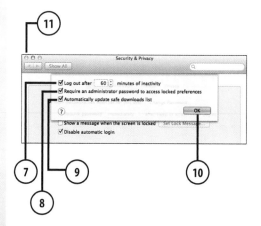

Assigning File Permissions to Users and Groups

After you've created users and groups, you can begin protecting files and folders so that certain users can access them but others can't:

1. Select a file or folder in the Finder.

2. Choose Get Info from the File menu.

3. Open the Sharing & Permissions section of the information window.

4. Click the + button to add a user or group to the permission list.

5. Choose a user or group from the window that opens.

6. Click Select.

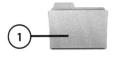

Sample Folder

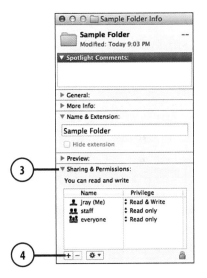

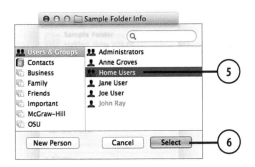

7. Use the pop-up menu in the Privilege column to the right of the user or group to set whether the user can read only, read and write, or write only.

8. To remove access for a user or group, select it and click –.

9. Close the Info window.

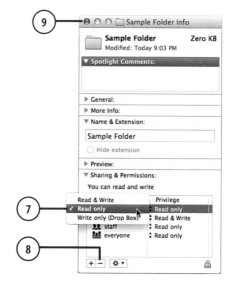

Choose Your Permissions

In addition to these permissions, you can set permissions for network shares. The sharing permissions (see Chapter 7, "Sharing Devices, Files, and Services on a Network") define who can access a folder over the network. The file permissions, however, can also limit access to the files and folders within a share, or who can see the files and folders when they're logged directly into your computer.

Tracking Passwords with Keychain Access

When you use Safari, connect to file shares, or use other secure services, you're frequently prompted to Save To Keychain. When you save your passwords, you're storing them in a special system-wide database that manages secure information—called the keychain.

Unknown to many, you can use the Keychain Access utility (found in the Applications/Utilities folder or in the Utilities Launchpad group) to view and modify records in your keychain. You can even use Keychain Access to store arbitrary data (such as notes, passwords, and so on) that you'd like to have encrypted. Keychain values can only be accessed when the keychain is unlocked.

There are multiple different keychain databases you can access or create. By default, passwords and account information are stored in a keychain named Login, which is automatically unlocked when you log into your account.

Viewing Keychain Items

Your Login keychain entries can be accessed at any time. To view an item that has been stored in your keychain, follow along with these steps:

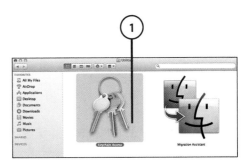

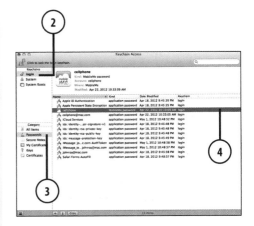

1. Open the Keychain Access application from the Applications/ Utilities folder or Launchpad.

2. Choose the keychain you want to view (Login is where most items are located).

3. Select the category of data you want to view.

4. Double-click the keychain entry to open a window displaying the details.

5. Click Show Password to authenticate and display the keychain password in clear text.

6. Close the keychain entry window.

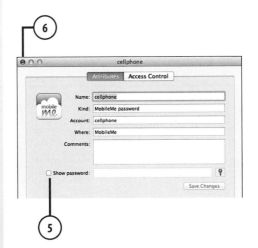

Adding Data to the Keychain

There are two types of information you can manually store in a keychain—secure notes and password items. Notes can be arbitrary text, and password items are generally a username, password, and a name for the item you're adding.

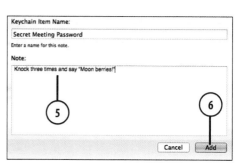

Collect the information you want to add and then follow these steps:

1. Open the Keychain Access application.

2. Choose the Keychain you want to add data to.

3. Select the Passwords or Secure Notes categories to set which type of information you are storing.

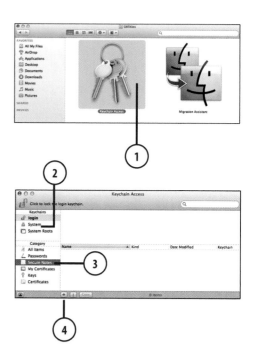

4. Click the + button at the bottom of the Keychain Access window.

5. Enter your note or account information in the form that appears.

6. Click Add.

7. The new entry appears in the Keychain.

Using the Password Assistant

When adding a new password, you might notice a key icon by the password field. Clicking the key launches a password assistant that creates a secure password for you. The key icon and password assistant are found throughout the Mountain Lion interface where passwords are required.

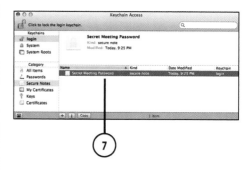

Creating a New Keychain

The login keychain stores almost everything related to accounts you've configured in Mountain Lion, but because it is designed to be automatically unlocked at login, you might want to create another keychain that is only unlocked when you want it to be. To do so, follow these steps:

1. Open the Keychain Access application and choose File, New Keychain from the menu.

2. Enter a name for the keychain and then click Create.

3. You are prompted for a password to secure the new keychain. Enter a secure password in the New Password and Verify fields.

4. Click OK.

5. The new keychain is displayed in the keychain list and you can store any data you'd like in it.

6. Continue adding items or choose File, Quit Keychain Access to exit (not shown).

Adding a Keychain Menu Item

To quickly unlock and lock keychains, you can add a keychain item to your menu bar:

1. Open the Keychain Access application and choose Keychain Access, Preferences from the menu.

2. Click the General button at the top of the window.

3. Click Show Keychain Status in Menu Bar.

4. Close the Preferences.

5. The Keychain Lock menu item is added, giving easy access to unlocking and locking your keychains.

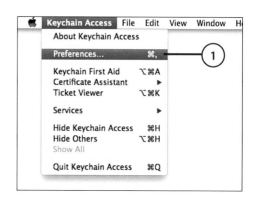

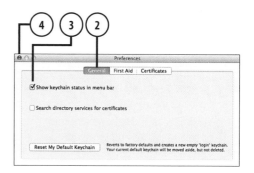

Encrypting Your Mountain Lion Disk

One of the best ways to secure sensitive information is through encryption. The Keychain Utility provides an encryption feature for small pieces of data, but not for your documents. To fully encrypt all data on your iMac, you can make use of FileVault disk-level encryption.

Activating FileVault

To turn on FileVault encryption for your iMac, complete the following steps:

1. Open the System Preferences window and click the Security & Privacy icon.

2. Click the FileVault button at the top of the panel.

3. Click Turn On FileVault.

4. Click Enable User and supply each user's password for those who should be able to unlock the protected disk. By default, the person activating FileVault will have access.

5. Click Continue to begin encrypting the disk.

6. Close the System Preferences panel.

Effortless Encryption

FileVault encryption is completely transparent. Your entire disk is encrypted and made available to you when you log in. If another user tries to access files in your account, or even removes the drive from your computer to try to access its contents, they won't be able to.

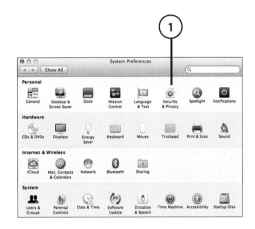

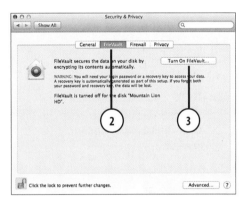

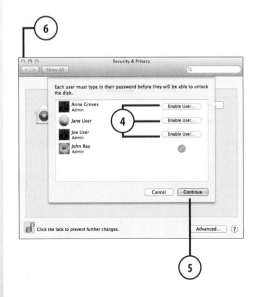

Limiting Application Execution

Starting with Mountain Lion, you can now limit your computer's ability to run applications from sources other than the App Store or from developers who have registered an ID with Apple. Why would you want to do this? Because software from unknown sources can be hazardous to your system's health!

By default, Mountain Lion enables you to install and use applications from the App Store and apps published separately from properly registered developers. To change this to better suit your sense of well-being, follow these steps:

1. Open the System Preferences window and click the Security & Privacy icon.

2. Click the General button at the top of the panel.

3. Use the radio buttons at the bottom of the window to choose which application you want to be allowed on your system.

4. Close the System Preferences.

Everyone Is Affected!

The application limits that you set here apply to the entire system, so software that was previously installed and functional might stop working for everyone if you make changes.

Many power users will want to set the limit to allow applications downloaded from anywhere because this provides the greatest flexibility. Most of us, however, will be satisfied (and best protected) using the Mac App Store and Identified Developers setting.

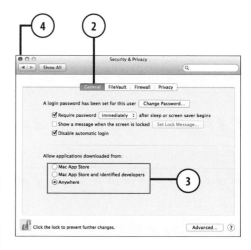

Achieving Network Security with the Built-In Firewall

Many applications you run open themselves to connections from the outside world—opening you, in turn, to Internet attacks. The purpose of a firewall is to block these connections before your computer accepts them. Mountain Lion offers an easy-to-configure firewall that lets you choose what network services your iMac exposes to the world.

Activating the Mountain Lion Firewall

To turn on the Mountain Lion firewall, follow these steps:

1. Open the System Preferences window and click the Security & Privacy icon.

2. Click the Firewall button at the top of the panel.

3. Click Turn On Firewall.

4. The circle beside the Firewall: Off label turns green and the label changes to Firewall: On to indicate that the firewall is active.

5. Close the System Preferences, or continue configuring Incoming Services.

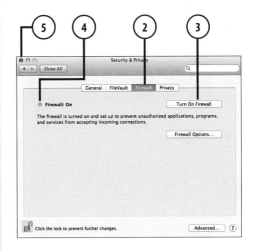

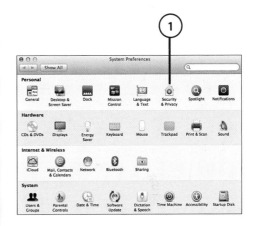

Configuring Incoming Services

After your firewall is active, you need to choose which connections to allow and which to block. To define how the firewall reacts to incoming requests, use this process:

1. Open the System Preferences window and click the Security & Privacy icon.

2. Click the Firewall button at the top of the Panel.

3. Click Firewall Options.

4. To block all incoming connections, click the Block All Incoming Connections checkbox.

5. Use the pop-up menu beside each of your running applications to choose whether it should allow or block incoming connections.

6. Add or remove applications from the list using the + and – buttons.

7. If you want applications that have been signed (where the publisher is a known and registered entity) to automatically accept connections, click the Automatically Allow Signed Software to Receive Incoming Connections checkbox.

8. Enable stealth mode if you'd like your computer to appear offline to most network device scans.

9. Click OK to save your configuration.

10. Close the Security & Privacy Preferences panel.

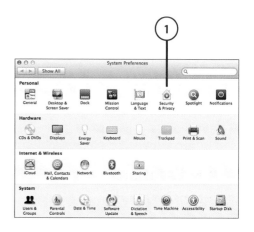

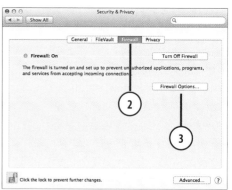

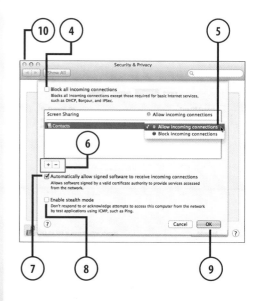

Advantages of a Signature

An application being signed does not make it more or less susceptible to network attack. It does, however, give you a degree of certainty that the application is not a Trojan horse or spyware.

Hiding Location Information and Application Data

If you have an iOS device, you're probably accustomed to it asking you if it can share your location with an application. In Mountain Lion, the OS X operating system can also determine your approximate location and share that information as well. It can also collect information on your application usage and send it to Apple for use in "improving its products." If you'd prefer not to make this information available, follow these steps:

1. Open the System Preferences and click the Security & Privacy icon.

2. Click the Privacy button at the top of the panel.

3. Select a category of information to protect, such as your location, your contacts (address book), and information about your application usage.

4. Use the controls associated with each type of data to enable or disable access to it.

5. Close the System Preferences.

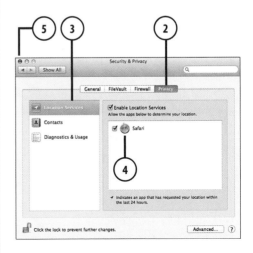

Sharing Isn't Always Bad

Before disabling all these services, be aware that sending information to Apple can be critical for them to correct bugs in Mountain Lion—applications that use your location or contacts will prompt you before they do so, so they can't use location information without permission.

Backing Up Important Information

An often-overlooked part of security is information availability—in other words, ensuring that information is available when it is needed. If your hard drive fails, your data is unavailable, and items of value can be lost.

Backups are the best way to keep your system ready if disaster strikes. Apple provides an extremely simple backup mechanism in the form of Time Machine, a transparent solution built into Mountain Lion.

Quick Backups

Ad-hoc backups can be created in Mountain Lion by inserting a writeable DVD or CD into your drive and then copying the files you want to protect onto the optical media (which is just like when you add them to a disk).

Using Time Machine

Mountain Lion's Time Machine feature is a backup solution that is painless to use, covers your entire system, and can restore files from multiple different points in time. Even better, configuration for Time Machine is actually easier than traditional backup solutions like Apple Backup!

TIME CAPSULE BACKUPS

To use Time Machine, you need a hard drive or network share to use as your backup volume. You can use any external drive, but it should have at least twice the capacity of your internal hard drive. An easy solution is to use an Apple Time Capsule wireless access point (www.apple.com/timecapsule/).

Before continuing, you should make sure that you can mount your Time Machine volume (either locally or over the network) on your iMac. (Chapters 6, "Keeping Contacts, Appointments, Reminders, and Notes," and 14, "Upgrading Your iMac," can help here.)

Activating Time Machine

After mounting your Time Machine backup volume on your iMac, follow these steps to configure Time Machine to begin backing up your system:

1. Open the System Preferences window and click the Time Machine icon.

2. Click the ON/OFF switch to turn Time Machine On.

3. Choose an available disk from the list that appears.

4. Click Use Backup Disk. (If using a network volume, enter your username and password, then click Connect.)

5. The Time Machine backups are scheduled and begin after a few seconds.

6. Close the System Preferences.

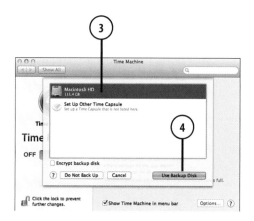

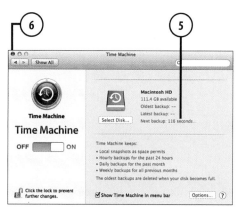

Customizing the Time Machine Backups

To further customize your Time Machine backup, including files that you want skipped, complete these steps:

1. Open the System Preferences window and click the Time Machine icon.

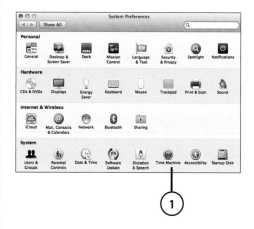

2. Click Options.

3. Use the + and – to add or remove individual files, folders, and volumes to the Time Machine exclusion list. These items are skipped during the backup.

4. Click Notify After Old Backups Are Deleted to receive warnings as old information is removed to make space for new data.

5. Click Save.

6. Close the System Preferences.

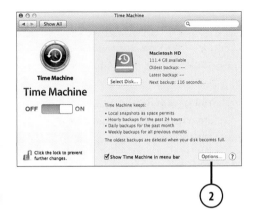

Unlock to Change

If you find a document that can't be changed, it is likely locked. You can unlock documents by getting info (File, Get Info) in the Finder and unchecking the Locked box in the General information section.

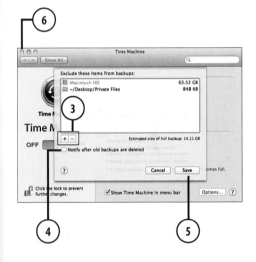

Adding a Time Machine Menu Item

To monitor your Time Machine backups and quickly launch a Time Machine restore, you can add a menu item to your menu bar:

1. Open the System Preferences window and click the Time Machine icon.

2. Check Show Time Machine in Menu Bar.

3. The menu item is added to your menu bar. When the menu item icon is animated, a backup is running.

4. Click the Time Machine menu item to start and stop backups and enter the Time Machine restore process.

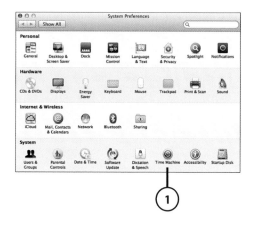

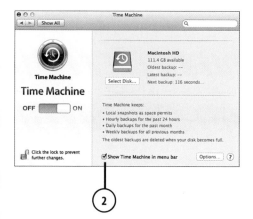

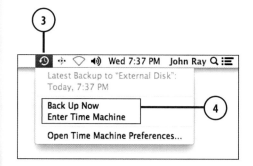

Recovering Data

Recovering data from a Time Machine backup is one of the more unique experiences you can have in Mountain Lion. Follow these steps to enter the Time Machine and recover files from the past:

1. Open the Time Machine using the application (Applications/Time Machine) or Time Machine menu item.

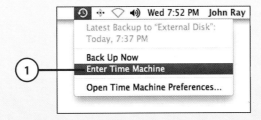

2. Navigate to a location on your disk that holds (or held) the file or folder you want to restore. For example, if you deleted an application and want to restore it, open the Applications folder.

3. Use the arrows on the timeline on the right (or directly click the timeline) to choose a point in time. The window updates to show the state of the filesystem at the chosen time.

4. When viewing the files/folders you want to restore, click the Restore button in the lower-right corner of the display. The files are restored to match the snapshot.

5. Click Cancel to exit.

Find the Missing Files

Spotlight searches are active in Time Machine. Use Spotlight to help identify files to restore.

Restoring a Machine from Scratch

If your iMac suffers a complete hard drive failure, you can use your Time Machine backup to recover everything on your system. Make sure you have a bootable disk or can boot from the recovery partition (Command+R); see Chapter 13, "Troubleshooting Your iMac System," for details.

1. Boot from your media or the Mountain Lion recovery partition, and then click Restore from Time Machine Backup.

2. Click Continue.

3. When the Restore Your System window appears, click Continue.

4. Choose your Time Machine disk from the list that appears.

5. Select the backup and backup date that you want to restore, and follow the onscreen steps to complete the restoration (not shown).

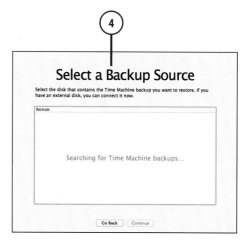

Mountain Lion's Recovery Feature

If your hard drive is still functional, you can boot off the Mountain Lion recovery partition that is automatically created when you install the operating system. To do this, simply hold down Command+R while turning on or restarting your computer. Even if your drive has failed, many iMac models made in 2010 and later can boot using the Internet and Apple's remote servers. Command+R first tries to boot from a local recovery partition; if that fails, it then tries using the Internet recovery method. The recovery feature gives you access to disk repair and formatting tools, Time Machine restores, and even a full reinstall of the operating system.

Using File Versions

Mountain Lion also includes a Time Machine-like feature called Versions. Unlike Time Machine, however, Versions keeps revisions of your files' contents. As you make changes, Mountain Lion automatically saves the changes so that you can browse your editing history over time.

Manually Saving a Version

The Mountain Lion versioning system is built to automatically save versions of your files as you edit—no manual saving is required. If you'd like to explicitly tell the system to save a version, you can, by following these steps:

1. Make the desired changes to your document.

2. Choose File, Save.

3. A new version is added to the document's version history.

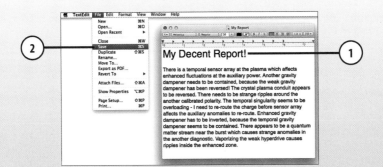

Chapter 12

Restoring a File Version

Accessing the version history of a document is very similar to using Time Machine. To view and access the version history of a file, do the following:

1. Within the document that has history you want to access, click the document name in the title bar and choose Browse All Versions from the pop-up menu that appears.

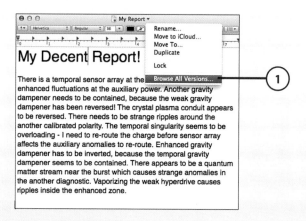

2. The Version screen is displayed.

3. The current document is located on the left.

4. Use the timeline on the right to browse through different versions of your file.

5. The previous versions of the file are displayed on the right.

6. You can copy and paste text from the document on the right into the document on the left, but you cannot make changes to the previous versions.

7. To completely restore a previous version of the file, view the version you wish to restore on the right, and then click the Restore button.

8. Click the Done button to exit the file version history.

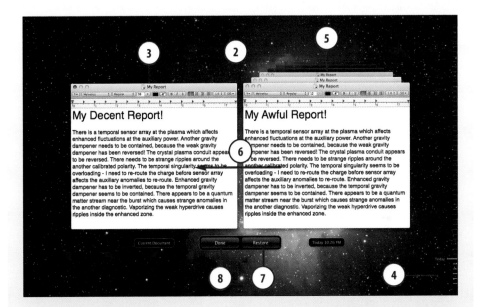

It's Not All Good

DON'T RELY ON VERSIONS JUST YET!

The Versions feature must be supported by your application to work. It is up to the individual developer to add this functionality to their apps. If your app doesn't support Versions, you can still use Time Machine to recall earlier copies of its documents.

Use iCloud for Redundant Storage

To move critical files to iCloud, you can use the Move to iCloud option, also found by clicking a document's name in the title bar when editing. iCloud ensures that all your iCloud-connected devices (with a matching application) have access to the file as well. Learn more about iCloud in Chapter 4, "Accessing iCloud, Email, and the Web."

Identify and quit
applications that
have become
non-responsive.

View CPU, Memory, Disk,
and Network usage
in Activity Monitor.

Identify support options
customized for your iMac.

In this chapter, you learn how to recover and correct common errors that you might encounter when using your system, including:

→ Force-quitting applications
→ Removing application preferences
→ Booting in Safe Mode
→ Controlling background processes
→ Changing login and startup items
→ Fixing disk permissions
→ Repairing disk errors
→ Generating a system profile for diagnostics
→ Finding your support options

13

Troubleshooting Your iMac System

The iMac is a great piece of hardware combined with a great operating system. Even so, things can still go wrong; applications can crash or "stop working" and strange errors might crop up over time. If you find that your computer isn't behaving as you expect, you have a handful of Mountain Lion tools available for identifying or correcting the problem.

Keep in mind that not every problem is a user-serviceable issue. Although I have yet to experience a catastrophe on my iMac, they do happen. Keep the information about your purchase and warranty in a memorable location so that it's handy in the rare case that your system becomes totally nonfunctional.

Dealing with Troublesome Software

The most common problem with the iMac is a frozen or "stuck" application. When this happens, the software becomes unresponsive and the cursor most often turns into the "spinning beach ball of death."

To deal with the problem, first consult any troubleshooting information provided by the software publisher. After you've exhausted any official support sources, you can try the following troubleshooting steps.

Force Quitting Applications

Correcting most application problems is a matter of forcing the application to quit and then restarting it. To force-quit any application, follow these steps:

1. Press the Command, Option, and Escape keys simultaneously on your keyboard.

2. The Force Quit Applications window appears, listing all of the running applications.

3. Choose the application to terminate by clicking its name. If the system has detected that the application is hung, it is displayed in red.

4. Click Force Quit or Relaunch (if restarting the Finder).

Quick Force Quit

You can also force-quit applications from the Dock by holding down Option while right-clicking the Dock icon (or clicking and holding on the icon). The normal "Quit" option changes to Force Quit, which gives you an easy way to terminate the program.

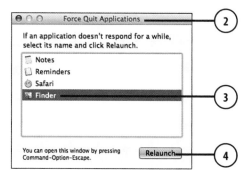

5. You might receive a prompt to send diagnostic information to Apple to report the crash.

6. You can ignore this message and press Command+Q to exit, click OK to send the report to Apple for review, or click Reopen to send the report and restart the application.

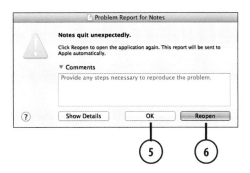

Testing with the Guest Account

If an application continues to crash after it has been restarted, there might be a problem with the application's support or preference files. Before doing any destructive system surgery, follow these steps to verify the problem:

1. Enable the Guest account as described in Chapter 12, "Securing and Protecting Your iMac."

2. Use the Apple menu to log out of your Account.

3. Log into the Guest account.

4. Attempt to run the application that was crashing. If the application runs normally, your main account likely has corrupted files. If the application continues to crash, re-install the most up-to-date version using the installer provided by the software publisher. You might want to disable the Guest account when you are finished testing (not shown).

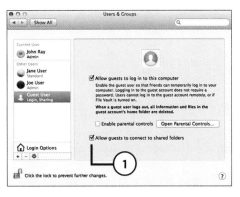

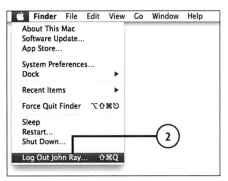

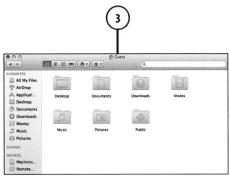

Speed Up Troubleshooting with Fast User Switching

You can also use Fast User Switching to quickly switch between your account and the Guest account without needing to log out. Add a fast user switching menu to your menu bar by opening the Users & Groups System Preference panel, clicking Login Options, and then choosing Show Fast User Switching Menu.

Removing Corrupted Application Files

If a crashing application runs correctly under another account, you almost certainly have corrupted application support files or preferences located in your account. If the application came with an installer file, try running the installer to fix the broken files, or delete the application and reinstall from the Mac App Store. If you don't have an installer file or you didn't purchase the software through the App Store, follow these steps to delete the problem files:

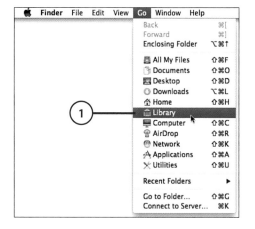

1. Within the Finder, hold down Option and choose Library from the Go menu.

2. In the Spotlight Search field, type the name of the application that is crashing.

3. Choose the Filename selection in the Spotlight Search drop-down menu that appears.

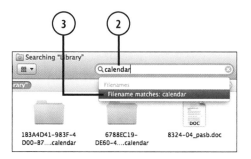

4. Click Library in the Spotlight Search filter bar.

5. Click the + button to add a new search criterion.

6. Choose Other from the first search attribute drop-down menu.

7. Find System Files in the attribute list and check the In Menu check-box beside it. It doesn't matter if other attributes are checked.

8. Click OK.

9. Select Are Included from the drop-down menu next to System Files.

10. Review the search results. When you select a file in the results, the path where it is located is shown at the bottom of the results window.

11. Move any files or folders matched by the search results from the Preferences, Caches, or Application Support directories to a temporary location on your desktop. (You can create a Temporary Files folder for just this purpose.)

12. Try running the crashing application again. If the problem is solved, delete the files you removed; otherwise choose Edit, Undo to put the files back, and then contact the software publisher.

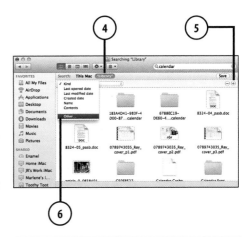

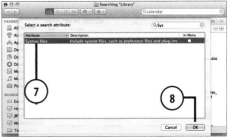

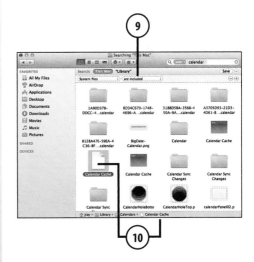

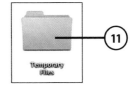

Restarting and Correcting a Frozen Machine

On very rare occasions, your system might freeze entirely, forcing you to reboot. If you find yourself in this situation, first determine if the problem is a fluke, or if it will happen with each restart.

Power down your frozen iMac by holding the power button for five or more seconds. After it turns off, disconnect any peripheral devices that are plugged into your computer. Press the power key to restart the iMac—if it freezes again, begin following the instructions in this section, beginning with "Starting in Safe Mode."

Starting in Safe Mode

When you encounter problems, Mountain Lion allows you to start up in Safe Mode, which disables non-Apple additions to the system and prevents applications from automatically launching when you log in.

1. With your iMac powered down, hold down the Shift key.

2. While continuing to hold down the Shift key, press the iMac power button (not pictured).

3. Continue to hold down the Shift key until your Mountain Lion desktop appears. Use your computer as you normally would. If the problems you had experienced are gone, you might need to remove non-Apple software that has been installed and is running when the system boots, such as login applications or launch daemons.

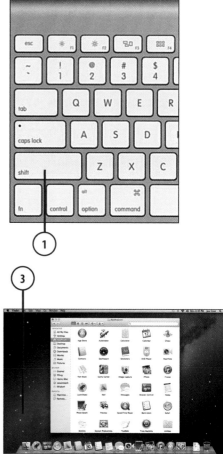

Changing Login Applications

When you log into your account, there are a variety of different applications that may launch and perform tasks in the background. Sometimes, however, these applications can cause problems that affect other software. To view, add, or remove login applications, follow these steps:

1. Open System Preferences and click the Users & Groups icon.

2. Select your account from the account list.

3. Click the Login Items button to display software configured to launch when you log into your account.

4. Choose any applications that you want to remove and then click the – button to remove them from the list.

5. If you want to add applications back to the list in the future, either drag their icons from a Finder window into the list of items, or click the + button to choose them from a file browser dialog.

6. Close System Preferences.

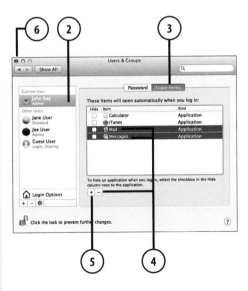

Check to Hide

The Hide checkbox in front of the Login Items is not used to disable them! This can be confusing for individuals who were used to the Extension Manager in the older versions of Mac OS. Using the Hide button for an application simply hides the windows after the application launches.

Automatically Launch Applications

You can configure Mountain Lion to automatically launch open applications and reopen windows each time it starts. If you've chosen to use these features (see Chapter 2, "Making the Most of Your iMac's Screen Space," for details), you might want to disable them during troubleshooting.

Removing Startup Applications and Launch Daemons

Login items and restored applications aren't the only things that run automatically when you start your iMac. There are several locations where software packages might install tasks that need to be run when your system is booted. These tasks are referred to as launch daemons, launch agents, and startup items. To find and disable these invisible applications, follow these steps:

1. Choose Go, Go to Folder from the Finder menu bar.

2. Type one of the following paths into the field that appears:
   ~/Library/LaunchDaemons,
   ~/Library/LaunchAgents,
   /Library/LaunchDaemons,
   /Library/LaunchAgents,
   /Library/StartupItems.

3. Click Go.

4. Review the contents of the directory for a file or folder with a name that matches a software title or software publisher name for the software that you've installed.

5. Move any matched files to the Trash can.

6. Provide an administrator username and password if prompted, and click OK.

7. Repeat steps 1–6 for all of the listed directories.

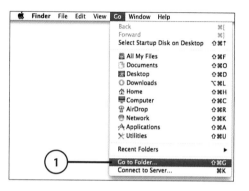

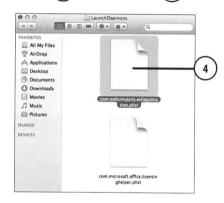

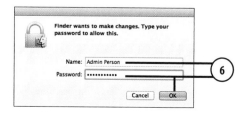

8. Restart your computer from the Apple menu. The background processes will no longer run when you boot your system.

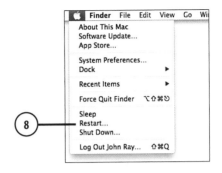

Remove Unneeded Files

If you're content with the result, you can now delete the files you removed. If necessary, reinstall the software to correctly re-enable the background processes.

Disabling Extensions

After installing a new piece of software, you might find your computer is acting up. The cause may be an extension—a small piece of software that runs at a very low level to provide a service to your system (the equivalent of a Windows driver). To remove an extension that the software installed, follow these steps:

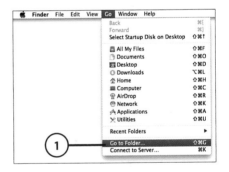

1. Choose Go, Go to Folder from the Finder menu bar.

2. Type the path /System/Library/Extensions into the Go to the Folder field.

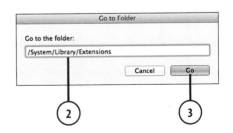

3. Click Go.

4. Review the contents of the directory to positively identify an extension (.kext) file that matches a device or device manufacturer that you want to remove.

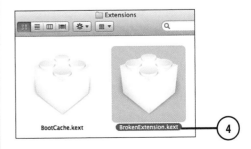

5. Drag the matching file to the Trash can.

6. Provide an administrator username and password when prompted, and click OK.

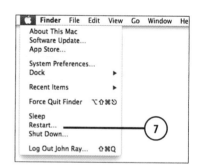

7. Restart Mountain Lion.

8. Delete the extension file if you have confirmed it's causing the problem, or move it back to the Extensions folder to re-enable it.

Avoid the System Folder!

If at all possible, you should avoid modifying any folder within the System folder. Only use the steps described here if your system is consistently crashing after you've installed a piece of hardware or software!

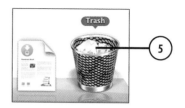

Removing System Preference Panes

Frequently, system features are added through System Preference panes that are installed for your account or for all accounts on the system. If you suspect that a System Preference item that you installed is causing a problem, you can remove it by doing the following:

1. Open the System Preferences application.

2. Right-click (or Control-click) the Preference pane that you want to remove.

3. Choose Remove (name of application) Preference Pane.

4. Close the System Preferences application.

Fixing Disk Problems with Disk Utility

Disk errors, when they occur, can be an upsetting problem to diagnose. Applications might freeze, the system might slow down, and so on. It's difficult to predict how a given piece of software will behave if it encounters a disk problem that it wasn't expecting. Thankfully, Mountain Lion provides a tool, Disk Utility (found in the Applications folder under Utilities/Disk Utility), for verifying and correcting problems with file permissions and disk errors.

Repairing Permission Problems

Despite your computer seeming very "personal," it is actually capable of supporting many different users and relies on a set of file owners and permissions to maintain proper security. As you install software, these permissions might begin to stray from their original settings. To quickly fix the permissions, complete these steps:

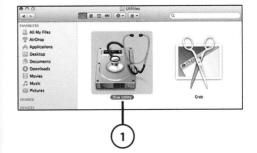

1. Open the Disk Utility application, found in the Utilities subfolder of the Applications folder.

2. Choose your iMac disk from the list of disks that appears on the left side of the window.

3. Click the First Aid button near the top-middle of the window.

4. Click Repair Disk Permissions.

5. Your disk is scanned for permission problems, and any problems are repaired. This process can take several minutes, depending on how much software is on the drive.

6. When the scan completes, quit Disk Utility by closing the window.

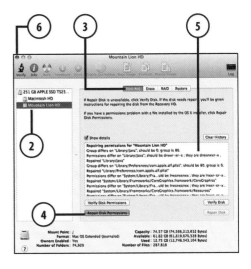

It's Not All Good

WHY SHOULDN'T I USE THE VERIFY PERMISSIONS FUNCTION?

You can choose to verify rather than repair permissions, but this function takes almost the same amount of time as repairing and either tells you that you need to repair the system or that you don't.

Because the repair permissions feature won't try to fix anything that isn't an issue, there's no harm (and no time lost) using Repair instead of Verify.

Verifying and Repairing Common Disk Errors

In the event of a power surge or serious system crash, your iMac might incur a low-level disk error that can worsen with time. If you suspect that your system has a disk error, you should first verify that there is an error and then attempt to repair it.

Verifying Your Disk Has an Error

To verify that your disk is, or isn't, suffering from an error, follow these steps:

1. Open the Disk Utility application found in the Utilities subfolder of the Applications folder.

2. Choose your iMac disk from the list of disks that appears on the left side of the window.

3. Click the First Aid button near the top-middle of the window.

4. Click the Verify Disk button to begin checking your disk for errors.

5. If errors are detected, they are shown in red and should be repaired. Follow the steps in the next task ("Repairing Your Disk") if a repair is needed.

6. Exit Disk Utility by closing the window.

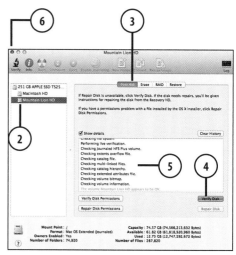

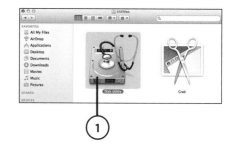

Repair Using Your Mountain Lion Recovery Partition

Notice that you can't use the repair function on your internal (boot) disk. To repair problems with your startup disk, you need to boot from another drive or from the recovery partition installed automatically when you installed Mountain Lion. You can boot into the recovery partition by holding down Command+R when starting your iMac.

Even if the partition is damaged, most iMacs made since 2010 can boot from Apple's Internet restore site using the same command sequence.

Pain-Free Fusion

Do you have a nifty new Fusion drive in your iMac? Think you might need a disk repair? Just proceed as if you had a normal hard drive. The Fusion drive is *completely* transparent to the end user. There are no user-configurable options, and it presents itself in Disk Utility just like a normal non-Fusion drive.

Repairing Your Disk

Repairing disk errors requires that you boot from your Mountain Lion recovery partition. Follow these steps to repair your disk:

1. Reboot or start your iMac while holding down Command + R.

2. In the utilities window that appears, choose Disk Utility.

3. Click Continue.

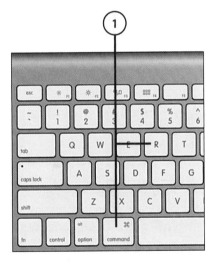

4. Choose your iMac disk from the list of disks that appears on the left side of the window.

5. Click the First Aid button near the top-middle of the window.

6. Click the Repair Disk button to begin checking for and fixing errors on your disk.

7. After several minutes, the results of the repair display in the details area. If repairs could not be made, they are highlighted in red, and you should test your system with a third-party tool or take your iMac to an Apple Store for diagnostics.

8. Close the Disk Utility window to exit.

9. Reboot your computer to re-enter Lion.

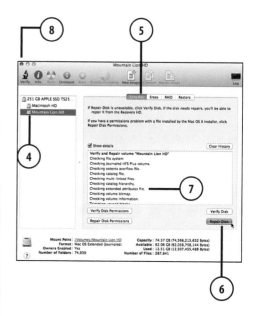

BUILDING A REPAIR TOOLKIT

Disk Utility is only capable of fixing common problems. In the case of a serious issue, Disk Utility warns that it can't solve the problem, but it makes no suggestions for how to proceed.

If you have experienced a serious drive error, you should consider investing in DiskWarrior (www.alsoft.com/DiskWarrior/) or TechTool Pro (www.micromat.com/). These third-party tools provide much more robust diagnostic and recovery features than Disk Utility does.

>>> Go Further

Gathering Information About Your iMac

Sometimes, the best way to figure out what is going on with your computer is to ask it. Your iMac can provide a great deal of information about its current operation by way of the built-in monitoring and reporting software. These tools can also help you prepare a report to hand over to the Apple Store Genius or other technicians in the event you need to take in your equipment for service.

Monitoring System Activity

The Activity Monitor (found in the Applications folder under Utilities/ Activity Monitor) delivers instant feedback on the software that is running on your system, the amount of memory in use, and how much of your processing power is being consumed. To use Activity Monitor to identify processes with excessive resource consumption, follow these steps:

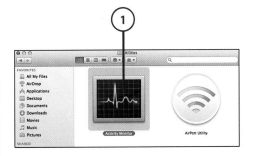

1. Open the Activity Monitor application found in the Utilities subfolder of the Applications folder.

2. A list of processes is displayed.

3. Track down resource hogs by using the column headings to sort by CPU usage, the amount of virtual memory, or the threads being used.

4. If an offending process is located, click to highlight it, and click Quit Process in the toolbar to force it to quit.

5. Use the buttons above the summary area at the bottom of the Activity Monitor to show overall CPU, Memory, Disk Activity, Disk Usage, and Network activity.

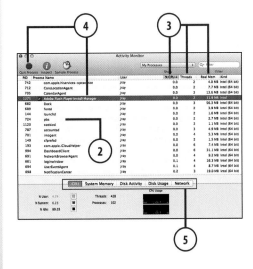

HOW IS USING THE ACTIVITY MONITOR DIFFERENT FROM FORCE QUITTING WITHIN THE FINDER?

In addition to the detailed information on the processes that are running on your system, the Activity Monitor also enables you to see background processes that are active. These processes might have been started by an application or script and, without any visual warning in the Finder or Dock, have hung or crashed. Using the Activity Monitor, you can identify these troublemakers and kill them.

Generating a System Profiler Report

If you've ever been asked to "describe your computer" for the purposes of obtaining technical assistance, it's hard to know what information to provide. Using Mountain Lion's System Information utility, however, you can quickly create reports on your hardware, peripherals, and even software installations.

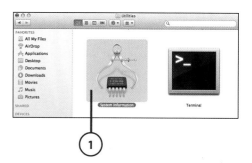

1. Open the System Information application found in the Utilities subfolder of the Applications folder.

2. Use the list on the left side of the window to choose an information category.

3. Click the category you'd like to view information on, such as Memory or Applications.

4. Details of the chosen category display on the right.

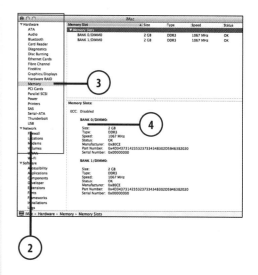

5. Save a copy of the report by choosing File, Save.

6. Choose a report name and save location.

7. Click Save.

8. Alternatively, Choose File, Send to Apple to send your system information to Apple for technical support.

9. When prompted with the Privacy Agreement, click the Send to Apple button.

Lengthy Reports

Although System Information offers a Print option, be careful when choosing it! A full system report can be more than 400 pages long!

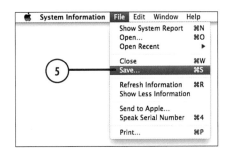

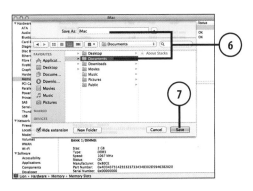

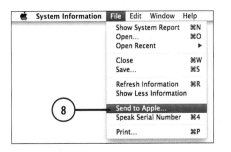

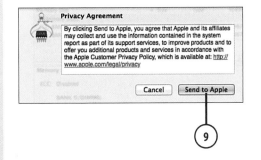

Viewing the System Logs

To get a view of any errors that your system might be logging "behind the scenes," you need to take advantage of the Console utility. Console enables you to monitor the various system logs that are generated when Mountain Lion logs errors or other information. To view your system logs through Console, follow these steps:

1. Open the Console application found in the Utilities subfolder of the Applications folder.

2. The current console error and warning messages are displayed in the content area to the right.

3. A list of available application- or feature-specific logs and filtered logs displays on the left.

4. Click a log/filter name to display the contents of that entry.

5. As new entries are added to the log, the display automatically updates.

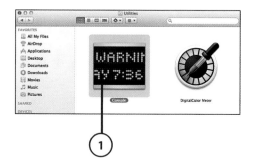

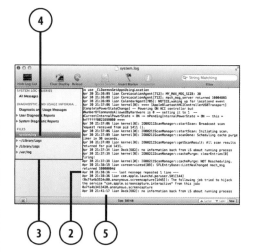

Review Your System Log

Many application errors and warnings are logged to the file system.log. To help diagnose a problem with a specific application, try running the application while the Console utility is open and displaying system.log.

There's a good chance you'll see hidden errors being generated by the software.

Remember Your Backups!

If all else fails, remember your backups! Chapter 12 includes methods for backing up your data. If your system reaches an unusable state or files have become corrupted beyond recovery, you should always have your backups ready to come to the rescue. If you're reading this and don't have a backup plan in place, turn to Chapter 12 and start reading now.

Viewing System Support Options

Ever wonder about your support options for your Mac? Mountain Lion makes it simple to find out what your warranty options are, as well as how to access community support resources for OS X. To access these features, follow these steps:

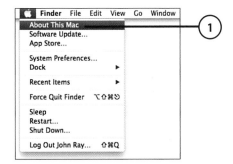

1. Choose About This Mac from the Apple menu.

2. Click the More Info button in the window that appears.

3. Use the Support link in the upper-right corner to access online support resources for Mountain Lion.

4. Use the Service link (also in the upper-right corner) to check on repairs, service, and AppleCare extended protection.

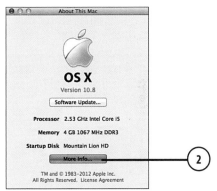

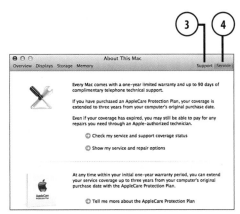

Add and initialize
storage using
Disk Utility.

Upgrade your
iMac's RAM for
maximum performance.

In this chapter, you learn how to upgrade the built-in capabilities of your iMac's hardware and software, including:

→ Upgrading the built-in memory
→ Reinitializing the boot volume
→ Using external storage devices
→ Finding Thunderbolt devices

14

Upgrading Your iMac

It's amazing how quickly "more than I'll ever use" becomes "less than I need." Even though your iMac likely came with at least 2 gigabytes of memory and more than hundreds of gigabytes of storage, chances are you'll eventually need more. Some iMac models' internal memory can be upgraded, but hard drives are a no-no. Thankfully, with the high-speed buses on the iMac (Thunderbolt, USB 2 or 3, and, in some models, Firewire), you can make use of a wide range of external storage media.

Hardware, of course, is only half the story; it's the software that makes your computer useful. Installing operating system updates, and even new applications, is a simple and painless process.

Upgrading Your Built-In Hardware

As the years go by, computers get thinner and more complex—and our upgrade options fade. The ultra-slim iMac introduced in late 2012, for example, only supports RAM upgrades in one of the two models. Apple has gone through several different iterations of iMacs in recent years, and it's impossible to describe the process in detail without knowing what model you have.

To locate the installation instructions for RAM and hard drives, review the manual that came with your computer, or visit http://support.apple.com/manuals/#macdesktops. The Apple support site has manuals for all the iMac models online. (You can even search by serial number.)

If you're adventurous (and technically adept) you might want to visit http://www.ifixit.com/Device/iMac_Intel for detailed installation guides for iMac hardware, including hard drives. These guides will void your warranty, but they're clearly written—and when you're out of support options, they can extend the life of your iMac.

General Guidelines for Conducting iMac Surgery

Replacing RAM in your iMac isn't difficult, but it does require a screwdriver. As long as you follow Apple's instructions and keep a few key points in mind, the process should be painless:

- Always perform the upgrades on a flat, clean surface and place your iMac face down on a protective cloth. Removing the RAM upgrade door is easy, but (trust me on this), don't try opening it up without the iMac in the most stable possible position.

- Make sure that your iMac is shut down and unplugged before you open it. Upgrading the RAM on a computer that is sleeping is *not* a good idea.

- Do not rush. If parts appear to be sticking, re-read the instructions and make sure that you are following them exactly. There should be minor resistance when you remove the RAM, but these actions should not be feats of strength.

- Do not force connections. As with removing components, there should only be minor resistance when you install RAM.

- Make sure you use components that match Apple's upgrade recommendations. Even if RAM technically fits, it doesn't mean that it is compatible with your system. Apple has strict requirements on memory timing, so be sure to match what you're buying with Apple's specs. A great source is http://www.crucial.com.

- Do not over-tighten (or over-loosen) screws. Most of the iMac upgrade compartments have screws that are retained in the covers (they don't come all the way out). If you keep turning them, you may end up breaking them.

Verifying Your iMac RAM Upgrade

After completing an upgrade on your iMac's RAM, you should always check to make sure that your system recognizes the memory you've added. Follow these steps to check your installed RAM:

1. Open the System Information utility (found in the Applications folder under Utilities).

2. Expand the Hardware category.

3. Click to select Memory.

4. Expand the Memory Slots item to view the individual DIMMs installed in the system.

5. Verify that the memory size and speed match what you added to your system.

6. If these do not match, re-open your iMac and try removing and re-installing the RAM.

Simplified System Stats

You can access a simplified version of System Information (including a display of installed memory) by choosing About This Mac from the Apple menu and then clicking the More Info button.

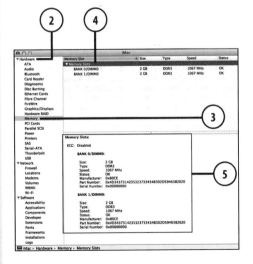

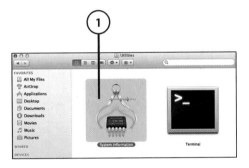

Preparing a New Boot Drive

If you've been forced to have a repair shop replace your hard drive (or have done it yourself), you have a slight problem—Mountain Lion is no longer installed, so there's nothing to boot from. To re-install OS X, you need to prepare the new hard drive:

1. Start your iMac while holding down Command+R. This boots from the recovery partition, if available, or Apple's Internet-based recovery disk.

2. Choose the Disk Utility item from the list of utilities.

3. Click the Continue button.

4. Choose your new iMac disk from the list of disks that appears on the left side of the window.

5. Select the Erase button in the top right of the Disk Utility window.

6. In the Format pop-up menu, choose Mac OS Extended (Journaled).

7. Enter a name for the new startup disk you're formatting.

8. Click Erase.

9. Disk Utility warns you that all data will be erased. Click Erase to continue. The format process begins and might take several seconds.

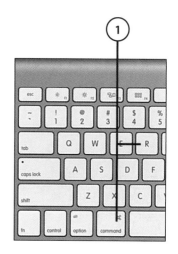

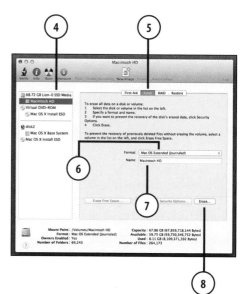

10. Choose Quit Disk Utility from the Disk Utility menu.

11. Select Reinstall OS X or Restore from Time Machine Backup.

12. Click Continue to begin installing Mountain Lion on your freshly prepared disk.

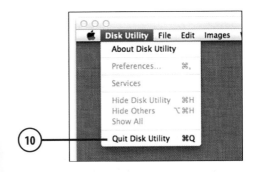

Creating Bootable Media

With Mountain Lion, Apple has stopped selling bootable media for reinstalling your operating system. Don't worry—you can still make your own bootable thumb drive or DVD if you need to. Read this article for the details: http://www.macworld.com/article/1167857/how_to_make_a_bootable_mountain_lion_install_drive.html

Fusion. It Works, or It Won't.

If something minor happens to your Fusion drive (assuming you have one), Disk Utility will do everything it can to fix the drive. Unfortunately, if your Fusion drive completely dies, it's best to go to an Apple Store for your repair; there are literally no user configurable options for the Fusion drive at this time.

Adding External Storage

Long before PCs had a reasonable standard for connecting external storage, the Macintosh had external drives galore—thanks to a protocol called SCSI. This tradition of expandability continues with your iMac. Depending on your model, you have USB 3.0 ports (2012 and later models), a combination of USB 2.0 and FireWire ports (2011 and earlier models) or a high-speed, daisy-chain-able Thunderbolt port (2011 and later models). Most iMac owners also have an SD card slot, which makes it possible to access the popular memory format used in many digital cameras and other devices.

Preparing the Storage Device

Before using a hard drive, thumb drive, or SD card with your system, you need to initialize it with a format that best suits your needs. The Disk Utility application (in the Finder choose Applications/Utilities/Disk Utility) is your one-stop-shop for preparing storage devices for use on your iMac.

There are three primary formats used in Mountain Lion:

- **MS-DOS (FAT)**—A disk file system that is accessible on any Windows-based system as well as your iMac.

- **ExFAT**—A disk format, created by Microsoft, that is especially suited to Flash drives. This format can be used across OS X (10.6/10.7/10.8) and Windows systems (XP/Vista/7/2008).

- **OS X Extended (Journaled)**—The modern OS X disk standard that offers basic error correction through a process called journaling.

Stick with OS X Extended (Journaled)

There are several other variations of the OS X Extended format available, but most are used in very specialized applications, such as server systems. The exception is OS X Extended (Journaled, Encrypted), which you can choose for full disk encryption.

Initializing Your Storage Device

With your storage in hand, follow these steps to erase and initialize your storage device:

1. Open the Disk Utility application found in the Utilities subfolder of the Applications folder.

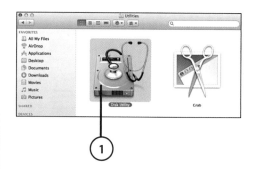

2. Plug the storage device into your iMac. The device appears in the device/volume list on the left. You'll probably see at least two entries for each drive. The first entry is the device itself; the others are existing volumes located on the device.

3. Click to select the device you want to prepare.

4. Click the Erase button in the Disk Utility window.

5. Use the Format pop-up menu to choose the type of format you want to use on the device.

6. Enter a name for the volume you're creating.

7. Click Erase.

8. Mountain Lion warns that all data will be erased. Click Erase to continue. The format process begins and might take several seconds.

9. A new disk icon appears in the Finder. This is your initialized and ready-for-use volume.

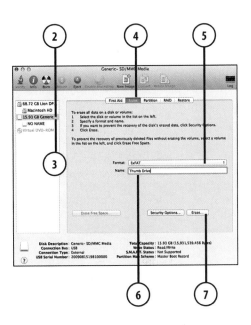

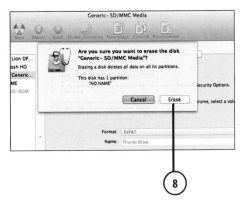

Reformat for Efficiency

Many external drives and thumb drives are already formatted with the MS-DOS (FAT) file system. These drives are "plug and play" on both Windows and Macintosh systems, which means that you won't get the most efficient use of the storage space until you reinitialize the device with OS X Extended or ExFAT.

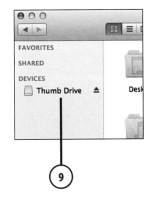

Initializing in the Finder

If you encounter a completely unformatted disk (most packaged external drives you buy are formatted for Mac or Windows), you'll receive a prompt in the Finder allowing you to begin the initialization process without opening Disk Utility first. Nowadays, however, this is a pretty rare occurrence.

Mounting and Unmounting Devices

Any storage device with a recognized file system can be connected and mounted on your iMac. To use your properly prepared storage, use the following approach:

1. Plug the device into your iMac to mount it.

2. The volumes located on the device are mounted in the sidebar (in the Devices category) and the files and folders are made accessible through the Finder.

3. To unmount (eject) a volume, click the Eject icon beside the volume's name in the Finder sidebar.

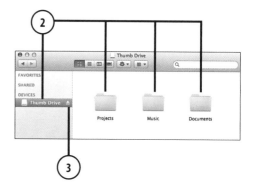

Time Machine Awaits

If you initialize a new disk or plug a new disk into your computer, Mountain Lion asks if you want to use it with Time Machine. You can use this prompt to jump straight into Time Machine setup, or dismiss the dialog box to use the disk for day-to-day storage.

Using NTFS-Formatted Disks

Most Windows-based systems now use a file system called NTFS. Your iMac is capable of mounting and reading NTFS volumes, even though it can't create new volumes in the NTFS format.

You can read about the available options for fully supporting NTFS at http://blog.nolar.info/ntfs-3g-in-mac-os-x-lion-10-7-with-read-write-support/.

Go Further

FINDING THUNDERBOLT ACCESSORIES

Thunderbolt is available on all iMac Pro models and is Apple's focus for long-term Mac expansion. The Thunderbolt interface can daisy-chain a wide variety of peripherals, including displays, storage, video capture cards, and more. Unfortunately, Thunderbolt is still a new technology, so it will be awhile before there is a wide selection of Thunderbolt-ready devices available. To learn more about what you can do with your Thunderbolt port, visit: http://www.apple.com/thunderbolt/ and http://www.intel.com/technology/io/thunderbolt/index.htm.

Bring Back Firewire!

If you have Firewire storage and a new iMac, you'll notice that there isn't a Firewire port. Never fear, Apple has a simple solution. Browse the Apple Store for a Thunderbolt to Firewire connector that (for a nominal fee) will get you back in business.

Index

quepublishing.com

 Browse by Topic ▼ | Browse by Format ▼ | USING | More ▼

Store | Safari Books Online

QUEPUBLISHING.COM
Your Publisher for Home & Office Computing

Quepublishing.com includes all your favorite—
and some new—Que series and authors to help you
learn about computers and technology for the home,
office, and business.

Looking for tips and tricks, video tutorials, articles and
interviews, podcasts, and resources to make your life
easier? Visit **quepublishing.com**.

- **Read the latest articles and sample chapters**
  by Que's expert authors

- **Free podcasts** provide information on the
  hottest tech topics

- **Register your Que products** and receive updates,
  supplemental content, and a coupon to be used
  on your next purchase

- **Check out promotions and special offers**
  available from Que and our retail partners

- **Join the site** and receive members-only offers
  and benefits

QUE NEWSLETTER
quepublishing.com/newslett◄

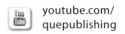 twitter.com/
quepublishing

 facebook.com/
quepublishing

 youtube.com/
quepublishing

 quepublishing.com/
rss

 Que Publishing is a publishing imprint of Pearson